Some aspects of the extraterritorial reach of the American antitrust laws

by

Hendrik Zwarensteyn, J.D., Ph.D.

Professor of Business Law
Michigan State University

Springer Science+Business Media, B.V. 1970

ISBN 978-90-268-0442-7 ISBN 978-94-017-4467-6 (eBook)
DOI 10.1007/978-94-017-4467-6

International Standard Book Number 90 268 0442 3
Library of Congress Catalog Card Number 72-130210

Originally published by Uitgeversmaatschappij AE. E. Kluwer, Deventer in 1970

TABLE OF CONTENTS

CHAPTER II

REMEDIAL AND OTHER PROCEDURAL ASPECTS OF THE AMERICAN ANTITRUST LAWS

CHAPTER III

THE SPECIAL CHARACTER OF THE AMERICAN ANTITRUST LAWS

CHAPTER IV

THE EXTRATERRITORIAL REACH OF THE AMERICAN ANTITRUST LAWS JURISDICTIONAL ASPECTS

CHAPTER V

THE EXTRATERRITORIAL REACH OF THE AMERICAN ANTITRUST LAWS REMEDIAL ASPECTS

CHAPTER VI

THE EXTRATERRITORIAL REACH OF THE AMERICAN ANTITRUST LAWS INTERNATIONAL LAW ASPECTS

CHAPTER VII
CONCLUSIONS

INTRODUCTION

General

While there is an abundance of literature dealing with the American antitrust laws, one can also observe that the application of this area of the law to foreign commerce is still in an evolutionary stage of development. To some extent this can be quantifiably explained by pointing out that the rapid rise of the interests of the American business community in foreign commerce is only a fairly recent phenomenon.[1] This participatory interest reveals a wide spectrum of commercial activities.

While the traditional concept of foreign commerce was often limited to thinking in terms of exports and imports, present commercial activities include also such marketing methods as the establishment of foreign branches or subsidiaries, or the location of manufacturing, processing, or assembly plants abroad.[2] To this array of arrangements, most of which contemplate a widening of the market potential, we may add the current merger movement, the conglomerate character of which has been termed its 'most unique characteristic'.[3] Little wonder that at least one author refers to the application of the antitrust laws to foreign commerce as being still somewhat of a 'frontier area of the law'.[4] Because of the rapidly expanding participation of the American business community in international commerce a gradual evolution of the international dimensions of the American antitrust laws seems therefore within the realm of justified expectations.

Most of the thinking so far can be described as centrifugal in its approach because of the apparent tendency to focus on the problems of the American entrepreneur who ventures out into the international business arena. As a result we find a primary emphasis on the extent to which the American antitrust

1. According to the U.S. DEPARTMENT OF COMMERCE, STATISTICAL ABSTRACT OF THE UNITED STATES, 1968, p. 791, the total of U.S. private investment abroad rose from $ 14,883 million in 1945 to $ 86,235 million in 1966, an increase of almost 600% over a period of 21 years.
2. *cf.* NOTE in 1 *Case Western Reserve J. Int'l Law* 132, 140 (1969)
3. *cf.* ANTITRUST DEVELOPMENTS 1955–1968, A SUPPLEMENT TO THE REPORT OF THE ATTORNEY GENERAL'S NATIONAL COMMITTEE TO STUDY THE ANTITRUST LAWS, MARCH 31, 1955, American Bar Association, 1968, p. 83 (hereinafter to be referred to as SUPPLEMENT). For an example of such a merger, see *U.S.* v *Jos. Schlitz Brewing Co.*, 385 US 37, 87 S Ct 240 (1966), affirming *per curiam* a decision of the Federal Distriot Court of Northern California, 253 F Supp 129, cited in SUPPLEMENT, p. 59
4. *cf.* FUGATE, W. L., FOREIGN COMMERCE AND THE ANTITRUST LAWS, Boston, 1958, p. IX

enforcement will apply to either the businessman himself or to his entrepreneurial decisions, or both.[5]

At least in the United States comparatively little attention has been given to the problems of American antitrust enforcement confronting the foreign businessman, i.e., the businessman located and substantially doing business outside the territorial boundaries of the United States, but who has diverted part of his commercial activities to the United States.[6] Partly this can be explained because of the newness of the problem, partly because of the complexity of the problems involved.[7]

During the last decade some notable contributions which focus on the problems of the foreign businessman have been made, both in the United States and abroad.[8] Notwithstanding the many important observations and statements made by the various authors during this last decade, we feel that there is still room left for additional study whereby in particular the legal problems pertaining to the foreign businessman who ventures into the American market are emphasized. As an illustration we mention the conceivable problems connected with the post-World War II efforts of foreign producers and exporters who combined their efforts in order to secure a foothold on the American market.[9] Combined efforts such as these often include agreements pertaining to uniform or standard quality, combined advertising, propaganda and public relations. It is furthermore, not at all unusual to also provide for united

5. The term 'businessman' should not be taken too literally, or in a narrow sense. The term, as we refer to it, pertains to the entrepreneur as we encounter him in any of the manifold ventures such as commercial, industrial, or financial institutions. Therefore, when speaking of the 'businessman', reference is made to that sector of society that is entirely, or in part, engaged in some form of commercial, industrial, or financing activity, involving either goods, or services. Furthermore, the term refers to both persons and institutions.

6. The term 'foreign businessman' when used hereafter will always be used in the above defined meaning. For the definition of the term 'businessman', see *n.* 1, *supra.*

7. For the difficulties involved in even such a seemingly simple task as the determination of the nationality of an enterprise, see *e.g.*, KRONSTEIN, H., 'The Nationality of International Enterprises', 52 *Col. Law Rev.* 983 (1952).

8. Specific mention should be made of the contributions made by KRONSTEIN, H., 'Conflicts Resulting From The Extraterritorial Effects Of The Antitrust Legislation Of Different Countries', in XXth CENTURY COMPARATIVE AND CONFLICTS LAW, Leiden, 1961, pp. 432, *seq.;* SCHWARTZ, I. E., DEUTSCHES INTERNATIONALES KARTELLRECHT, Köln, 1962; the position papers of RIEDWEG, A. J. ('The Extra-Territorial Application of Restrictive Trade Legislation – Jurisdiction and International Law'), and OLIVER, C. T. ('The Range of Effect of the Anti-Trust Laws of the United States') at the FIFTY-FIRST CONFERENCE OF THE INTERNATIONAL LAW ASSOCIATION HELD AT TOKYO IN 1964; REHBINDER, E., EXTRATERRITORIALE WIRKUNGEN DES DEUTSCHEN KARTELLRECHTS, Baden-Baden, 1967; NOTE ('An Introduction to the Extraterritorial Application of the American Antitrust Laws'), 1 *Case Western Reserve Journal of International Law* 132 (1969).

9. Examples are: the Irish Linen Guild, the Swiss Watchmakers Association, the Dutch Bulb Growers Association, the Holland Herring Fisheries Association.

sales efforts[10], use of the same agents, and uniform prices.
It so happens that horizontal agreements which have as objective to provide for uniform prices – as would agreements which would in other ways unduly restrict competition, such as tying arrangements, market division among competitors, quota restrictions, production restrictions, exclusive territorial dealership arrangements, exclusive licensing agreements – are subject to scrutiny by the American antitrust enforcement agencies, if for no other reason than that the pertinent provisions of the American antitrust laws make specific reference to the trade or commerce with foreign nations.[11] Of these legal provisions we mention in particular:

(1) *The Sherman Act:*[12]

(a) Sec. 1: Every contract, combination in the form of trust or otherwise, or conspiracy, in restraint of trade or commerce among the several States, *or with foreign nations,* is hereby declared to be illegal...
Every person who shall make any contract or engage in any combination or conspiracy hereby declared to be illegal shall be deemed guilty of a misdemeanor, and, on conviction thereof, shall be punished by fine not exceeding fifty thousand dollars, or by imprisonment not exceeding one year, or by both said punishments, in the discretion of the court.

(b) Sec. 2: Every person who shall monopolize, or attempt to monopolize, or combine or conspire with any other person or persons, to monopolize any part of the trade or commerce among the several States, *or with foreign nations,* shall be punished by fine not exceeding fity thousand dollars, or by imprisonment not exceeding one year, or by both said punishments, in the discretion of the court.

(c) Sec. 8: That the word 'person,' or 'persons,' wherever used in this act shall be deemed to include corporations and associations existing under or authorized by the laws of either the United States, the laws of any of the Territories, the laws of any State, *or the laws of any foreign country.*

10. Advertising, propaganda and public relations should be understood as referring to the meaning usually given to these terms in the area of Marketing: they are all aspects of 'impersonal selling'.
11. With regard to the reference in the American antitrust laws to the trade or commerce with foreign nations, mention should be made of the statement by REHBINDER that the antitrust provisions of the European Economic Community do not contain such a 'foreign commerce clause'; *cf.* REHBINDER, *op. cit.*, p. 36
12. Act of July 2, 1890, as amended by the Act of August 17, 1937, and the Act of July 7, 1955 (Italics supplied).

(2) *The Clayton Act:*[13]

(a) Sec. 2: That it shall be unlawful for any person engaged in commerce, in the course of such commerce, either directly or indirectly to discriminate in price between different purchasers of commodities of like grade and quality, where either or any of the purchases involved in such discrimination are in commerce... and where the effect of such discrimination may be substantially to lessen competition or to create a monopoly in any line of commerce, or to injure, destroy, or prevent competition with any person who either grants or knowingly receives the benefit of such discrimination, or with customers of either of them.

(b) Sec. 4: That any person who shall be injured in his business or property by reason of anything forbidden in the antitrust laws may sue therefor in any district court of the United States in *the district in which the defendant resides, or is found, or has an agent,* without respect to the amount in controversy, and shall recover threefold the damages by him sustained, and the cost of the suit, including a reasonable attorney's fee.

(3) *The Robinson-Patman Act:*[14]

Sec. 3: It shall be unlawful for any person engaged in commerce, in the course of such commerce, to be a party to, or assist in any transaction of sale, or contract to sell, which discriminates to his knowledge against competitors of the purchasers, in that any discount, rebate, allowance, or advertising services charge is granted to the purchaser over and above any discount, rebate, allowance, or advertising service charge available at the time of such transaction to said competitors in respect of a sale of goods of like grade, quality, and quantity; to sell, or contract to sell, goods in any part of the United States at prices lower than those exacted by said person elsewhere in the United States for the purpose of destroying competition, or eliminating a competitor.

Even a summary perusal of the American judicial decisions shows clearly that the American antitrust laws are applied to the foreign businessman, i.e., the businessman located and substantially doing business outside the territorial boundaries of the United States, but who has diverted part of his commercial activities to the United States. On the basis of this observation one could therefore, state that the American antitrust laws have an extraterritorial reach, be-

13. Act of October 15, 1914, as amended by the Act of June 19, 1936, the Act of June 25, 1948, the Act of December 29, 1950, the Act of July 7, 1955, and the Act of July 23, 1959 (Italics supplied).
14. Act of June 19, 1936.

cause they reach out to, i.e., bring under the purview of these laws behavior that occurred outside the national boundaries. Thus, we find in an opinion of the United States Supreme Court the statement that, 'A conspiracy to monopolize or restrain the domestic or foreign commerce of the United States is not outside the reach of the Sherman Act just because part of the conduct complained of occurs in foreign countries'.[15]

Our statement that the antitrust laws of the United States have an extraterritorial reach may need some clarification. The terminology as used by us is no more than a statement-of-fact and conveys no more than the factual observation that these antitrust laws are applied to behavior outside the territorial boundaries of the United States; the context in which we have used the term does not imply a legal connotation or value judgment, be it approval or rejection. Nor does the use of the term suggest under which circumstances or conditions the application of these laws to behavior abroad will (or is likely to) occur. The term 'extraterritorial' as used by us is therefore, not a normative but merely a descriptive adjective.[16]

Our statement then, that the American antitrust laws have an extraterritorial reach as a matter-of-fact implies a distinction between what is being done and what may be done.[17] Because no normative aspects are implied, use of the term leaves unanswered the question under which circumstances these laws were (or will be) applied to the foreign businessman. Nor does it answer the question whether the application of these laws under the circumstances was justified, i.e., whether the norms used are compatible with the generally recognized and accepted principles of law, both domestic and (more importantly) international. Finally, it leaves entirely open to question the expediency and the adequacy of the existing norms themselves, particularly when seen against the background of a possible collision between the antitrust laws of the United States and those of other nations, with regard to the protection and the preservation of the interests of the international community of nations.[18]

There is still another aspect of the term extraterritorial reach which needs clarification. The statement that the American antitrust laws reach out to the foreign businessman refers to two different ways of 'reaching out':

a. the so-called legislative reach, suggesting the existence of legislative enact-

15. *Continental Ore Co.* v *Union Carbide & Carbon Corp.*, 370 US 690, 82 S Ct 1440 (1962)
16. Similarly, REHBINDER, *op. cit.*, p. 28: 'Die Bezeichnung 'extraterritorial' enthält also keine Bewertung...' For a narrower construction, see SCHWARTZ, I. E., *op. cit.*, p. 190, who uses the term in the sense of *rechtliche Wirksamheit.*
17. *cf.* HOLLAND, T. E., THE ELEMENTS OF JURISPRUDENCE, 6th Ed., Oxford, 1893, pp. 101, *seq.*, distinguishing between 'acts' (something that is done, be it lawful or unlawful) and 'juristic acts' (the rights creating activity, within the limits of the law).
18. *cf.* 1 *Case West. Res. J. Int'l Law* 132, 149 (1969): 'Traditional principles of international law are not sufficiently adaptable to meet the pressing needs of the new types of business organizations which exist today'.

ments which state under which circumstances persons or behavior abroad shall be subject to the provisions of the particular law;

b. the so-called judicial reach, i.e., judicial or quasi-judicial proceedings involving or behavior abroad.

In either case there may be an extraterritorial reach, but in the former the initiative lies with the legislature, while in the latter the initiative lies with the judiciary.[19] We do not think that we have to elaborate that these different possibilities need a separate examination.

Possible approaches

A study contemplating an inquiry into the legal problems of the foreign businessman who ventures onto the American market can be undertaken along several approaches. Of these we mention the following:

(1) a description of what factually can be observed, i.e., that the American antitrust laws are applied to persons or conduct outside the territorial boundaries of the United States;

(2) an analysis of the normative aspects of the factually observed behavior, i.e., the jurisdictional competency. This jurisdictional competency, in turn, can be approached from two different vantage points:

  (a) the legislative jurisdictional competency, i.e., the legality of a State to legislate who or what (foreign) conduct shall come under the reach of its national laws, not only in accordance with the State's domestic law, but also with the generally recognized and accepted principles of international law;

  (b) the judicial jurisdictional competency, i.e., the legality of a State's judiciary or quasi-judiciary to hear and decide cases or controversies involving persons or conduct abroad, not only in accordance with the State's domestic law, but also with the generally recognized and accepted principles of international law;

(3) an examination of the possible differences in antitrust enforcement depending on the qualifications of the defendant, or the *locus* of the conduct, or both. This approach would result in:

  (a) an analysis of the application of the American antitrust laws to American businessmen venturing onto foreign markets;

  (b) an analysis of the application of these laws to foreign businessmen venturing onto the American market place.

  Each of these analyses could, in turn, be approached along the lines suggested above *sub* (1) and (2), i.e., alternately dealing with the descriptive and the normative aspects of the topic under consideration. It is obvious

19. Or even with the quasi-judiciary, i.e., the executive branch of government.

that each of these alternate approaches requires a different treatment of the subject matter.

It is our intention to focus on the application of the American antitrust laws to the foreign businessman venturing onto the American market place, specifically with regard to the jurisdictional competency of the United States, not only in accordance with its domestic law, but also in accordance with the generally recognized and accepted principles of international law, to enforce its national antitrust laws against foreign defendants or conduct outside the territorial boundaries of the United States.

This approach will necessitate an examination of the instances in which the American antitrust laws are applicable (i.e., against whom or with regard to what kind of conduct), as well as an examination of the instances in which these laws have actually been applied against persons, or conduct, or both. It will furthermore, be necessary to examine the extent to which this application can be squared with the generally recognized and accepted principles of international law.

We hope that on the basis of our findings we will be able to suggest a generally acceptable formula for the solution of methods of antitrust enforcement in cases involving trans-national business. This means that we do not propose to solely limit ourselves to an inquiry into the legality (either at the domestic or the international law level) of the extraterritorial reach of the American antitrust laws; we also plan to inquire into the expediency of the ways in which this extraterritorial reach is carried out (including the possibility of alternate solutions).

Identification of the problems

While a study as presently contemplated may reveal a host of problems, all in need of further examination, two problems present themselves at the outset. Because of their importance we single them out for special consideration. They are:

(1) the legality of the extraterritorial reach, i.e., are the substantive provisions and the procedural aspects of the American antitrust enforcement with regard to foreign conduct, or foreign defendants[20], or both, in accordance with the principles of the domestic law of the United States and the principles of international law?

(2) the 'alternate solutions' problem, i.e., are there alternatives to the presently followed methods of antitrust enforcement which would make for better international relations? In other words, while it may be legally acceptable to do what the United States is doing, is it also expedient when

20. A foreign defendant is an alien defendant domiciled outside the United States.

viewed against the background of the international community of nations?

Methodology

(1) The historical development and the philosophical bases

We propose to first, approach the area of the American antitrust enforcement in general, viewed from its historical and philosophical development bases, in order to portray how the legal sphere (i.e., the *Sherman Act* and subsequent Acts) is but a reflection of the economic and political spheres. Indeed, we consider a proper understanding of the historical development of the antitrust laws indispensable for a proper insight into some of the problems of antitrust enforcement. For instance, this will show that antitrust enforcement grew out of a settling of relationships between citizens which they asked the courts to enforce, not out of a government dictate of how these relationships should be. In other words, American antitrust law grew out of tort and contract law, not out of a relationship based on government decrees.

Furthermore, a historical approach will make the battle in the courts (during the years 1890–1911) with regard to the wording 'every contract in restraint of trade', as used in the *Sherman Act,* more meaningful: it was from this battle that the 'rule of reason' doctrine (re-)emerged which holds that only the *unreasonable restraint* of trade is counter to the provisions of the *Sherman Act,* and *not every restraint* of trade, as the wording of the Act would suggest. To appreciate this legal battle one should be conversant with contracts in restraint at common law, i.e., the situation prior to the enactment of the *Sherman Act.*

Equally important is it to portray how the prevailing political and economic concepts during the many decades preceding 1890 lead up to the statutory enactments known as the American antitrust laws. These political and economic ideas made themselves also felt where the foreign commerce of the United States was affected; an understanding thereof is therefore important to our inquiry into the extraterritorial reach of antitrust enforcement.

On the basis of the above we suggest that to commence a study of the American antitrust laws with the *Sherman Act* of 1890 would constitute serious error. We find support for our view in the fact that we do not know of one leading American handbook that does not deal with antitrust enforcement in its historical and philosophical perspectives. The historical background is furthermore, important when viewed against the background of a possible comparative study of the antitrust laws of other nations. Thus, we find that authors who compare the American antitrust laws with those of other countries are quick to point out that there are historical and historic-economic differences.[21]

(2) The remedial and procedural aspects

Following the portrayal of the historical and the philosophical foundations of the American antitrust laws we propose to subsequently, direct our attention to the remedial and procedural aspects thereof. Our main reason for doing so is that while it is commonly known in the civil law countries that the common law countries are characterized by the case law system, it is not always understood how the cases are used for understanding the law. It is standard practice in American legal education to study the cases by looking for an answer to the question: who is sueing whom for what? The question purports to force the respondent to identify the relationships in which the plaintiff and the defendant are pitched against each other, as well as the remedy which the plaintiff asks the court to grant.
Failure to approach the common law system from the vantage point of the remedies asked for is tantamount to failure to understand the common law system.[22]
A discussion of the remedial and other procedural aspects of antitrust enforcement will first, show which remedies are available and second, which agencies or institutions are empowered to instigate legal proceedings in case of violations of the antitrust laws.
Furthermore, it will reveal that the extraterritorial reach exists both with regard to the Government and the private litigant, because not only the Government, but also a private party, or even the Government-acting-as-a-private-party can litigate against American and foreign businessmen.
We propose to first, deal with the remedial and other procedural aspects of antitrust enforcement in general, and then, where possible, with regard to persons or conduct abroad.

(3) The special character of the antitrust laws

Because the antitrust laws are an amalgam of private law, criminal law, and

21. *cf.* SCHWARTZ, I. E., *op. cit.*, p. 2, for the comparison with the German laws: SILBIGER, T., 'Dutch Antitrust Laws – Some Developments and Comparisons', 1 *Am. Bus. Law Journal* 35, 36 (1963), for the comparison with the Dutch laws; KANAZAWA, Y., 'The Regulation Of Corporate Enterprise: The Law Of Unfair Competition And The Control Of Monopoly Power', in VON MEHREN, A. T., LAW IN JAPAN, Cambridge, 1963, pp. 480, *seq.*, for the comparison with the Japanese laws.
22. *cf.* MAITLAND, F. W., FORMS OF ACTION AT COMMON LAW, Cambridge, 1962, p. 78: 'This dependence of right upon remedy it is that has given English law that close texture to which it owes its continuous existence despite the temptations of Romanism.' A further substantiation might be found in the way the law of contracts is taught in many American Law Schools: by way of studying the available remedies in case of breach of promise.

administrative law, each with different jurisdictional problems, we propose to show that they should be considered as a separate area of the law. We feel encouraged in our thinking because of the similarity of opinion expressed elsewhere.[23]

It seems evident that our suggestion will have a definite impact on the general theme of our study, the extraterritorial reach of the antitrust laws. Recognition of these laws as a separate area of the law would also introduce the notion that attention ought to be given (as we propose to do) to the creation of a special antitrust judiciary, both at the national and the supra-national level.

(4) The jurisdictional aspects

The jurisdictional aspects of antitrust enforcement will be dealt with respectively, from the legislative jurisdictional competency and the judicial jurisdictional competency angles (including the quasi-judicial jurisdictional competency), with special emphasis on persons or conduct abroad. We suggest that recognition of the antitrust laws as a special area of the law will give the jurisdictional aspects special relevance when the extraterritorial reach of the antitrust laws is considered.

(5) The extraterritorial reach

Only after the various aspects of the American antitrust laws (i.e., in terms of history, philosophy, remedies, procedure, special character, and jurisdiction) have been reviewed will a discussion of the extraterritorial reach thereof be appropriate and beneficial. We trust that by that time we shall have laid sufficient a foundation to suggest that while the extraterritorial reach by necessity has aspects peculiar to the nature and the function of antitrust enforcement, still, these aspects must be in harmony with the general principles of the American domestic law as well as the generally recognized and accepted principles of international law. We shall in this connection have to determine whether the American legislative and judicial practices are justified when viewed against the background of the international community of nations. And even if our findings are that these practices are legally justified, we still will have to consider whether they are advisable in the light of the rapid increase in international trade and the concomitant interdependence of nations.

23. *cf.* REHBINDER, *op. cit.*, p. 57: 'Wie fast alles Wirtschaftsrecht läszt sich das Gesetz gegen Wettbewerbsbeschränkungen als ganzes weder dem Verwaltungsrecht, noch dem Privatrecht, noch dem Strafrecht zuordnen. Es enthält vielmehr Elemente aller drei Rechtsgebiete.' Also, see SCHWARTZ, I. E., *op. cit.*, p. 4, recognizing, '. . . dasz das Kartellrecht teils aus privatrechtlichen, teils aus verwaltungsrechtlichen und teils aus wirtschaftsstrafrechtlichen Normen besteht.'

(6) The limitiations

It seems appropriate to also point out which limitations we will impose upon the study which we propose to undertake. In general these limitations can be stated as follows:

(a) With regard to the American antitrust laws only the federal laws will be considered. It would go beyond reasonable expectations to include a discussion of the antitrust laws of the several States.

(b) With regard to the antitrust laws of other countries, only the American laws will be considered. Our reasons for this limitation are the following:

(1) In the first place, we do not intend to engage ourselves in a comparative study of the antitrust laws, not even of the extraterritorial reach thereof. There would be little reason to do so because a comparative study of the antitrust laws of some 17 countries has been made and published.[24]

(2) Second, tthe extraterritorial reach of antitrust enforcement – which is the topic of our study – has not reached that stage of development in other countries that a comparison on that point would yield valuable results. Even foreign authors themselves admit that much.[25]

The same observation could have been made with regard to antitrust enforcement in the European Economic Community up until the middle of 1969. On July 24, 1969, however, the Commission of the E.E.C. handed down its decree in the so-called *Aniline* case, which has extraterritorial aspects.[26] An appeal from the decree has been taken to the European Court of Justice. It is therefore, too early to predict whether the

24. *cf.* EDWARDS, C. D., CONTROL OF CARTELS AND MONOPOLIES – AN INTERNATIONAL COMPARISON, New York, 1967, comparing the American antitrust laws with those of Austria, Belgium, Denmark, Finland, France, Germany, Ireland, Israel, Japan, The Netherlands, New Zealand, Norway, Spain, Sweden, Switzerland, The United Kingdom, Union of South Africa.

25. *cf.* SCHWARTZ, I. E. *op. cit.*, p. 1: '. . . das internationale Kartellrecht [hat] bisher nur in den Vereinigten Staaten erhebliche praktische Bedeutung erlangt.' *Idem*, p. 2: 'Einbezogen werden vielmehr auch die Rechtsprechung der Vereinigten Staaten als der einzigen, die bisher über den internationalen Anwendungsbereich eines Kartellrechts existiert. . .' *Idem*, p. 14: '. . . gegenwärtig die Mehrzahl der Autoren eine Auffassung vertritt, die der amerikanischen Konzeption sehr nahe verwandt ist.' Also, see REHBINDER, *op. cit.*, pp. 34, 35: 'Schlieszlich wird in neuerer Zeit zunehmend auf das amerikanische Antitrustrecht verwiesen.'

26. PUBLIKATIEBLAD VAN DE EUROPESE GEMEENSCHAPPEN, Vol. 12, nr. L-195/11, August 7, 1969

views of the Commission will be upheld by the Court.[27] If they do, then, it seems that there is not too great a discrepancy between the law within the E.E.C. and the prevailing doctrine in the United States. Even so, we suggest that one case does not provide sufficient material for a valid comparison. The only conclusion we have arrived at is that the problems in the E.E.C. and in the United States seem to parallel each other, thus leading to similar judicial results.

Summary

Summarizing the preceding observations with regard to the study under consideration we should like to stress the following aspects as justification for this study:

(1) The American antitrust laws, because they reach out to persons and conduct outside the territorial boundaries of the United States, have an extraterritorial reach. However, the legality (i.e., according to both the domestic law of the United States and the generally recognized and accepted principles of international law) and the expediency (i.e., the wisdom in view of the interdependence of nations, the possibilities of retaliation, and the requirements of international commerce) will need further examination.

(2) The history and philosophy, as well as the remedial and other procedural aspects of antitrust enforcement, suggest that the antitrust laws should be considered as a separate area of the law, answerable to its own rules of substance and procedure, legislatively and judicially.

(3) In view of the special character of the antitrust laws as a separate area of the law, a codification of these laws into one comprehensive Antitrust Code will be a desirable if not necessary step. The continuation and possible proliferation of provisions in a number of Acts, such as the *Sherman Act*, the *Wilson Tariff Act*, the *Clayton Act*, the *Federal Trade Commission Act*, the *Robinson-Patman Act*, the *Celler-Kefauver Act*, the *Antitrust Civil Process Act*, is confusing and does not make for a systematic attack on what the antitrust laws purport to preserve and protect. Furthermore, codification of the hitherto separate provisions into one comprehensive Antitrust Code (similar to, e.g., the Uniform Commercial Code) would provide a systematic regulation of business practices and economic power.

(4) In addition to advantages at the national level resulting from a comprehensive Antitrust Code, some additional advantages could be obtained. We mention the following:

27. At the time of this writing no decision by the Court was published; however a decision has been announced to be forthcoming shortly.

(a) Such a Code might serve as an inspiration to similar legislative efforts in other countries;

(b) The emerging of a number of national Antitrust Codes might lead to a special regulation of the extraterritorial aspects of antitrust enforcement in an internationally accepted Uniform Code of Antitrust Enforcement Involving Transnational Business Practices and Relations. This is less remote a possibility than might appear, because of the efforts to arrive at a harmonization of antitrust laws at the international level, as evidenced by the fact that this aspect of antitrust enforcement has become a topic of active interest among scholars and practitioners.[28]

(5) The recognition of antitrust enforcement as a separate area of the law could furthermore, lead to the creation of a special judiciary for antitrust matters, capable of expertly dealing with the special exigencies of modern domestic and transnational business practices.

(6) The creation of a special judiciary for antitrust matters in the various countries could in turn, lead to the establishment of a supra-national Court for Antitrust Matters, to which decisions of national antitrust courts could be submitted for review. It follows that the establishment of such an international tribunal, to be meaningful and relevant, implies that not only the decisions of the national courts of the member nations, but also the national laws themselves will be subject to scrutiny against the background of generally recognized and accepted principles of international antitrust law; this means that the member nations would have to recognize the supremacy of this supra-national tribunal in matters of antitrust enforcement in the international community of nations.

28. *cf.* OLIVER, C., 'The Harmonization of Laws and the Development of Principles for the Resolution of Conflicts of Enforcement Jurisdiction as to Transnational Monopolistic and Restrictive Trade Practices', in REPORT OF THE FIFTY-FIRST CONFERENCE OF THE INTERNATIONAL LAW ASSOCIATION HELD AT TOKYO, 1964, London, 1965, pp. 544, *seq.* (hereinafter to be referred to as *1964 Tokyo Proceedings*)

CHAPTER I

HISTORICAL AND PHILOSOPHICAL SOURCES OF THE AMERICAN ANTITRUST LAWS

The Historical Sources

While government concern with monopolistic behavior has a respectable history, going back to the *Codex Iustiniani,*[1] we feel justified in viewing the historical development of the American antitrust laws only as it evolved through the English common law courts down to the present-day situation. In so doing we can divide this historical evolution into four periods:

(1) The period beginning with the Anglo-Saxon Common Law of the Middle Ages, which is part of the American legal heritage, through the years of American Independence down to the *Sherman Act* of 1890;[2]

(2) The period beginning with the *Sherman Act* of 1890 down to the *Report of the Attorney General's National Committee to Study the Antitrust Laws* of 1955;

(3) The *Report of the Attorney General's National Committee to Study the Antitrust Laws*, March 31, 1955;

(4) The period after 1955.

The Early Period

In order to obtain a proper perspective of the American antitrust laws it seems to us of paramount importance to trace the development thereof by way of a review of the older judicial decisions dealing with the subject. This method will show us that the *Sherman Act* of 1890 was not the result of a spur-of-the-moment action but rather, the result of a centuries old gradual development, even though the rapid industrialization of the United States, following the Civil War (1861-1865), and the concomitant emergence of the large industrial enterprise was an important contributing factor leading to the enactment of antitrust legislation.[3]

1. *cf.* MULDER, A., & MOK, M. R., KARTELRECHT, Alphen a/d Rijn, 1962, p. 5.
2. MULDER & MOK, *op. cit.*, p. 6, refer to this act as 'the first real, modern antitrust law.' However, see FORTAS, A., 'American Antitrust,' 45 *Progress, The Magazine of Unilever* 244 (1957) who states that the act 'was copied from the English Statute of Monopolies (1623).'
3. *cf.* THORELLI, H. B., THE FEDERAL ANTITRUST POLICY – ORIGINATION OF AN AMERICAN TRADITION, Baltimore, 1955, pp. 564, *seq.*: 'Antitrust did not become institutionalized overnight. Neither was the Sherman Act itself the result of a momentary flurry of public opinion and legislative activity. Some of its roots – all closely intertwined – may be traced back several centuries, while others became more clearly distinguishable after the Civil War.'

In turning to the early cases we will find that these cases deal with the right to compete. It is important to keep this aspect of the legal heritage in mind, because it has been repeatedly stated that the antitrust laws are aimed at the preservation of the competitive system.[4]

As one of the early cases dealing with the right to compete we find an anonymous case of 1410, the *Schoolmaster Case.*[5]

> Two masters of a grammar school at Gloucester brought a writ of trespass against another master, and counted that the defendant had started a school in the same town, so that whereas the plaintiffs had formerly received 40*d.* or two shillings a quarter from each child, now they got only 12*d.* to their damage, etc.

The fact that the action is for trespass, makes the action one sounding in tort. That means that there must be a wrongful act, causing damage. Damage, if not caused by a wrongful act, would be *damnum absque iniuria*, and the result would be that the case would be dismissed.

The question, therefore, before the court was whether the starting of a second school was a wrongful act.

In his opinion, Judge Hankford stated that 'the instruction of children is a spiritual matter; and if one retains a master in his house to teach his children, it is a damage to the common master of the town, yet, I think, he will have no action.'

Judge Hill concurred with this opinion, and stated: 'The plaintiffs have no estate, but a ministry for the time; and though another equally competent with the plaintiffs comes to teach the children, this is a virtuous and charitable thing, and an ease to the people, for which he cannot be punished by our law.'

If we analyze the case, we find that there are apparently situations in which an action alleging trespass would be successful. That would be if the plaintiff had 'a freehold and inheritance in the market.' But inasmuch as this condition does not present itself in the case at bar and because the public interest, in the opinion of the court, is not hindered by the opening of a second school, the right to compete is recognized. In other words, it is clear that competition leads, somehow, to restraint of somebody else's trade. Restraint of trade, in turn, may lead to an action for trespass, but only if the restraint is unlawful (*quod non* in the case at bar). We may summarize the rule of the case as follows: competition

4. *cf. Report of the Attorney General's National Committee to Study the Antitrust Laws,* Washington, 1955, p. 1: 'The general objective of the antitrust laws is promotion of competition in open markets.' (We will hereafter refer to this publication as *Att'y. Gen. Report.*)

5. Court of Common Pleas, Hilary Term, 1410. Y. B., 11 Hen. IV, f. 47, pl. 21. The case is quoted from HANDLER, M., CASES AND MATERIALS ON TRADE REGULATION, 4th ed., Brooklyn, 1967, p. 143. For a different, more incisive historical evaluation, see LETWIN, W. L., 'The English Common Law Concerning Monopolies,' 21 *University of Chicago Law Review* 355 (1954).

is not wrongful *per se*; it can become unlawful if some additional element makes it so.

From this rule we may abstract the principle, by an *argumentum e silentio*, that *unlawful restraint of trade will lead to a cause of action.*

The second case we should like to mention in our historical survey is an anonymous one of 1415, the so-called *Dyer's Case.*[6] In this case one person had bound himself to another person to refrain from practicing his art of a dyer's craft in the town of Dale, for a period of six months.

When the plaintiff claimed a violation of the promise, and sued on the bond, the following remark was made from the bench: '. . . the obligation is void because the condition is against the common law, and *per Dieu*, if the plaintiff were here, he should go to prison till he paid a fine to the King.' The conclusion that can be drawn from this case is that it would be against the Common Law to prevent another person to practice his trade, even if that other person has made a contract to that effect.

The next case, cited in this sequence is a case of 1602, the so-called *Case of Monopolies*, also referred to as *Darcy v. Allein:*[7]

> A royal patent granted Bowes the power to buy playing cards overseas, import them and sell them; also, Bowes had the exclusive right to manufacture playing cards within the realm. This exclusive right was originally granted for a period of twelve years, later extended for another period of 21 years. Darcy claimed exclusive rights under the patent, based on an arrangement between him and Bowes. Allein, a member of the Society of Haberdashers of London, in alleged violation of this exclusive right, made and sold cards for *20s.* per gross, while Darcy sold them for *35s.* per gross.

In the arguments we find references to both the *Schoolmaster Case* (to the effect that as long as no wrong was done, incurring losses would not lead to a cause of action), and to the *Dyer's Case* (where restraining a person not to use his trade in the town of Dale for half a year was a void condition, the argument being that restraining men from using their trade for a period of 21 years, throughout the whole realm, certainly would be void).

Indeed, Chief Justice Popham, speaking for the entire Bench, stated that the grant to the plaintiff of the sole making of cards within the realm was utterly void, because:

(a) this was a monopoly and against the common law, for the following reasons:

6. Y. B., 2 Hen. V. vol. 5, pl. 26, 1415. The case is quoted from HANDLER, *op. cit.*, p. 142.
7. Court of King's Bench, 11 Coke 84, 77 Eng. Rep. 1260, 1602. The case is quoted from HANDLER, *op. cit.*, p. 846. Also, see SCHWARTZ, L. B., FREE ENTERPRISE AND ECONOMIC ORGANIZATION, 3rd ed., Brooklyn, 1966, p. 33; OPPENHEIM, S. C., & WESTON, G. E., FEDERAL ANTITRUST LAWS, 3rd ed., St. Paul, 1968, p. 645, referring to additional literature on the subject.

1) all trades which prevent idleness and keep men in labour are profitable to the commonwealth; the exclusive grant to the plaintiff is therefore against the common law and the benefit and liberty of the subject;
2) any monopoly is both a damage to others in the same trade, as well as to other members of the community, because of the danger that it will lead to:
   a) a raise in price;
   b) a deterioration of the quality;
   c) an impoverishment of the working classes, who previously by their labour had maintained themselves and their families, and who now of necessity would be forced to live in idleness and beggary;
3) the Queen was deceived in her grant;
4) never before had such a grant been awarded by letters patent, and therefore it was a dangerous innovation;

(b) it was against several acts of Parliament for the advancement of the freedom of trade and traffic.

The *Case of Monopolies* was followed, in 1610, by a royal decree, declaring 'all monopolies contrary to the laws of the realm.'[8]

Nevertheless, many grants and monopolies were obtained in the years after 1610. To counter the practice of granting monopolies notwithstanding the royal decree of 1610, Parliament enacted in 1623 the *Statute of Monopolies.*[9]

The major provisions of this Statute were:

1. All monopolies and all commissions, grants, licenses, charters and letters patent . . . are contrary to the laws of the realm, and therefore utterly void.
2. All monopolies ought to be examined, heard, and determined by and according to the common laws of the realm.
3. Violations causing damage to any person or persons will lead to an action for treble damages.
4. Exceptions are recognized for:
   (a) letters of patent and grants of privilege during fourteen years (or less) for new manufacturing processes or inventions for new manufacturing processes, as long as they are not contrary to the public interest;
   (b) the city of London, or other incorporated cities, for grants or licenses for or concerning customs used by them;
   (c) corporations or associations of craftsmen or merchants erected for

8. Reference to this royal decree of 1610 can be found in the preamble of the *Statute of Monopolies, infra*, n. 9; *cf.* SCHWARTZ, L. B., *op. cit.*, p. 32.
9. 21 Jac. I, c. 3, 1623. For the text of the *Statute of Monopolies, cf.* HANDLER, *op. cit.*, 848, or SCHWARTZ, L. B., *op. cit.*, p. 32 (condensed versions).

the maintenance, enlargement, or ordering of any trade or merchandise;

(d) letters of patent or grants of privelege concerning printing, the digging, making or compounding of saltpeter or gunpowder, or the making of ordnance or shot;

(e) letters of patent or commissions for the keeping of any tavern or selling of wines to be drunk in the mansion house or other place in the tenure or occupation of the party so selling.

A comparison with our present-day antitrust laws will show an interesting similarity.[10]

The next case that needs careful attention is one decided by the Court of King's Bench in 1711, the case of *Mitchell* v. *Reynolds.*[11]

The case is important for several reasons:

(a) it establishes the so-called 'rule of reason': restraints limited either to a certain time, or to a certain geographical area are to be analyzed and adjudged in accordance with the reasonableness of the restraint;

(b) a judicial analysis of previous cases, leading to the one at bar, is given in a comprehensive manner.

Reynolds, a baker, had sold his business to Mitchell. In addition, he assigned his five-years lease of the building to Mitchell, and promised not to compete with the latter in the parish of St. Andrews Holborn during those five years. As security, Reynolds gave Mitchell a bond of 50 pounds. When Reynolds breached his promise, Mitchell sued on the bond. Reynolds defended with the argument that he was a baker by trade and the obligation, therefore, void in law.

The court occupied itself with the question: Is a bond given in restraint of trade a valid obligation?

In their attempts to arrive at a satisfactory solution, the judges of the Court of King's Bench found the case 'very troublesome' because of the 'seeming disagreements of the resolution of the books.' They found that in every case, beginning

10. The importance of a historical approach even to a study of the extraterritorial reach of the antitrust laws may be demonstrated by a recent article in which the author intimates that the treble damage action is one of the modern tools with which the American antitrust enforcement agencies threaten the European entrepreneurs; *cf.* GLEISS, A., 'Die Gefahren des US-Antitrustrechts für europäische Unternehmen," XV/12 *Auszenwirtschaftsdienst des Betriebs-Beraters* 499 (1969). Without engaging in a detailed discussion of the article (we consider the incisive and penetrating studies by SCHWARTZ, I. E., and REHBINDER more relevant), we should like to state that the treble damage action is not a recent invention of antitrust enforcement, but was one of the remedies provided for in the (British) *Statute of Monopolies* of 1623. (One would almost answer the final query of the author, 'Is this fairyland or the courthouse?' with the statement: 'Neither, Sir, it is history, based on "gesundenes Volksempfinden".')

11. I. P. Williams 181, 24 Eng. Rep. 347, 1711. The case here discussed is quoted from HANDLER, *op. cit.*, p. 144. Also, see SCHWARTZ, L. B., *op. cit.*, p. 33; OPPENHEIM & WESTON, *op. cit.*, p. 5.

with the *Dyer's Case* of 1415, up through the *Case of the Taylors of Exeter*, of 1585, there had been a question of some restraint of trade. Yet, in some of the cases the bond given in restraint was held to be invalid, while in other cases the court upheld the obligation. In addition to the *Dyer's Case*, the following cases were reviewed and analyzed by the court:[12]

1. *Anonymous Case of 1578*[13]
   An apprentice had covenanted not to employ the craft of a mercer in the city of Nottingham for a period of four years. The covenant was held invalid.
2. *The Blacksmith's Case of 1587*[14]
   A blacksmith had promised another blacksmith not to exercise his craft in the same town, therefore giving a bond as security. The bond was declared illegal.
3. *Colgate v. Bacheler*[15]
   Bacheler had covenanted not to engage in the trade of haberdasher, for a period of four years, within the county of Kent or the cities of Canterbury or Rochester. The covenant was secured by a bond.
   The obligation was held void (Reasoning: 'This condition is against law, to prohibit or restrain any to use of a lawful trade at any time or at any place; for as well as longer time and more places, which is against the benefit of the commonwealth.')
4. *Rogers v. Parrey*[16]
   Parrey had promised not to exercise the trade of carpenter in a shop conveyed to him by Rogers, for a period of twenty-one years; in return for this promise Rogers had paid Parrey a sum of money.
   The agreement was upheld by the court, thereby drawing a distinction between a general restraint and one restricted 'for a time certain and in a place certain.'
5. *Broad v. Jollyfe*[17]
   Jollyfe sold his stock of textile goods; part of the sale price was allegedly in return for Jollyfe's promise not to keep a mercer's shop in Newport.
   The court upheld the agreement because:
   a) the promise was voluntary;
   b) the promise was supported by a valuable consideration;
   c) the restriction was limited to a particular place.

12. These cases can be found in HANDLER, *op. cit.*, p. 145, who refers for more detailed analysis to OLIPHANT, H., CASES ON TRADE REGULATION, St. Paul, 1923, pp. 34-42.
13. Moore 115, 72 Eng. Rep. 477, 1578.
14. 3 Leo. 217, 74 Eng. Rep. 643, 1587.
15. Cro. Eliz. 872, 78 Eng. Rep. 1097, 1596.
16. 2 Bulst. 136, 80 Eng. Rep. 1012, 1613.
17. Cro. Jac. 596, 79 Eng. Rep. 509, 1620.

6. *Prugnell v. Gosse*[18]

Mrs. Gosse had promised Prugnell that if the latter would marry her daughter, she would:

a) pay him a sum of money;
b) assign her shop to him;
c) not engage in the same trade in the town of Basingtooke.

The agreement between mother-in-law and son-in-law was upheld by the court, because:

a) the restraint was limited to a particular place;
b) the agreement in restraint of trade was supported by consideration.

To avoid misunderstanding, the court noted that a general restraint, even if supported by consideration, would be bad.

7. *Clerk v. Governor & Company of Taylors of Exeter*[19]

A covenant, secured by a bond, stipulated that Clerk would not use his trade of tailor in the town of Exeter. When the plaintiffs sued on the bond, Clerk defended with the argument that he had been vexed by the association and that he had signed the bond to avoid this vexation. On the other hand, the association argued that the obligation was valid because it was limited to a particular place.

The court held the obligation void, because it considered the bond a penal one, thereby making the following distinction.

a) assumpsits on promises for good consideration not to engage in a trade in a particular locality are enforceable;
b) yet, in some of the cases the court upheld the obligation, while in other instances the court denied recovery.

In arriving at its decision in the principal case, *Mitchell* v. *Reynolds* [20] the court proceeded to an analysis of the 'jarring opinions' on the question wether a bond given in restraint of trade constituted a valid obligation. In the *Dyer's Case,* the *Anonymous* (mercer's) *Case*, the *Blacksmith's Case,* the *Colgate* v. *Bacheler* (haberdasher) *Case*, and the *Clerk* v. *Governor & Company of Taylors Exeter* (tailor's) *Case*, the promise not to engage in the particular trade was held void. But in the *Rogers* v. *Parrey* (carpenter) *Case*, the *Broad* v. *Jollyfe* (textile merchant) *Case*, the *Prugnell* v. *Gosse* (mother-in-law) *Case*, the court upheld the obligation. Upon further analysis, the Court of King's Bench found that the former category all consisted of involuntary contracts, while the latter consisted of voluntary restraints by agreement of the parties.

Having made this distinction, the court stated:

a) involuntary restraints lack the prerequisite of mutual assent, and, therefore, do not qualify as valid obligations.

18. Aleyn 67, 82 Eng. Rep. 919, 1648.
19. 3 Lev. 241, 83 Eng. Rep. 670, 1685.
20. *supra*, p. 18, n. 11.

b) voluntary restraints seemingly satisfy the prerequisite of mutual assent. However, these voluntary restraints can be subdivided into two groups:
   1) general restraints, or unlimited restraints: these are void;
   2) particular restraints, or limited (either in time or place) restraints; these can be, again, subdivided into:
      a) particular restraints without consideration: these agreements are void;
      b) particular restraints upon a good and valuable consideration: these can be held valid, provided the agreement is reasonable in terms of time, place, and the interest to be protected.

In other words: to hold an agreement binding, the court has to be satisfied that the agreement is:

(a) supported by a good and valuable consideration;
(b) that the restraint is reasonable with regard to time, place and the interest to be protected. The degree of needed protection can be determined, either from the vantage point of the parties involved, or from that of the community as a whole.

For instance, in the case at issue the agreement between bakers Mitchell and Reynolds may enable the seller, presumably 'an old man,' to receive more money for his shop so that upon retirement he can 'procure to himself a livelihood, which he might probably have lost' (i.e., protection in the interest of the parties), or the agreement may be 'useful and beneficial as to prevent a town being overstocked' (i.e., protection of the community in terms of livelihood for its members). Applying this line of reasoning to the case at hand, the court found the restraint reasonable and ruled in favor of Mitchell.

With the above case we find the introduction of the *rule of reason* in cases of restraint of trade.

The adherence to this *rule of reason* is well expressed in the opinion of Lord MacNaghten in *Nordenfelt* v. *Maxim Nordenfelt Guns and Ammunition Co.*:[21]

> A corporation was organized to acquire the business and patents of Thorsten Nordenfelt, inventor of various improvements in arms and ammunition. Thorsten was paid the equivalent of well over a million dollars and was given a five year contract as managing director of the company. He agreed that he would not, during the term of twenty-five years from the date of the incorporation of the company, engage except on behalf of the company either directly or indirectly in manufacturing guns or ammunition or in any business competing or liable to compete in any way with that of the company.
>
> The company was then amalgamated with another munitions firm, the Maxim Nordenfelt Guns and Ammunition Co. When Nordenfelt's connec-

21. A.C. 535, 1894. The case is cited in HANDLER, *op. cit.*, p. 147; SCHWARTZ, L. B., *op. cit.*, p. 35; OPPENHEIM & WESTON, *op. cit.*, p. 4.

tion with that company terminated, the British courts enjoined him from reentering the munitions business, even abroad.

In upholding the world-wide scope of the restrictive covenant (notwithstanding the reasoning of the court in *Mitchell* v *Reynolds*, to the effect that general restraints were bad), Lord MacNaghten stated:

> '...The public have an interest in every person's carrying on his trade freely: so has the individual... That is the general rule. But there are exceptions: restraints of trade and interference with individual liberty of action may be justified by the special circumstances of a particular case.'

SCHWARTZ, L. B., in his analysis of the case, states that the opinions of the judges reveal a responsiveness to British imperial policy not 'to encourage unfettered competition in the sale of arms of precision to tribes who may become her antagonists in warfare.'[22]

So much for the historical development at common law, which we consider the first phase. The reason why we need to know of this development is that, 'The common law of England has (thus) always been the common law of the colonies and states of North America . . .'[23]

The Period After 1890

After 1890, antitrust enforcement in the United States had a development peculiarly its own. We therefore, now turn to the second phase of the historical development of the American antitrust laws, to wit, the development on the American continent. This phase commences with the *Sherman Act* of 1890 and terminates with the *Report of the Attorney General's National Committee to Study the Antitrust Laws* of 1955.

In 1890 the United States Congress enacted an 'Act to Protect Trade and Commerce Against Unlawful Restraints and Monopolies,' the so-called *Sherman Act.*[24]

From the wording of the *Sherman Act*, quoted in our introductory chapter, we may, by way of paraphrasing state, that sec. 1 reads, in a much simplified version: *every contract, combination, or conspiracy, in restraint of trade or commerce, is illegal.* As we have indicated in the first part of this chapter, the common law considered illegal only those contracts in restraint of trade where the restraint was unreasonable.

The language of the *Sherman Act* declares *every* contract in restraint of trade

22. *op. cit.*, p. 36.
23. *Ohio* v. *Lafferty*, Tappan (Ohio) 113 (1817)
24. Act of July 2, 1890, as amended by the Act of August 17, 1937, and the Act of July 7, 1955. 'It was called the Sherman Act for no better reason, according to its draftsman, than that Senator Sherman had nothing whatever to do with it."; *cf.* FORTAS, *l.c.*, p. 244.

illegal. The question which resulted from the text of the *Sherman Act*, was whether the wording of the new Act should be taken literally, or whether the interpretation should follow the by-then-accepted common law concept (i.e., that only contracts which *according to the common law* were in unreasonable restraint of trade should be considered illegal).

In 1897, the question came to a head in the *Trans-Missouri Case:*[25]

> Eighteen freight carriers had formed an association for the purpose of regulating the prices charged for freight traffic to and from the West Coast. The defendants claimed that the major point of determination should be whether the combination acted in unreasonable restraint of trade or commerce.

In a 5-4 split decision, the majority of the United States Supreme Court rejected the view that the language of the *Sherman Act* should be construed in the light of what was considered the law of the land at the time; in other words, the majority of the Court refused to interpret the *Sherman Act* as being declaratory of the Common Law, by stating:

> 'When, therefore, the body of an act pronounces as illegal every contract or combination in restraint of trade or commerce among the several States, etc., the plain and ordinary meaning of such language is not limited to that kind of contract alone which is in unreasonable restraint of trade, but all contracts are included in such language, and no exception or limitation can be added without placing in the act that which has been omitted by Congress.'

The dissenting opinion, written by Mr. Justice White, claimed that the Court should consider 'The spirit which vivifies, and not the letter which killeth,' by stating:

> 'It is, I submit, not to be doubted that the interpretation of the words "every contract in restraint of trade," so as to embrace within its purview every contract, however reasonable, would certainly work an enormous injustice and operate to the undue restraint of the liberties of the citizen. But there is no canon of interpretation which requires that the letter be followed, when by so doing an unreasonable result is accomplished.'

A year later, Judge Taft, of the Sixth Circuit of the United States Court of Appeals, stated rather tersely:

> 'The contention on behalf of the defendants is that the association would have been valid at common law, and that the federal antitrust law was not intended to reach any agreements that were not void and unenforceable at common law. It might be a sufficient answer to this contention to point to the decision of the Supreme Court of the United States in *United States* v. *Trans-Missouri Freight Ass'n*, 166 *U.S.* 290, 17 *Sup. Ct.* 540, in which it

25. *United States* v. *Trans-Missouri Freight Association*, 166 US 290, 17 S Ct 540 (1897).

> was held that contracts in restraint of interstate transportation were within the statute, whether the restraints would be regarded as reasonable at common law or not.'[26]

It was not until 1911 that the United States Supreme Court retreated from the view as expressed in the *Trans-Missouri* case, in an opinion written by Mr. Chief Justice White, who had led the dissenters in that case.[27]

After having suggested that one should interpret the language of the Act 'guided by the principle that where words are employed in a statute which had at the time a well-known meaning at common law or in the law of this country they are presumed to have been used in that sense unless the context compels to the contrary,' the opinion states,

> 'That the context manifests that the statute was drawn in the light of the existing practical conception of the law of restraint of trade . . .'

With this case, the United States Supreme Court adopted the 'rule of reason' in the adjudication of cases in restraint of trade.

This view was upheld in another case of the same year, where we find in the opinion of the Court the following statement:

> 'Applying the rule of reason to the construction of the statute, it was held in the *Standard Oil Case* that as the words "restraint of trade" at common law and in the law of this country at the time of the adoption of the antitrust act only embraced acts or contracts or agreements or combinations which operated to the prejudice of the public interests by unduly restricting competition or unduly obstructing the due course of trade or which either because of their inherent nature or effect or because of the evident purpose of the acts, etc., injuriously restrained trade, that the words as used in the statute were designed to have and did have but a like significance.'[28]

Based on the authority of both the *Standard Oil* case and the *American Tobacco* case, one can state that the *Sherman Act* should be viewed in the light of the preceding history.

However, it soon became clear that the Act left other aspects of government regulation of business open to divergent views. In fact, the language of the Act 'gave rise to a variety of judicial interpretations, and many critics argued that it created more problems than it solved . . .'[29]

26. *U.S.* v. *Addyston Pipe & Steel Co.*, 85 F. 271 (1898); aff'd. 175 US 211, 20 S Ct 96 (1899).
27. *Standard Oil Co. of New Jersey* v. *United States*, 221 US 1, 31 S Ct 502 (1911). For a comprehensive analysis of the case, 'in the light of modern developments, rather than old debates,' see *Att'y Gen. Report*, pp. 5, *seq.*
28. *U.S.* v. *American Tobacco Co.*, 221 US 106, 31 S Ct 632 (1911)
29. HOUGHTELING, J. L. & PIERCE, G. G., THE LEGAL ENVIRONMENT OF BUSINESS, New York, 1963, p. 810

For instance, contracts or combinations[30] that could not be proven to be in restraint of trade but still, would have a potential effect to injure, destroy, or prevent competition were not covered by the *Sherman Act.* Thus, it would be possible for a single person to acquire so much stock of a corporation that this would in fact create a controlling force in that corporation. But if a person could acquire such power, then, what about a corporation doing the same thing? Would that purchase of stock control come within the reach of the Sherman Act? If not, then, through the device of having a holding company purchase stock control over a corporation one could evade the reach of the *Sherman Act.* In 1904 the U.S. Supreme Court split five to four on this issue.[31] Mr. Justice HARLAN, writing for the Court, held that the ownership of stock by a holding company in competing interstate carriers fell within the reach of the Act. But mr. Justice HOLMES in his dissenting opinion argued differently.[32]

One could state that the *Sherman Act* attacked specific transactions when the deleterious effects upon competition could be proved. But this left open those practices where such effects could not be proved, yet where the practical result would be a potential stifling of competition.[33]

In order to cope with the problem of the 'incipient' restraint of trade practices (i.e., where the effect *may be* a lessening of competition) Congress, in 1914, enacted the *Clayton Act.*[34]

Further curbing of practices which were considered undesirable and which the *Sherman Act* or the *Clayton Act* did not satisfactorily curtail lead to subsequent legislative action. Thus, to effectively deal with such practices as discriminatory pricing, Congress, in 1936, enacted the *Robinson-Patman Act.*[35]

Furthermore, in order to entrust the administration of the antitrust laws to an effective governmental agency Congress, in 1914, established the Federal Trade Commission.[36] This agency was empowered to interpret and enforce the provisions of the various antitrust laws, such as the *Clayton Act*, the *Robinson-Patman Act*, the *Unfair Trade Practices Act* (jurisdiction over the *Sherman Act* remained exclusively with the federal judiciary).

In fact, the period between 1890 and 1962 is characterized by a great number

30. At common law, the distinction is that 'contracts' would apply to arrangements which restrain the trade of the contracting parties, while 'combinations' would apply to arrangements which restrain the trade of other people.
31. *Northern Securities Co.* v. *United States,* 193 US 197, 24 S Ct 436 (1904)
32. For a synopsis of this case, see SCHWARTZ, L. B., *op. cit.*, pp. 105, *seq.* The common law distinction between 'contracts' and 'combinations' can be found there, because it was one of the arguments advanced by Mr. Justice HOLMES.
33. *cf.* OPPENHEIM & WESTON, *op. cit.*, p. 21
34. Act of October 15, 1914. For some of the provisions of the Act, see INTRODUCTION, *supra*, pp. 3.
35. Act of June 19, 1936; the provisions of this Act became sec. 2 of the *Clayton Act.*
36. Act of September 26, 1914.

and variety of enactments dealing with aspects of antitrust enforcement.[37]

In addition to these enactments the courts continued to refine their views of practices and agreements in restraint of trade. It would go far beyond the scope of our historical review to either elaborate on the substantive provisions of the separate Acts or of the various court decisions which were handed down during this period. The existing handbooks supply ample reading material with respect thereto. Only those statutory provisions and judicial and quasi-judicial decisions that have a direct bearing on our topic will be discussed, albeit separately, at a later time.

Suffice it to state that an apparent continuous governmental and judicial concern with effective antitrust enforcement can be observed in the years following 1890. The extent of this governmental concern can best be summarized by stating that by 1955 practically every field of economic activity had been brought within the reach of antitrust enforcement.

In the meantime the desirability of a thorough study of the antitrust laws had become manifest. In 1953, in an address before the United States Court of Appeals for the Fourth Circuit the Attorney General of the United States, H. BROWNELL, Jr., announced his intention 'to establish a National Committee to Study the Antitrust Laws.'[38] After nineteen months of meetings the final draft of the Committee's study was printed and transmitted to the Attorney General, on March 31, 1955.[39]

The Period After 1955

It seems natural to consider the period following the publication of the Report as the third phase in the development of the American antitrust laws. This statement appears to be particularly valid with regard to the present study, dealing with the extraterritorial reach of the American antitrust laws, in view of the opinion expressed in the Report, that there might be a need to coordinate the governmental policies 'touching on the foreign trade and national security programs of the United States' with the antitrust provisions, 'in order to avoid or minimize any policy conflict.'[40]

37. For a comprehensive chart of the federal antitrust laws, see OPPENHEIM & WESTON, *op. cit.*, pp. 903, *seq.* (Appendices A – E). We mention specifically: The *Sherman Act* of 1890; the *Wilson Tariff Act* of 1894; the *Federal Trade Commission Act* of 1914; the *Clayton Act* of 1914; the *Shipping Act* of 1915; the *Webb-Pomerene Act* of 1918; the *Capper-Volstead Act* of 1922; the *Norris-LaGuardia Act* of 1932; the *Robinson-Patman Act* of 1936; the *Miller-Tydings Act* of 1937; the *Wheeler-Lea Act* of 1938; the *Lanham Act* of 1946; the *Celler-Kefauver Anti-merger Act* of 1950; the *McGuire Act* of 1952; the *Celler-Kefauver Act* of 1955; the *Antitrust Civil Process Act* of 1962.
38. *cf. Att'y Gen. Report*, p. IV
39. *ibid.*, p. VI.
40. *ibid.*, p. 66.

Although the Report expresses itself against 'any proposal for blanket exemption of foreign commerce from the antitrust laws,' it considers it opportune to establish 'procedures for coordinating antitrust with related government policies.'[41]

There is another reason to consider the period commencing with the Attorney General's Report as a new phase in the historical development of the antitrust laws. Substantiation of this assertion may be found in the words of the President of the United States, conveying his hope that as a result of the study to be undertaken the group would 'provide an important instrument to prepare the way for modernizing and strengthening our laws to preserve American free enterprise against monopoly and unfair competition.'[42]

In its Report, the Committee viewed the assignment in a way which can best be summarized by a quotation from the Report:

> '. . . a backward look across the 64 years since the Sherman Act reveals on the whole a healthy process of growth through which antitrust fundamentals have gained in strenght and effectiveness . . . A large body of antitrust doctrine has thus developed. A principal task of the Committee is to analyze the main course of this antitrust policy, its interpretations and decisions. From this analysis, an evaluation of antitrust developments is made in light of established antitrust goals. On this evaluation the Committee bases its conclusions and recommendations as future guides to enforcement agencies, Congress, and the courts . . .'[43]
>
> '. . .this Committee's primary task is to mark out as clearly as possible the path antitrust has traveled and what it augurs for the future . . . Our hope is that from such clarification will emerge more practical guides for business seeking to comply with the antitrust laws and for Government officials charged with enforcing their prohibitions.'[44]

The Report is interesting, furthermore, because we find in it a conscious effort to blend legal and economic concepts. For instance, we find reference to the fact that the existence of monopoly power has to be determined by the power in the relevant market. This observation is followed by the words:

> 'Although the word "market" does not appear in the statute, it is a necessary element of the concepts of monopoly and of certain restraints of trade upon which the statute rests.'[45]

The necessity to blend law and economics is, furthermore, demonstrated by the statement that 'actual or probably market consequences must be determined as part of the test of their legality. Such determination, in turn, involves resort to economic analysis.'[46]

41. *ibid.*, p. 66.
42. *ibid.*, p. IV.
43. *ibid.*, p. 3.
44. *ibid.*, p. 4.
45. *ibid.*, p. 44.
46. *ibid.*, p. 315.

At the same time, the Report emphasizes the difficulty of effectively blending law and economics, by stating:

> 'An important difficulty in making economics of aid to the antitrust law is nomenclature. This confusion has occurred largely because both law and economics have borrowed so much of their respective vocabularies from common speech before making of them works of art. Words like "monopoly", "competition", "discrimination", etc. are used in economics which may have a very different meaning in law, and vice versa.'[47]

With regard to our specific inquiry into the extraterritorial reach of the American antitrust laws, we find in the Report the following observation:

> 'In addition to marking out the limits of antitrust policy, we consider its coordination with our programs for national security and promoting foreign trade, as well as our relations with ohter countries. Antitrust proceedings involving activities abroad by American foreign firms may, of course, affect a variety of related Government programs. In such situations, the Committee recognizes that the Attorney General and the Federal Trade Comission, charged with enforcing our antritrust laws, cannot resolve all complex interrelations of our national interest. Decisions of a delicate nature may be involved beyond the authority of antitrust enforcement agencies alone to make.'[48]

This suggestion for the exploration of ways and means to arrive at a closer cooperation between the various government agencies has had tangible results, as may be concluded from the establishment, in 1962, by the Antitrust Division of the Department of Justice, of a Foreign Commerce Section, to provide 'liaison between the Department of Justice, the State Department, and other Government agencies in connection with all matters relating to foreign commerce, nationals, or governments.'[49]

Also, outside the United States a closer cooperation has been established between the Justice Department and other nations in antitrust matters, through the Organization for Economic Cooperation and Development (OECD), as illustrated by the following: A Committee of Experts on Restrictive Business Practices of the Paris-based OECD meets twice a year in Paris. Member countries have been advised to share information on restrictive business practices. Furthermore, a member country 'contemplating an investigation of such a practice involving the important interests of another member should first give it an opportunity to express its views, undertake its own action, or participate in coordinated action.'[50]

This 'advise' given to the member countries seems to have had practical results, as may be concluded from the contents of a number of bilateral treaties signed

47. *ibid.*, pp. 315, 316.
48. *ibid.*, p. 92
49. *cf.* SUPPLEMENT, p. 61.
50. *ibid.*, pp. 61, 62.

by the United States, providing for consultation concerning anticompetitive practices and even coordinated action to eliminate the practices.[51]

Finally, we should mention that as result of the Committee's recommendation to give the penalties a more deterrent character, the criminal penalties were substantially increased. Since the enactment, in 1890, of the *Sherman Act* the maximum fine for a criminal violation had remained $5,000. Using the period from 1946 through 1953 as a basis for its inquiry, the Committee disclosed that the average fine assessed during that period was approximately $2,600, while 'numerous fines of $100, $150, $200, $250, $350, $400, and $500 were imposed.'[52]

The Committee recommended that a new ceiling of $10,000 be established. Congress, however, raised the ceiling to the present $50,000.[53]

Before concluding this part of our historical survey we may ask ourselves whether the Committee had, indeed, come close to the hope expressed by the President of United States, 'to prepare the way for modernizing and strengthening our laws to preserve American free enterprise against monopoly and unfair competition.'[54]

An answer to this question can probably best be given by quoting some of the statements by the dissenting members of the Committee. We find the following observations:

> '. . .the Report fails in my view to meet the duties imposed upon our Committee . . . Our Report is largely a review and restatement of the substantive doctrines of antitrust law . . .
>
> '. . .the principal theme of the Report, on which we are unanimous, is that Congress and the Courts have developed a reasonably unified and consistent corpus of antitrust law, directed at protecting the economy against substantial and significant limitations on competitive conditions . . .
>
> '. . .we conclude that by and large our antitrust law is adequate to its task.
>
> 'While I welcome and agree with the general tenor of this analysis, I deplore the failure of the Committee to have carried it forward in certain respects, in order to provide clear-cut answers as to ways in which the

51. *ibid.*, p. 62, *n.* 7. As an example we mention the treaty with Italy which provides: 'The two High Contracting Parties agree that business practices which restrain competition, limit acces to markets or foster monopolistic control, and which are engaged in or made effective by one or more private or public commercial enterprises or by combination, agreement or other arrangement among public or private commercial enterprises may have harmful effects upon the commerce between their respective territories. Accordingly, each High Contracting Party agrees upon the request of the other High Contracting Party to consult with respect to any such practices and to take such measures as it deems appropriate with a view to eliminating such harmful effects.'; *cf.* FUGATE, *op. cit.*, p. 275.
52. *Att'y Gen. Report*, p. 352.
53. *Celler – Kefauver Act* of 1955, referred to *supra*, p. 26, *n.* 37.
54. *Att'y Gen. Report*, p. IV

antitrust law needs modernizing and strengthening . . .'[55]

'The Majority Report would weaken the antitrust laws in a number of respects, and, even more important, it fails to adopt necessary measures for strengthening the law so as to create a truly competitive economy in this country.'[56]

Nevertheless, the Report was hailed even by some of the dissenters, 'as a commendable accomplishment.'[57]

Personally, we do not question but that the Attorney General's Report is an important milestone in the historical development of the American antitrust laws. It is also important in that both in the literature and the judicial decisions many references to the Report are made. At the same time, we agree with some of the dissenters that, with regard to the extraterritorial application of the antitrust laws, the Report lacks clear directives of how to deal with foreign defendants and conduct abroad. On the positive side, the Committee states:

(1) '. . .the Sherman Act applies only to those arrangements between Americans alone or in concert with foreign firms, which have such substantial anticompetitive effects on this country's "trade or commerce with foreign nations" as to constitute unreasonable restraints.'

(2) '. . .conspiracies between foreign competitors alone should come within the Sherman Act only where they are intended to, and actually do, result in substantial anticompetitive effects on our foreign commerce.'[58]

No reference is made to the *incipiency* aspects of agreements in restraint of trade, or large mergers, or stock purchases, as covered by the provisions of the *Clayton Act.* Also, what the 'intention' must amount to in order to come under the reach of the *Sherman Act* is not elaborated upon. We will discuss some of these topics, in sofar as they apply to the present study, and in sofar as further developments of the law have occurred.

Furthermore, the statement that, 'we must assume . . . that Congress did not intend the "general words" of the *Sherman Act* to be read "without regard to the limitations customarily observed by nations upon the exercise of their powers"[59] is admittedly only an assumption. Even if one were to read the statement as a recommendation, the Committee fails to clearly indicate what these limitations are or should be. Certainly a general statement that one should adhere 'to the Supreme Court rule that broad and sympathetic standards must be applied in applying regulatory statutes to cases involving any interference with the sovereignty of another nation'[60] falls short of a clear delimitation of the assertion of jurisdictional competency.

It seems only natural to ask what further developments have occurred since the

55. *ibid.*, pp. 388, 389, containing the 'Concluding Statement of Partial Dissent by Eugene V. ROSTOW.'
56. *ibid.*, p. 390, containing the 'General Dissent by Louis B. SCHWARTZ.'
57. *ibid.*, p. 389.
58. *ibid.*, p. 76
59. *ibid.*, p. 77
60. *ibid.*, p. 77

publication of the Report. In response to such a question we could mention that several new topics of legislative activity have found their way in the antitrust laws; of these we mention the *Bank Merger Acts* of 1960 and 1966, and the *Antitrust Civil Process Act* of 1962.[61] Furthermore, we should mention that merger and private damage litigation have gained much greater importance than was the situation prior to 1955.[62]

In view of our current concern with the historical development of the antitrust laws we consider as one of the important developments the 'updating project' of the 1955 *Report of the Attorney General's National Committee* by the Section of Antitrust Law of the American Bar Association. This two-years project was completed in 1968.[63]

With regard to the extraterritorial reach of the American antitrust laws the findings of the Committee can be summarized as follows:

(1) The requirements pertaining to the assumption of personal jurisdiction over alien defendants, both as to venue and service of process, constitute a practical limit on the extraterritorial reach of the antitrust laws.[64] The major limitation is caused by the language of the *Clayton Act* which provides:

    (a) with regard to venue: that proceedings under the antitrust laws can be brought in the judicial district where the defendant may be found or transacts business;

    (b) with regard to service of process: that the service of process may be done wherever the defendant may be found.

    These provisions apply both to persons and corporations.

    Thus, before a court can assume jurisdiction over the person (i.e., the defendant) it must convince itself that the requirements were properly met, to wit, that the defendant was properly *found* (with regard to the service of process), and that he was *either found or transacting business* in the jurisdictional area of the court (for purposes of venue).

    The interpretation of the wording of the *Clayton Act* by the courts, with regard to the requirements of venue and service of process, is illustrated by the Committee with three important cases:

61. See *infra*, p. 64.
62. We wonder whether it was this increase in private damage litigation that moved GLEISS, A., to write his earlier cited article in XV/12 *Auszenwirtschaftsdienst des Betriebs-Beraters* 499 (1969)
63. ANTITRUST DEVELOPMENTS 1955-1968, A SUPPLEMENT TO THE REPORT OF THE ATTORNEY GENERAL'S NATIONAL COMMITTEE TO STUDY THE ANTITRUST LAWS, Chicago, 1968 (hereinafter to be referred to as SUPPLEMENT)
64. *ibid.*, p. 40. In this respect we should point out that a distinction is made between the jurisdiction *in personam* (i.e., whether the defendant has properly been brought under the authority of the court) and the jurisdiction over the subject matter (i.e., whether the court has the authority to adjudicate the subject matter); *cf.* SCHWARTZ, I. E., *op. cit.*, p. 154.

(a) *U.S.* v *Scophony Corp.*[65]

In this leading case the United States Supreme Court found that venue and the service of process in New York on Scophony, Ltd., a British corporation, were proper.

Scophony Ltd. (British Scophony) had entered into a series of agreements with two American corporations for the purpose of securing American capital to develop in the United States a manufacturing and selling business based on its television patents. As a result a third American corporation, American Scophony (as distinguished from British Scophony) was organized. One of the directors of British Scophony was to become president and a director of American Scophony; British Scophony was also entitled to elect a majority of the directors, as well as the vice-president and treasurer. American Scophony was to receive from British Scophony its equipment and patents and to exploit the patents by licensing. Furthermore, territorial divisions of the world market were made between British Scophony and its American partners. Because of the requirement in the charter that to constitute a quorum at least one of the directors elected by an American partner had to be present, British Scophony did not have effective control of American Scophony: all it would take to prevent a decision was for the American directors to be absent. As it happened, the American partners soon caused the resignation of its directors, thus leaving American Scophony unable to transact business.

British Scophony and the other defendants were prosecuted for violations of the antitrust laws.[66]

Although the District Court had held that British Scophony was not 'found' in the Southern District of New York, the United States Supreme Court reversed the District Court. The Supreme Court held that British Scophony was doing business in New York, because the activities were *of a substantial character* and largely, if not exclusively, *the only business in which it could engage at the time.* The statement was clearly in response to the argument advanced by British Scophony that it was merely an investor in the United States as distinguished from being engaged in the business of manufacturing and selling television equipment.

The Supreme Court stated that with regard to venue the test was the

65. 333 US 795, 68 S Ct 855 (1948).

66. For a synopsis of the case, see SUPPLEMENT, pp. 41, 42. For a more detailed analysis, see FUGATE, *op. cit.*, pp. 58, *seq.* SCHWARTZ, I. E., too, refers to this case; *cf. op. cit.*, pp. 155, 156. REHBINDER only mentions the case to illustrate how the requirements of venue and service of process have to be satisfied; *cf. op. cit.*, pp. 334, 335.

'practical everyday business or commercial concept of doing or carrying on business *of any substantial character.*' With regard to the service of process the Supreme Court intimated that, at least as to alien corporations, service of process might be sustained wherever venue was proper.[67]

(b) *Hoffman Motors Corp.* v. *Alfa Romeo S.p.A.*[68]
In this case, an action was brought against an Italian manufacturer by its former American franchisee. Process was served at the defendant's Italian headquarters by registered letter, and by personal service on its general manager in Italy by a court-designated Italian attorney.[69]
Because the court found that the Italian manufacterer had transacted business in New York (the suit was one arising out of those transactions), venue was proper. Furthermore, service of process was sustained under the so-called New York long-arm statute.

(c) *U.S.* v. *Watchmakers of Switzerland Information Center, Inc.*[70]
This so-called *Swiss Watchmakers* case involved a civil suit by the United States against a number of Swiss and American defendants, alleging that the defendants had unreasonably restrained the American trade in Swiss watches, watch parts, and watchmaking machinery. All of the Swiss defendants were parties to a 'Collective Convention,' regulating the production, sale, and export of watches and watch parts. Sanctions were imposed for violations of the terms on members or their foreign affiliates. American companies were compelled to restrict the manufacture and export of American made watches and parts in order to be allowed Swiss watches and parts.
Two of the Swiss defendants, Fédération Suisse des Associations de Fabricants d'Horlogerie (FH) and Ebauches, S.A., (Ebauches) were sued by virtue of service of process on their jointly owned American subsidiary, Watchmakers of Switzerland Information Center, Inc. (Information Center). In response to the argument that the court had no jurisdiction in view of the rule that a parent's complete commercial and financial domination of its subsidiary still would not bring the parent within the jurisdiction, the court stated that this rule would hold only 'as long as the formal separation between parent and the subsidiary was scrupulously maintained.' In the present instance, the court found that the Information Center's annual budget of about $70,000 was approved annually by FH and

67. *cf.* SUPPLEMENT, p. 41
68. 244 F Supp 70 (1965)
69. For a synopsis of the case, see SUPPLEMENT, p. 42 and p. 45
70. 133 F Supp 40 (1955); *reargument refused,* 134 F Supp 710 (1955). For a synopsis of the *Swiss Watchmakers* case, see SUPPLEMENT, pp. 42, *seq.*

Ebauches; furthermore, that the Information Center made monthly reports to FH and Ebauches, and that its principal purpose was to perform advertising, promotional, and consumer liaison for FH and Ebauches. The court then went on to state that 'where the substance of corporate independence is not preserved and the subsidiary acts as an agent of the parent, this corporate separation has been found without significance.' Examining the purpose and operations of the Information Center in detail, the court came to the conclusion that 'realistically appraised the Information Center has no business of its own. Its principal purpose was the advancement of the programs of FH and Ebauches . . . It is a mere adjunct of its parents and its activities will be regarded as theirs."

On this basis the Swiss parents were deemed 'found' within the United States and properly served there.

Similarly was the Swiss defendant Eterna, G.A., held to have been properly served through its exclusive American distributor (a New York corporation), because the complete domination by the defendant made the distributor a mere agent.

(2) The assumption of jurisdiction over the subject matter involving foreign conduct of alien defendants is limited to cases involving the 'deliberately engaging in conduct the natural and probable consequences of which is restraint of trade or monopoly.'[71]

The statement purports to harmonize the apparent difference between the guideline contained in the 1955 Committee Report recognizing the assumption of jurisdiction if the anticompetitive effects resulting from foreign conduct were *intended,*[72] and the corresponding provision in the *Restatement* which recognizes the assumption of jurisdiction over foreign conduct if the effect occurs as *a direct and foreseeable result* of such conduct, because 'intent means deliberately engaging in conduct the natural and probable consequences of which is restraint of trade and monopoly.'[73]

The above classification does not indicate what the right to the assumption of jurisdiction is if the foreign conduct is authorized, or even encouraged by a foreign government. In addressing itself to this problem the Committee first, distinguishes between conduct that is *authorized* and conduct that is *required*. With regard to authorized conduct the Committee quotes with apparent approval the uniform view of the American courts that 'authorization standing alone is no defense',[74] but that 'extraterritorial

71. SUPPLEMENT, p. 49.
72. *cf. Att'y Gen. Report,* p. 76
73. SUPPLEMENT, pp. 48, 49
74. *ibid.,* p. 49

acts which are *required* of a defendant by a foreign government' cannot be held illegal.[75] Support for the latter statement is found in the opinion of the Court in the *Swiss Watchmakers* case[76] where the Court by way of *dictum* stated:

> 'If, of course, the defendants' activities had been required by Swiss law, this court could indeed do nothing.'

So that there would be no misunderstanding as to the court's interpretation of the word 'required', the court stated that the test would be 'direct foreign governmental action compelling the defendants' activities.'[77]

Nevertheless, the Committee comes to the conclusion that 'the law is insufficiently developed to permit the extraction of useful guides as to what type of requirements by a foreign government would cause our courts to refuse jurisdiction . . .'[78]

(3) The scope of decree provisions involving extraterritorial activities should display judicial restraint, both with regard to the activities themselves and the production of foreign located documents (*subpoenas duces tecum*).[79] The rationale for this proposition is that a defendant should not be caught between the American judgment on one side and the operation of the foreign law in those countries where it is doing business on the other side.[80]

Thus, we find that decree provisions with regard to activities abroad state that a defendant shall not be prohibited to perform any act which is required of it in that foreign country. With regard to disclosure proceedings under a *subpoena duces tecum* the practice is that a defendant will not be held in contempt of court if good faith is used in attempting to comply with the discovery order, i.e., that an honest attempt be made to 'secure the waiver of any foreign law prohibiting disclosure'[81] (such as, for instance, a waiver from the Netherlands Government exempting a defendant from compliance with article 39 of the Economic Competition Act of 1956).

However, the Committee concludes (and we agree) that the law is not sufficiently developed to predict with even a reasonable degree of certainty how in a given case the courts will act to avoid conflicts with foreign law.[82]

75. *ibid.*, p. 50
76. 1963 Trade Cas. Nr. 70,600 (SD-NY), *order modified* 1965 Trade Cas. nr. 71, 352 (SD-NY), cited in SUPPLEMENT, pp. 47, 50; the citations are taken from there.
77. *cf.* SUPPLEMENT, p. 50. Of course, since the statements are only *dictum* and not *holding*, they are not entirely authoritative.
78. SUPPLEMENT, p. 50
79. *ibid.*, p. 53
80. *ibid.*, p. 53, citing *Att'y Gen. Report*, p. 76
81. SUPPLEMENT, pp. 53, 54
82. *ibid.*, p. 55

Our summary of the present state of the law is: the United States has come a long way but still has far to go. For instance, the entire problem of mergers and conglomerate mergers is only slightly touched upon.[83] More attention to this aspect of antitrust enforcement will be inevitable in the years to come, particularly where foreign corporations are involved.

The Philosophical Sources

In whatever words the purposes of the American antitrust laws are expressed they all suggest that the preservation of the competitive system is the final goal. This is in contrast to aims and purposes of restrictive trade legislation in a number of other countries or group of nations. Thus, we find that the final goal of the German antitrust laws is the 'promotion of the welfare and the freedom of the citizens.'[84] In Sweden the purpose is 'to achieve the best possible utilization of the resources of society.'[85]

In the European Economic Community the aim is to 'establish a system of free competition between all enterprises that exercise their activities within the Common Market.'[86]

In the United States the desire for the maintenance of a competitive system is partly based on a rejection of concentration of power, be it economic or political. The Attorney General's National Committee opens its Report with the words:

> 'The general objective of the antitrust laws is the promotion of competition in open markets. This policy is a primary feature of private enterprise. Most Americans have long recognized that opportunity for market access and fostering of market rivalry are basic tenets of our faith in competition as a form of economic organization . . . 'Antitrust is a distinctive American means for assuring the competitive economy on which our political and social freedom under representative government in part depend.'[87]

The eulogy goes so far as to state that of the many forces which have contributed to the creative American economy, 'the antitrust laws remain one of the most important.'[88] Indeed, the image Americans have of their national economy is a form of economic organization characterized by a free enterprise system.

The existence of a free enterprise system suggests the continuous presence of rivalry between competitive forces. Terms such as 'free trade', 'free enterprise',

83. *ibid.*, p. 59
84. *cf.* SCHWARTZ, I. E., *op. cit.*, p. 36
85. *cf.* RIEDWEG, A. J., 'The Extra-Territorial Application Of Restrictive Trade Legislation – Jurisdiction And International Law', in 1964 *Tokyo Proceedings*, at p. 385
86. *cf.* VAN GERVEN, W., PRINCIPES DU DROIT DES ENTENTES DE LA COMMUNAUTE ECONOMIQUE EUROPEENNE, Bruxelles, 1966, p. 5
87. *Att'y Gen. Report*, pp. 1, 2
88. *ibid.*, p. 2

'competition', are part of the folkloric vocabulary of the American people. Of these three, competition is probably the most typical.

But competition as an ideal for a free enterprise society is not the same as competition in its everyday practical application. The problems arrive when the ideal has to be implemented and applied.[89] On that basis one might even consider the introductory language of the *Attorney General's Report* general hortatory language commonly found in preambles of documents of a political nature. We submit that it would be error te come to such a conclusion when reading the language with which we commenced this section. On the contrary, in the statement that the purpose of the law is the preservation of the competitive system lies the answer to many questions that may be posed when one tries to analyze the actions of the antitrust enforcement agencies.

Preservation of the competitive system does not suggest a protection of individual competitors. At the same time, while individual competitors may be eliminated, the process may not lead to the ultimate victory of one sole contender.[90] The preservation of the competitive system is wanted because of the belief that through competition prices will be held down and, consequently, consumers will be given a greater variety of choices for the available spending money; furthermore, such a system would conceivably provide for the most efficient allocation of available capital and labor resources.[91]

That the preservation of the competitive system would keep prices down and provide for the most efficient allocation of capital and labor resources was not a startlingly new discovery. As far back as *Dyer's* case[92] the courts considered a promise to refrain from practicing one's trade against the common law. And in the *Case of Monopolies*[93] we find the observations (a) that it is desirable to keep people gainfully employed, and (b) that a monopoly may cause a raise in the prices and unemployment.

But the maintenance of competition had been achieved through the mechanism of private litigation, i.e. through actions based on contract law and tort law. This was possible as long as the litigants were about equal in economic strength.

What was new was the emergence of big enterprise in the 19th century (the railroads, the banks, the oil companies, large industrial firms).[94] To rely on private litigation by the economically weak against the economically powerful

89. *cf.* FRIEDMANN, W., LAW IN A CHANGING SOCIETY, Berkely, 1959, p. 263: 'Of all the basic ideals of modern liberal democracy, that of freedom of trade is perhaps the most ambiguous, and the most elusive.' The author illustrates his statement with a number of examples.
90. *cf. ibid.,* p. 264: 'Every industrial society needs some competition; but none can afford to let it develop without interference, lest a surfeit of competition should lead to the destruction of all competition.'
91. *cf. Att'y Gen. Report,* p. 318
92. *supra,* p. 16
93. *supra,* p. 16
94. see *infra,* p. 71

would not be realistic. Additional safegueards were called for, in order to combat these emerging power blocs.[95] Thus, we find a new dimension added to the already established idea that free competition in open markets should be preserved: the prevention of excessive concentration of economic power in private hands.

Competition suggests the rejection of excessive concentration of economic power, because it would jeopardise the free entry into the market place of potential competitors. And it is precisely the presence of more than one seller that is required in order to have rivalry, i.e. competition.

It is an interesting phenomenon that, while the right to compete was by the year 1890 a firmly anchored concept in the American legal lore, the popular sentiment against the rapidly growing industrial combinations and their practices called for the passing of special legislation.[96]

It seems fair to suggest that the emergence of the powerful commercial and industrial enterprises caused fear, particularly in a country of pioneers where no widespread sympathy for monopolists existed.[97]

This antipathy against monopolies and monopolists found its expression in the antitrust laws, because through these laws a mechanism was established to oppose those who would or could wield the power to control and dominate interstate trade and commerce to such an extent that it could lead to the exclusion of actual or potential competitors.[98]

The ultimate result of the struggle between those who could control the economic order and those who were opposed to excessive concentration of power was the kind of legislation which many people, following THORELLI's suggestion, have described as 'economic egalitarianism.'[99]

No wonder that the *Sherman Act* has been termed 'a charter of freedom,' with 'a

95. The suspicion against concentration of power is a characteristic American phenomenon. This is even visible in government, through the device of the so-called 'balance of powers'.
96. *cf.* BREWSTER, K., Jr., ANTITRUST AND AMERICAN BUSINESS ABROAD, New York, 1958, p. 19: 'The Sherman Act was passed in the wake of widespread popular and journalistic outcry against the rapidly growing power of trusts, combines, and looser combinations of businesses and their allegedly predatory practices.' For a similar statement, see FUGATE, *op. cit.*, p. 10.
97. *cf.* THORELLI, *op. cit.*, p. 568: 'It is significant that the Boston Tea Party took place at the expense of a hated monopoly. The tremendous importance of the frontier in the history of American ideas is well-known to everyone. Its spiritual climate was one of intense individualism and radicalism at once. Would-be monopolists could not expect sympathetic treatment in the land of the pioneer.'
98. *cf. American Tobacco Co.* v. *United States,* 328 US 781, 66 S Ct 1125 (1946).
99. *cf.* THORELLI, pp. 566, *seq.*, who considers this composite body of thought a conglomerate of component parts which under close examination might not even be found to be fully compatible. '. . . economic egalitarianism struck a middle way between the dichotomy of the Gospel of Wealth and the Social Gospel.'

generality and adaptability comparable to that found to be desirable in constitutional provisions.'[100]

The reason for fear of excessive power in the hands of a few was well expressed in the opinion of Mr. Justice DOUGLAS, expressing the spirit and the philosophy of the *Sherman Act*:

> '. . .power can be utilized with lightning speed. It can be benign or it can be dangerous. The philosophy of the Sherman Act is that it should not exist. For all power tends to develop into a government in itself. Power that controls the economy should be in the hands of elected representatives of the people, not in the hands of an industrial olichargy. Industrial power should be decentralized. It should be scattered into many hands so that the fortunes of the people will not be dependent on the whim or caprice, the political prejudices, the emotional stability of a few self-appointed men. The fact that they are not vicious men but respectable and social minded is irrelevant. That is the philosophy and the command of the Sherman Act. It is founded on a theory of hostility to the concentration in private hands of power so great that only a government of the people should have it.'[101]

We have referred to the opinion of Mr. Justice DOUGLAS only because it states clearly what the *Sherman Act* purports to achieve. We could not even consider the statement dictum because it appears in a dissenting opinion. In fact, in the case itself the majority of the Supreme Court allowed United States Steel Corporation (the largest producer of rolled steel products in the United States) to acquire (through its wholly-owned subsidiary, the Columbia Steel Company) a manufacturer of fabricated steel plates.

What this case points up to is the apparent or seeming dichotomy between the philosophy of the *Sherman Act* (the prevention of excessive concentration of economic power in private hands) and the observable phenomenon that big enterprise not only continues to exist, but even tends to become bigger. We might even add that the modern conglomerate merger movement is clearly an example of excessive concentration of economic power in private hands.

All we have to offer as explanation for this re-occuring phenomenon is our conjecture that only big business has the resources (financially and otherwise) to risk and wage a battle in the courts. Small companies succumb in the initial stages of a threateningly protracted government litigation: they give in to the wishes of the government to prevent litigation.

This might lead to the partly erroneous conclusion that it is only big business that is being attacked by the government. We submit that the government attacks as a matter of principle all forms of stifling of competition and excessive concentration of economic power in private hands. But the cases we hear about

100. *cf. Appalachian Coals, Inc.* v. *United States,* 288 US 344, 53 S Ct 471 (1933).
101. *U.S.* v. *Columbia Steel Co.*, 334 US 495, 68 S Ct 1107 (1948)

are the cases which involve big business. The problem is partly explained in the Government's contention in one celebrated case where the Government stated that it was not attacking the firm 'because of its size but because of its abuse of the power that went with such size.'[102]

To which we add that if the powerful big company has been successful in its battle in the courts and emerges victoriously, it will tend to become bigger still. That this may lead to a troublesome situation is only stating the obvious.

We have one other explanation for the seeming incongruity between what we can see before our eyes and the philosophy of the antitrust laws: the (by necessity) imperfect mechanism to combat the ills that are the subject of the attack. With regard to the prevention of excessive concentration of economic power in private hands, the law fails to indicate what shall constitute such concentration. As a result we find that in one case the court will use a different yardstick than in another case, as may be illustrated by the following cases:

(a) in the *Alcoa* case[103] the court stated that, while a control of 90% of the market would be enough to constitute a monopoly, 'it is doubtful whether sixty or sixty-four per cent would be enough; and certainly thirty-three per cent is not.'

(b) in the *Philadelphia Bank* merger case[104] the Court stated that the merger of 2 banks in a metropolitan area of 42 commercial banks (which would result in a single bank's controlling about 30% of the commercial banking business in the four-county Philadelphia metropolitan area), would pose an undue threat to concentration of economic power. 'Without attempting to specify the smallest market share which would still be considered to threaten undue concentration, we are clear that 30% presents that threat.'[105]

(c) in the *Brown Shoe* case[106] the Court held that the merger between a manufacturer of shoewear who produced 4% of the nation's total footwear production with a retail chain that accounted for 2.3% of the nation's total retail shoe outlets might tend to substantially lessen competition.

(d) in the *Timken* case[107] the Court held that one American corporation could restrain interstate and foreign commerce, by the device of subisidiaries in two foreign countries (Great Britain and France) with which it formed joint ventures, even though the corporation asserted that this was the only method by which it could succesfully participate in international com-

102. *U. S.* v. *New York Great Atlantic & Pacific Tea Co.*, 173 F 2d 79 (1949)
103. *U. S.* v. *Aluminum Co. of America*, 148 F 2d 416 (1945)
104. *U. S.* v. *Philadelphia National Bank*, 374 US 321, 83 S Ct 1715 (1963)
105. For the different percentages that may be considered posing a threat to concentration of economic power, see HANDLER, *op. cit.*, p. 746, *n.* 20, and the literature there quoted.
106. *Brown Shoe Co.* v. *U. S.*, 379 US 294, 82 S Ct 1502 (1962)
107. *Timken Roller Bearing Co.* v. *U.S.*, 341 US 593, 71 S Ct 971 (1951)

> merce. The Court adopted the view that 'parent and subsidiary corporations must accept the consequences of maintaining separate corporate entities,' and that consequence is conspiracy to restrain trade.'

With regard to the principle that the antitrust laws purport to encourage free competition in open markets, there is also uncertainty as to what is meant with this term. In the above mentioned *Timken* case, the Court apparently gave a different interpretation thereto than did the corporation. The law fails to spell out what constitutes free competition. It is in fact, highly questionable that the term 'free competition' should be taken in its literal sense.

Thus, it is left to the courts to determine whether competition should take the form of perfect competition, or pure competition, or imperfect competition, or non-price competition, or predatory competition, or effective or workable competition. Furthermore, the courts will have to choose between the economic concept of competition (focussing particularly on the result of a given situation) and the legal concept (focussing on the activities and practices).[108]

Furthermore, it seems obvious that a successful competitor will acquire a more powerful position than his less successful adversary. But the philosphy of the antitrust laws directs us to hold that performance (which results from competition) may not unduly upset the structure (which indirectly results from competition), because the change in structure may lead to a concentration of economic power beyond the allowable limit.

In addition, we should not forget that only where large concentrations of economic power exist, are the resources available for research and development, which in turn lead to greater wealth, and to greater employment possibilities.

Therefore, it seems to us that what the antitrust laws really intend to combat is the abuse of economic power and the abuse of the competitive process. To recognize this would be particularly relevant to the extraterritorial reach of the antitrust laws, because the desire to combat abuse will generally be perceived as fair and just.

With regard to the excessive concentration of economic power in private hands, it seems to us that the courts are largely guided by this abuse factor.

With regard to the encouraging of free competition in open markets, there seems to be a consensus that the so-called effective or workable competition is the desirable form of competition. While our own interpretation of the term would be the absence of an abuse situation, economists generally interpret the term as referring to a market structure whereby no one seller, or a group of sellers acting in concert, has the power to choose its level of profits by giving less and charging more.[109]

There are two other topics that merit consideration when the philosophical bases of the antitrust laws are under discussion:

108. *cf. Att'y Gen. Report*, pp. 339, 340
109. *ibid.*, p. 320

(1) the activities covered by the reach of the law;
(2) the special character of the antitrust laws as a separate area of the law.

ad (1): the activities covered by the reach of the law.

If the preservation of the competitive system and the prevention of excessive concentration of economic power in private hands are the major politico-economic objectives of the antitrust laws, then, it follows that activities of the business community that could thwart these objectives are of concern to antitrust enforcement agencies. Patents, trademarks, licensing of know-how, unfair methods of competition are all topics with antitrust aspects. For instance, the use of a patent or trademark can prevent competition in open markets, either through a process of exclusive cross-licensing agreements, or by non-use licensing agreements.[110] Furthermore, patents are considered 'assets', the acquisition of which may not lead to a substantial lessening of competition or tend to create a monopoly.[111] In other words, the use made by an industrial property owner of his rights may subject him (and his grantee) to investigation by the antitrust enforcement agencies, or private litigation under the provisions of the *Clayton Act.*

In view of the above we too, shall consider topics of patents, trademarks, licensing, and unfair methods of competition within our subject if the particular activity would bring the person or the conduct within the reach of the antitrust laws. Consultation of the various handbooks, as well as the *Report of the Attorney General's National Committee to Study the Antitrust Laws* and the SUPPLEMENT, all follow this same approach.

ad (2): the special character of the antitrust laws as a separate area of the law.

Because the preservation of the competitive system (i.e., a positive purpose) and the prevention of excessive concentration of economic power in private hands (i.e., a negative purpose) are the major politico-economic objectives of the antitrust laws, the methods applied to achieve these objectives display (almost inevitably so) a plurality of approaches which lead to consider the antitrust laws as a separate area of the law. We have earlier indicated that we propose to show the validity of this suggestion.[112] While we still intend to do so we do not feel this to be the proper place and time; we consider it appropriate to deal with this topic

110. For an example, see *U.S.* v. *Singer Mfg. Co.*, 374 US 174, 83 S Ct 1773 (1963), cited in SUPPLEMENT, pp. 56, *seq.* For a similar example, but then pertaining to the European Economic Community, see *Consten-Grundig* v. *Commission of the E.E.C.*, decision of the European Court of Justice of July 13, 1966, cited in VAN GERVEN, *op. cit.*, pp. 275, *seq.;* the case is extensively discussed in 15 *Sociaal Economische Wetgeving* 162 (1967).

111. *Clayton Act*, section 7. For support of this statement, we refer to *U.S.* v. *Lever Bros. Co.*, 216 F Supp 887 (1963) (S.D.-N.Y.), cited in SUPPLEMENT, p. 169

112. *cf.* INTRODUCTION, p. 9, where we also referred, in support of our suggestion, to the statement by SCHWARTZ, I. E., *op. cit.*, p. 2, to the effect that the American antitrust laws had a history, system, and legal technique peculiarly its own.

after we have discussed the remedial and procedural aspects of antitrust enforcement.

We would be remiss, however, not to point at this peculiar character of the antitrust laws when the philosophical bases thereof are under discussion.

CHAPTER II

REMEDIAL AND OTHER PROCEDURAL ASPECTS OF THE AMERICAN ANTITRUST LAWS

General

The preceding survey of the historical and philosophical sources purported to show how and why the preservation of the competitive system and the prevention of excessive concentration of economic power in private hands became the major objectives of the American antitrust laws. In this chapter we will examine the methods of implementation of these objectives. It goes without saying that any short answer such as 'by the enforcement of the antitrust laws' only begs the question. A further exploratory search seems indicated. This search can be undertaken in different ways:

(1) The doctrinal approach:
This approach would require an analysis of the various acts either on the basis of a pre-existing doctrine, or by an examination of these acts in order to determine whether or to what extent they fit into a doctrinal system. Following this analysis one could, then, determine whether the acts and the doctrine make a unified whole, or whether there are shortcomings and what these are. In a legal system where doctrinal principles are an important factor for legislation – as appears to be the case in most civil law nations – this might be a useful method. But in a legal system where doctrinal principles often come about as a result of judicial decisions – as appears to be the case in the common law nations – this method would not be useful. It has often been asserted that the common law courts do not decide principles but cases,[1] thus continually providing for new solutions to new problems.[2] To build a doctrinal structure on the basis of separate acts and judicial decisions would be an elusive if not impossible undertaking.

(2) The functional approach:
This approach would require an analysis of the mechanism by which the

1. *cf.* LLEWELLYN, K. N., THE BRAMBLE BUSH, New York, 1951, p. 42. Also, see BERMAN, H. J., & GREINER, W. R., THE NATURE AND FUNCTIONS OF LAW, 2nd ed., Brooklyn, 1966, p. 477
2. *cf.* LAWSON, F. H., A COMMON LAWYER LOOKS AT THE CIVIL LAW, Ann Arbor, 1953, p. 18: '... solutions to the new problems had to be worked out on the spot, partly no doubt by applying customary ideas, but much more by hardy invention and by the gradual elaboration of a legal grammar of independent origin.'

objectives of the antitrust laws are implemented. Three different ways of doing this can be suggested:

(a) The institutional approach:

This method consists of an analysis of the various agencies (and institutions) empowered to enforce the antitrust provisions. Thus, we would find that proceedings (be they formal or informal) can be initiated by:

(1) the Department of Justice, through civil and criminal actions;
(2) the Federal Trade Commission, through administrative procedures, encouraging voluntary compliance or compelling involuntary compliance;
(3) other regulatory agencies, through a system of miscellaneous sanctions;
(4) injured individuals, through private actions seeking injunctive relief and/or treble damages.[3]

A number of publications deal with the various forms of antitrust enforcement by reviewing subsequently, the jurisdictional powers and procedures of the Department of Justice, the Federal Trade Commission, injured private parties.[4]

(b) The litigation approach:

This method consists of an analysis of the various forms of litigation in relation to the particular topic of antitrust under discussion.[5] Most of the leading textbooks in the United States follow this approach.[6]

(c) The remedial approach:

This method consists of an analysis of the remedies available under the antitrust laws. To some extent this method is closely related to the litigation approach; the difference is that the remedies are considered without regard to a particular topic of antitrust. It is to a lesser extent related to the institutional approach, because the remedies are primary point of consideration, while the institutions entitled to these various remedies are of secondary importance.

A cursory review of the multiplicity of statutory remedies available

3. *cf.* VAN CISE, J. G., THE FEDERAL ANTITRUST LAWS, rev. ed., Washington, 1955, pp. 39, 40
4. *cf. Att'y Gen. Report,* pp. 343, *seq.;* SUPPLEMENT, pp. 218, *seq.;* VAN CISE, *op. cit.,* pp. 41, *seq.* For the inevitability of overlapping jurisdiction, see OPPENHEIM, S. C., 'Federal Antitrust Legislation: Guideposts to a Revised National Antitrust Policy', 50 *Mich. Law Review* 1139 (1952)
5. Examples: litigation in cases of horizontal price fixing; litigation by private parties
6. *cf.* HANDLER, *op. cit.;* OPPENHEIM & WESTON, *op. cit.;* SCHWARTZ, L. B., *op. cit.* For a different approach (analyzing the market effects the parties attempted to achieve), see BLAKE, H. M., & PITOFSKY, R., CASES AND MATERIALS ON ANTITRUST LAW, Brooklyn, 1967

will confirm the view of at least one author that these laws 'entail multiple damnations of forbidden restraints, one punishment sure if another fails.'[7]

The Remedial Aspects of Antitrust Enfocement

Among the above indicated methods of approach we have selected the remedial approach. Rather than deal with a listing of the various institutions and their jurisdictional competency, or an enumeration of actions appropriate to specifically identified aspects of antitrust provisions, we prefer to deal with the remedies-as-such, viewed in the light of their purported goals, and then, indicate which institution can instigate the proceedings.[8] We have earlier indicated that it is important to a proper understanding of the common law that one systematically analyze the problem by looking at the remedy asked for.[9] The remedial approach is also important because it will show the great number and variety of actions and remedies available; furthermore, that the maintenance of competition in open markets is promoted by a system of public and private enforcement, i.e., actions avaible to governmental agencies (either by way of the judicial or administrative process) and private individuals (by way of appropriate court proceedings).

The remedial approach is furthermore important because of the following:

(1) this method will show more clearly why our suggestion to consider the antitrust laws as a special area of the law merits consideration;

(2) this method will better help us to understand why the extraterritorial reach of the antitrust laws needs a closer examination than has hitherto been afforded to it;

(3) this method will help to show under which circumstances matters pertaining to patents or trademarks, or licensing of know-how, or unfair methods of competition, or false advertising are part of the antitrust laws. We say so because it is on the basis of the procedural aspects (particularly, the remedial aspects) that we determine whether we are dealing with antitrust enforcement or with another area of the law.
For instance, adulteration of food and drugs is a matter of concern to the Food and Drug Administration. But unfair or deceptive practices in com-

7. *cf.* VAN CISE, *op. cit.*, p. 40, drawing a parallel between the statutory remedies of the antitrust laws and the biblical text in Galatians.
8. To a limited extent, a similar approach is followed by OPPENHEIM & WESTON, *op. cit.*, pp. 826, *seq.*
9. *cf.* INTRODUCTION, p. 9. We submit that the same reason must have moved the authors who adhere to the litigation approach, because they too, deal with the various topics of antitrust from the viewpoint of the applicable forms of litigation.

merce[10], or false advertising[11] are matters of concern to the Federal Trade Commission. As a result, the false advertising of food and drugs comes under the jurisdiction of the Federal Trade Commission.[12] This, in turn, renders the false advertising of food and drugs part of the antitrust laws because of the language of these laws, such as, for instance, the *Antitrust Civil Process Act.*[13]

We propose to handle the remedial approach by first, classifying the various actions in civil, criminal, and regulatory (administrative) remedies and then, deal with them in that order.

We admit that our classification is an arbitrary one for the following reasons:

(1) a sharp distinction is difficult to make because the question: what is civil? what is criminal? what is regulatory? is not an easy one to answer;

(2) some of the remedies which we will qualify as civil, could just as well be classified as regulatory, while some of the remedies which we will qualify as criminal, could just as well be classified as civil.

Recognizing the arbitrary aspect of our classification, we consider our method defensible.

We consider a remedy 'civil' if it is available to private parties (the action for damages, and the injunction). Therefore, where the government litigates in the same manner as a private litigant, we consider the remedy a civil remedy.

We consider a remedy 'criminal' if it aims at punishment of the offender, and if only the government can avail itself of the action. In this category we include actions which aim at imprisonment, fine, civil penalty, forfeiture. We include the civil penalty in this group because (a) only the government can initiate the action, and (b) because it aims at punishment. The formal difference with other criminal remedies (such as fine and imprisonment) is of a procedural nature: in a criminal procedure the guilt of the defendant must be proved 'beyond a reasonable doubt', while in a civil procedure the burden of proof is only to the extent of the 'preponderance of the evidence'. It is obvious that the latter is less onerous.

A similar argument can be made for the forfeiture: only the government is entitled to the action, while the purpose thereof is punishment.

We consider a remedy 'regulatory' if (a) only the government is entitled to the

10. *cf.* Section 5 (a)(1) *Federal Trade Commission Act:* 'Unfair methods of competition in commerce, and unfair or deceptive acts or practices in commerce, are hereby declared unlawful.'
11. *cf.* Section 12 (a) *Federal Trade Commission Act:* 'It shall be unlawful for any person, partnership, or corporation to disseminate, or cause to be disseminated, any false advertisement.'
12. *cf.* Section 14 (a) *Federal Trade Commission Act*
13. *cf.* Section 1311 (a)(2) of the *Antitrust Civil Process Act* of 1962: '. . . (a) The term "antitrust law" includes: (1) . . .; (2) The Federal Trade Commission Act . . .' Also, Section 1311 (d) of the same Act: '(d) The term "antitrust violation" means any act or omission in violation of any antitrust law. . .'

action, and (b) the primary purpose is not to punish but to regulate or to correct a situation.

One might argue with our classification, because all law has ultimately a regulatory effect. This is readily conceded. There are however, differences:

(1) the remedies which we designate as 'civil' are equally available to a private litigant and the government (acting as a private party); the remedies which we designate as 'regulatory' are available to the government only;
We reiterate that this distinction is arbitrary and therefore, subject to attack; but for the purpose of our approach we consider it expedient;

(2) where the government acts as a private party (as in actions for damages, or injunctions), it is subject to the same procedural rules as a private party. But when the government acts *as government* in an administrative procedure it has all the weight of its authority behind it; furthermore, the procedural rules are different.

The above argument (i.e., that all law is regulatory) holds also true in the case of the injunction, be it a mandatory one (ordering the defendant to do something) or a restraining one (prohibiting the defendant to continue doing what he was doing): no matter who asks for the remedy, the injunction aims at the regulation of relationships. Our reason for classifying it as a civil remedy is based on the ground that both a private litigant and the government can avail themselves thereof, on the same procedural bases.

Where the government alone is entitled to enforce policies (on behalf of its aggregate citizenry) through judicial or quasi-judical proceedings, the situation is different: the purpose of the action is to obtain judicial sanction to compel a party to comply with the order, but the government alone can seek to obtain the order from the court. In other words, our concept of regulatory jurisdiction has to be viewed not only from the angle of the consequential results, but also in the light of the institution entitled to maintain the action.[14] Also, where the government seeks to obtain enforcement through quasi-judicial proceedings (often called the adjudicative process, in contrast to the judical process), even if they take place through informal proceedings aimed at voluntary compliance, we will speak of regulatory jurisdiction because of the objectives which the government seeks to obtain.

Civil Remedies

The questions which will need an answer with regard to the civil remedies in antitrust litigation are:

14. BLACK'S LAW DICTIONARY, 4th Ed., St. Paul, 1951, p. 1451, defines the concept of regulatory as 'power to prescribe rules by which commerce is to be governed, and embraces prohibitory regulations.' On that basis the injunction could just as well be classified as regulatory; we have followed a different classification because the action is also available to private litigants.

(1) which courts have jurisdiction?
(2) who are entitled to bring an action?
(3) which actions or remedies are available?

(1) Which courts have jurisdiction?

In responseto the above question we can state that the jurisdictional competency for civil suits is entrusted to the federal courts.[15] This follows from the language of Sec. 4 and Sec. 4A of the *Clayton Act,*[16] which read in part as follows:

Sec. 4: '. . .any person who shall be injured in his business or property by reason of anything forbidden in the antitrust laws may sue therefor in any district court of the United States in the district in which the defendant resides or is found or has an agent . . .'

Sec. 4A: 'Whenever the United States is hereafter injured in its business or property by reason of anything forbidden in the antitrust laws it may sue therefor in the United States district court for the district in which the defendant resides or is found or has an agent . . .'

(2) Who are intitled to instigate legal proceedings?

The above quoted sections of the *Clayton Act*, in addition to indicating where lawsuits are to be brought, also provide an answer to our second question: who are entitled to bring an action? From the wording of the act we can conclude that civil suits can be brought either by private parties who are injured in their business or property, or by the government (i.e., the Department of Justice), under similar conditions. Yet the text leaves unanswered the question whether a corporation, a state, or a municipal corporation are entitled to bring an action for damages. With regard to corporations, sec. 1 (last paragraph) of the *Clayton Act* states specifically:

'The word "person" or "persons" wherever used in this Act, shall be deemed to include corporations and associations existing under or authorized by the laws of either the United States, the laws of any of the Territories, the laws of any State, or the laws of any foreign country.'

With regard to a State, the U.S. Supreme Court held in 1942 that a State may bring an action for damages under the *Sherman Act* to protect its proper interests.[17] With regard to municipal corporations, the U.S. Supreme Court held that they too, may sue for damages.[18]

(3) Which actions or remedies are avaible?

Having indicated who may bring an action, we now turn to the query: what are

15. Our statement refers to federal antitrust litigation only. Where litigation occurs pertaining to state antitrust laws the state courts would have jurisdictional competency.
16. Act of October 15, 1914, as amended; *cf. supra*, p. 4, *n.* 13
17. *Georgia* v. *Evans*, 316 US 159, 62 S Ct 972 (1942); *cf.* OPPENHEIM & WESTON, *op. cit.*, p. 875. The reference to the *Sherman Act* pertains to former sec. 7, which was repealed in 1955, and superseded by sec. 4 of the *Clayton Act; cf.* OPPENHEIM & WESTON, *op. cit.*, p. 874, *n.* 90.
18. *Chattanooga Foundry & Pipe Works* v. *Atlanta*, 203 US 390, 27 S Ct 65 (1906); *cf.* OPPENHEIM & WESTON, *op. cit.*, p. 875.

the remedies available in a civil suit? Part of our answer can, again, be found in the text of sections 4 and 4A of the *Clayton Act*, stating:

Sec. 4: '. . .any person . . .shall recover threefold the damages by him sustained, and the cost of suit, including a reasonable attorney's fee.'

Sec. 4A: '. . .the United States shall recover actual damages by it sustained and the cost of suit.'

A comparison between the amounts of damages available to parties under the above quoted sections of the *Clayton Act* reveals that persons, including corporations, states, or municipal corporations, may recover *treble* damages, whereas the United States can only claim *actual* damage.[19]

The fact that the remedy referred to consists of damages (be they treble or actual), signifies that we are dealing with a *tort action*. The significance of this will become clear when we are dealing with the foreign aspects of antitrust enforcement, because torts belong to the area of private law.[20]

Suffice it at this time to state that the action for damages is a civil remedy *at law* (in contrast to the civil remedy *in equity*), entitling an injured party to claim monetary recompense for the injury suffered.

In addition to the civil remedy *at law* there is also a civil remedy *in equity*, the so-called *injunction*. We find reference thereto in the following legal provisions:

Sherman Act, Sec. 4: 'The several district courts of the United States are hereby invested with jurisdiction to prevent and restrain violations of this act; and it shall be the duty of the several district attorneys of the United States, in their respective districts, under the direction of the Attorney General, to institute proceedings.'

Clayton Act, Sec. 16: '. . .any person, firm, corporation, or association shall be empowered to sue for and have injunctive relief, in any court of the United States having jurisdiction over the parties, as against threatened loss or damage by a violation of the antitrust laws, including sections two, three, seven, and eight of this Act, when and under the same conditions and principles as injunctive relief against threatened conduct that will cause loss or damage is granted by courts of equity, under the rules governing such proceedings, and upon the execution of proper bond against damages for an injunction improvidently

19. The difference seems to be founded on the desirability of encouraging private persons to bring actions which, 'though brought to enforce a private claim, will nonetheless serve the public interest in the enforcement of the antitrust laws. . .'; *cf.* OPPENHEIM & WESTON, *op. cit.*, p. 875, n. 96.

20. Thus, we find that SCHWARTZ, I. E. (*op. cit.*, p. 143) and REHBINDER (*op. cit.*, p. 308) refer to *Kartellzivillprozesse.*

> granted and a showing that the danger of irreparable loss or damage is immediate, a preliminary injunction may issue . . .'

The difference in wording between sec. 4 *Sherman Act* (prevent and restrain) and sec. 16 *Clayton Act* (injunctive relief), suggests that the *temporary injunction* would only be available to the U.S. Government and not to private parties, for the simple reason that sec. 16 *Clayton Act* only provides for injunctive relief which is final, and not expressly for temporary injunctions.[21]

We can, then, summarize that the two civil remedies available are the (treble) damage suit (tort action) and the (temporary) injunction (equity action). We can also state that these civil remedies are open both to private parties and to the Government.

In addition to the above remedies there are several others that are open only to the Government, also with jurisdiction entrusted to the federal courts. We are thinking of such remedies as dissolution, divestiture and divorcement, or the consent decree. Inasmuch as we are looking at these remedies from the vantage point of the objectives sought to be accomplished, we will discuss them when dealing with the regulatory jurisdiction: the effects of these remedies are much more of a regulatory nature, as we hope to demonstrate. The sole purpose for mentioning them at this time is to demonstrate that we are not unaware of the possible objections that others might raise against our admittedly arbitrary classification.

Criminal Remedies

Turning to the area of criminal remedies, we can forego the question 'who are entitled to bring an action?' It is obvious that only the Government can initiate a criminal prosecution. The second question is more relevant: 'Which actions or remedies are available?' We find the following remedies:

(a) a fine of $50,000 maximum for violation of sections 1, 2 or 3 of the *Sherman Act*;[22]

21. *cf.* OPPENHEIM & WESTON, *op. cit.*, p. 23. Interesting to note is that in the second edition (St. Paul, 1959), at p. 1034, the statement is made that 'such relief is generally considered to be within the scope of the section.' In the third ed. (St. Paul, 1968) we find, at p. 892, that, 'For a number of reasons the courts have been very reluctant to order drastic relief in private cases.' While this statement does not negate the validity of the above quoted earlier assertion, it does seem to reduce its possible availability.

22. Sec. 1 makes the making of any contract, or engaging in any combination or conspiracy, in restraint of trade, a misdemeanor. Sec. 2 makes monopolizing, or attempts thereto, either singly or in combination or conspiracy with others, of any part of trade or commerce, a misdemeanor. Sec. 3 extends the reach of sec. 1 to any Territory of the United States or the District of Columbia.

(b) a fine of $25,000 maximum for violation of sec. 10, paragraph 4, of the *Clayton Act;*[23]

(c) a fine of $5,000 maximum for violation of sec. 3 of the *Robinson-Patman Act,*[24] sec. 10, paragraph 4, second sentence, of the *Clayton Act,*[25] sec. 14 of the *Clayton Act;*[26]

(d) a civil penalty of $5,000 maximum to be recovered in a civil action, for violation of sec. 11, sub (1), of the *Clayton Act,*[27] or sec. 5, paragraph (6), sub (l) of the *Federal Trade Commission Act;*[28]

(e) a fine of $5,000 maximum for violation of sec. 14, paragraph (a), of the *Federal Trade Commission Act*, to be increased to a maximum of $10,000 in case of a subsequent violation after a first conviction;[29]

(f) a fine of a minimum of $1,000 and a maximum of $5,000 for violation of sec. 10, paragraph 1 and 2, of the *Federal Trade Commission Act;*[30]

23. Sec. 10, par. 4, declares common carriers guilty of a misdemeanor, if they have any dealings in securities, supplies, or other articles of commerce, or make or have contracts for construction or maintenance in excess of $50,000 in any one year, with another corporation, firm, partnership, or association, if any of the members of the board of directors is an executive, or has substantial interests, in any such other business enterprise (unless as a result of open competitive bidding).

24. Sec. 3 declares it unlawful for persons engaged in commerce to be in the course of such commerce a party to, or assist in, any sales transaction which they know to discriminate against competitors of the purchaser, in respect to sales of goods of like grade, quality, and quantity; or to sell goods at lower prices in certain parts of the United States (as compared with their prices charged elsewhere), for the purpose of destroying competition; or to sell goods at unreasonably low prices for the purpose of destroying competition or eliminating a competitor.

25. Sec. 10, paragraph 4, second sentence, declares directors, agents, managers or officers of common carriers, guilty of a misdemeanor, if they act in contravention of the prohibitions noted *supra, n.* 23

26. Sec. 14 declares directors, officers, or agents of corporations personally guilty of a misdemeanor for corporate violations of the penal provisions of the antitrust laws.

27. Sec. 11, sub (1) holds out this liability to anyone who violates any order issued by the Interstate Commerce Commission, Federal Communications Commission, the Civil Aeronautics Board (where applicable, respectively, to common carriers, to common carriers engaged in wire or radio communication or radio transmission of energy, to air carriers and foreign air carriers), the Federal Reserve Board (where applicable to banks, banking associations, and trust companies), or the Federal Trade Commission (with reference to all other character of commerce).

28. Sec. 5, paragraph (6), sub (l), holds out this liability to any person, partnership, or corporation who violates an order of the Federal Trade Commission to cease and desist.

The violations of sec. 11, sub (1) *Clayton Act* and sec. 5, paragraph (6), sub (l) *Federal Trade Commission Act* are considered separate offenses for each separate violation, or for each day of continuance through continuing failure or neglect to obey the final order.

29. Sec. 14, paragraph (a), declares it a misdemeanor to disseminate false advertising for the purpose of inducing the purchase of food, drugs, devices, or cosmetics, if the commodity may be injurious to health.

30. Sec. 10, paragraphs 1 and 2, declare it an offense against the United States to neglect or refuse to testify, or to produce documentary evidence, or to make false statements or entries in corporate records, or to willfully mutilate or remove documents out of the jurisdiction of the United States.

(g) a forfeit of $100 per day for violation of sec. 10, paragraph 3, of the *Federal Trade Commission Act,* recoverable in a civil suit in the name of the United States;[31]

(h) imprisonment for a maximum of one year for violation of sections 1, 2 and 3 of the *Sherman Act,*[32] sec. 10, paragraph 4 (second sentence), of the *Clayton Act,*[33] sec. 14 of the *Clayton Act,*[34] sec. 3 of the *Robinson-Patman Act,*[35] sec. 10, paragraph 1, of the *Federal Trade Commission Act;*[36]

(i) imprisonment for a maximum of three years, for violation of sec. 10, paragraph 2, of the *Federal Trade Commission Act;*[37]

(j) imprisonment for a maximum of six months, for violation of Sec. 14, paragraph (a), of the *Federal Trade Commission Act,* to be increased to a maximum of one year in case of a subsequent violation following a first conviction;[38]

(k) forfeiture of property, in accordance with sec. 6 of the *Sherman Act.*[39]

In other words, the criminal sactions consist of either a fine, or imprisonment, or both, the penalties ranging all the way from $100 per day to a maximum of $50,000, while the imprisonment ranges from a minimum of six months to a maximum of three years; also, as indicated above, forfeiture of property is a possibility, even though rarely used.

Inasmuch as we look at the American antitrust laws primarily through the *Sherman Act*, the *Clayton Act*, and the *Federal Trade Commission Act*, as amended from time to time, we do not find it opportune to also investigate what criminal remedies are available under the authority of other pertinent legislation. Such an undertaking would go beyond the scope of our undertaking. The major purpose of this section is merely to demonstrate that, in addition to civil jurisdictional

31. The forfeiture is held out for failure to file any required annual report within the time fixed for such filing. While technically not a criminal action, we have included the forfeiture in the group of criminal sanctions because of the clearly penal character thereof.
32. *cf. supra, n.* 22
33. *cf. supra, n.* 25
34. *cf. supra, n.* 26
35. *cf. supra, n.* 24
36. *cf. supra, n.* 30
37. *cf. supra, n.* 30
38. *cf. supra, n.* 29
39. Sec. 6 states: 'Any property owned under any contract or by any combination, or pursuant to any conspiracy (and being the subject thereof) mentioned in section one of this act, and being in the course of transportation from one State to another, or to a foreign country, shall be forfeited to the United States, and may be seized and condemned by like proceedings as those provided by law for the forfeiture, seizure, and condemnation of property imported into the United States contrary to law.' Interesting is this observation: 'Although it has frequently been suggested that this method of enforcement should be widely employed, the libel action has been rarely used and in each instance the issues were settled out of court before the cases went to trial.' *cf.* OPPENHEIM & WESTON, *op. cit.*, p. 24.
For the character of the forfeiture proceedings, see *supra, n.* 31

remedies, the Government can also resort to criminal sanctions to ensure compliance with the antitrust laws.

We should, however, point to the fact that sec. 11, sub (1), of the *Clayton Act* calls for a forfeiture of a civil penalty of $5,000 for each violation, while sec. 5, paragraph 6, sub (1), of the *Federal Trade Commission Act* calls for a similar civil penalty. While this would justify a classification of these remedies under the heading 'civil jurisdiction,' this has not restrained us from classifying these civil penalties under the heading of criminal jurisdiction.[40]

In other words, just as we have decided, for reasons of looking at the remedies in the light of their objectives, to classify the dissolution, divestiture, divorcement, and consent decree as regulatory remedies, so have we, for the same reasons, classified the civil penalties and the forfeiture as criminal remedies. Again, we are not unaware of the objections that might be raised against our arbitrary classification; however, because of our classification of remedies on the basis of their objectives, we feel justified in doing so.

Regulatory Remedies

Much like the criminal remedies, we can with regard to the regulatory remedies forego the question 'who are entitled to bring action?' It is obvious that regulatory jurisdiction is a Government matter.

More complicated is the answer to the question: 'which actions or remedies are available?' We say so, because we are including in this category remedies which are, *sensu strictu*, rather within the civil jurisdictional sphere. But, as indicated earlier, we feel justified in dealing with these remedies at this time because of our system of classification according to objectives.

The remedies to be discussed in this section are:[41]

(1) Dissolution, Divestiture, and Divorcement;
(2) the Department of Justice Consent Judgment and Decree;
(3) the Federal Trade Commission Stipulation;
(4) the Federal Trade Commission 'Administrative Treatment';
(5) the Federal Trade Commission Consent Order;
(6) the Cease-and-Desist Order;
(7) Advance Clearance by the Federal Trade Commission;
(8) the Federal Trade Commission Trade Practice Conference.

ad (1): Dissolution, Divestiture, and Divorcement.[42]

40. For our justification, see *supra*, p. 47
41. For a concise synopsis of these various remedies, *cf.* OPPENHEIM & WESTON, *op. cit.*, pp. 22-27.
42. *cf.* OPPENHEIM & WESTON, *op. cit.*, pp. 858, *seq.;* SCHWARTZ, L. B., *op. cit.*, pp. 191, *seq.* Some authors refer to these measures as 'the three D's of Antitrust'; cf. WILCOX, C., PUBLIC POLICIES TOWARD BUSINESS, Homewood, 1960, p. 112; OPPENHEIM & WESTON, *op. cit.*, p. 858.

Dissolution, divestiture, and divorcement are, formally speaking, civil remedies; they are available in equity proceedings. We have classified them as regulatory because only the Government (the Attorney General) is entitled to the action, while the objectives can be termed regulation of structural relationships.[43]

The right to invoke these remedies is based on the language of Section 4 of the *Sherman Act*[44] and the almost identical language of Section 15 of the *Clayton Act* giving the Attorney General the power to initiate an action 'to prevent and restrain' violations, by way of a prayer that such violations be 'enjoined or otherwise prohibited.' This language marks the proceeding as one in equity; the result is that the court has a wide discretion to make the order fit the requirements of the particular case.[45]

Dissolution aims at the dissolving of an allegedly illegal combination or association, as a result of which the enterprise breaks up into separate units.

Divestiture requires defendants, when found guilty of transgression of the law, to divest themselves of property, securities, or other assets in other enterprises. Divorcement aims at the specific ways in which certain types of divestiture have to be carried out, such as the separation of vertically integrated manufacturing and distribution activities.[46]

In *Schine Chain Theatres* v. *U.S.*[47] the United States Supreme Court made the following statement:

> 'Divestiture or dissolution must take account of the present and future conditions in the particular industry as well as past violations. It serves several functions: (1) It puts an end to the combination or conspiracy when that is itself the violation. (2) It deprives the antitrust defendant of the benefits of their conspiracy. (3) It is designed to break up or render impotent the monopoly power which violates the act.'

The *Attorney General's Report* notes that 'over the 60 odd years of Sherman Act history, courts have in only 24 litigated cases entered decrees requiring divorcement, divestiture or dissolution.'[48] A shift in attitude seems to have developed since 1955; we say so because in some recent decisions the United States Supreme Court has indicated that 'divestiture should be foremost in the court's mind since it is relatively easy to administer and is certain to achieve its intented result."[49]

No cases of dissolution, divestiture, or divorcement involving foreign business firms have been reported. It is conceivable however, that, absent considerations

43. For our justification, see *supra*, p. 48
44. *cf. supra*, p. 50
45. *cf.* OPPENHEIM & WESTON, *op. cit.*, p. 859
46. *cf.* OPPENHEIM & WESTON, *op. cit.*, p. 858; WILCOX, *op. cit.*, pp. 112, 113
47. 334 US 110, 68 S Ct 947 (1948)
48. *cf. Att'y Gen. Report*, p. 354
49. *cf.* SUPPLEMENT, p. 225, citing five cases, all from 1960 or later, in support of the conclusion that a shift in attitude seems to have developed.

of international law and/or expediency, cases will be heard involving foreign conduct and foreign parties. That so far no cases have been reported involving foreign defendants seems only to suggest that this area of the law is still in a stage of evolutionary growth.

The view of the Supreme Court is that 'divestiture is a remedy to restore competition and not to punish those who restrain trade . . .'[50]

The following guidelines have been suggested:[51]

(1) it should not be decreed as a penalty;

(2) it should not be invoked where less drastic remedies will accomplish the purpose of the litigation;

(3) the effect of a possible resultant disruption upon the industry involved, its cognate markets, and the public needs in peace and war, should be considered;

(4) once divestiture has been ordered, account must be taken of its effect on the public as well as on the defendant and persons interested in it, as investors, customers and employees.

ad (2): The Department of Justice Consent Judgment and Degree.

The utilization of the Department of Justice consent judgment and decree has been termed 'an extremely significant device in the enforcement of the antitrust laws.'[52]

This procedural device, which is not expressly authorized in the antitrust laws, consists of an agreement between the litigating parties.[53] Approval of the court is necessary for the agreement to become binding upon the parties; once the approval has been given by the court, the agreement has the same force as if it were a judgment or decree in a litigated case.[54] Consequently, if a defendant were to ignore his obligation, he might expose himself to contempt proceedings.[55]

How important the device is may quantitatively be demonstrated by showing that between 1935 and 1955, 72 per cent of the terminations of 'civil actions' ended in consent decrees;[56] this percentage has continued in approximately the same proportion during the period 1955-1968 (70%).[57]

With regard to the extraterritorial reach of the antitrust laws, consent decrees give recognition to the possibility that foreign defendants may be required to

50. *Timken Roller Bearing Co.* v *U.S.*, 341 US 593, 71 S Ct 971 (1951), in the concurring opinion of Mr. Justice REED.
51. *cf. Att'y Gen. Report*, pp. 355, 356
52. *cf.* OPPENHEIM & WESTON, *op. cit.*, p. 843
53. *ibid.*
54. A judgment results from an action 'at law', while a decree results from an action in equity.
55. *cf.* OPPENHEIM & WESTON, *op. cit.*, p. 844
56. *cf. Att'y Gen. Report*, p. 360
57. *cf.* SUPPLEMENT, p. 226

perform acts in their own country counter to the provisions of the consent decree.[58] Sometimes this occurs as a (subsequent modification of the decree, a possibility which exists because the civil action ending in a consent decree is a procedure in equity, giving the court the opportunity to modify the decree on the basis of changed circumstances.[59]

This was demonstrated in the *Swiss Watchmakers* case,[60] where the court granted the motion to modify the judgment after the Government had obtained the consent of the defendants to acquiesce if the judgment were modified 'to remove possible conflicts between the decree and the exercise of sovereignty by the Swiss Confederation.'[61]

Similarly, a consent judgment was entered in *U.S.* v. *United Fruit Co.,*[62] after United Fruit had claimed that what it did in foreign countries was done pursuant to measures adopted by those foreign nations.

The advantage to a private party is that (in addition to saving expense in a long-lasting trial) the consent decree may not be introduced by a private plaintiff as *prima facie* evidence in a treble damages action.[63] To the government there is advantage (in addition to saving expenses) because it avoids 'the characteristic complexities of antitrust litigation.'[64] All of this may seem strange in the light of an argument used in an important case that, 'jurisdiction cannot be conferred by consent;. . .jurisdiction can exist only if the transactions complained of are in fact violations of the act . . .'[65] We should add that the Supreme Court rejected this argument; it made, however, with regard to the authority of the Attorney General the following statement:

> 'His authority to make determinations includes the power to make erroneous decisions as well as correct ones.'

ad (3): The Federal Trade Commission Stipulation

The Federal Trade Commission stipulation consists of a document which specifies the acts or practices under consideration, and which contains the agreement that the party whose acts or practices are being scrutinized will cease and desist from same; the document is signed by the party involved and the Chairman and Secretary of the Federal Trade Commission. While the document lacks the force of an enforceable order to cease and desist, it still can give rise to a formal

58. 'Consent decrees occasionally exclude from their scope conduct required by the law of the place of performance.'; *cf.* HANDLER, *op. cit.*, p. 1171, *n.* 13, and the cases there cited.
59. *cf.* OPPENHEIM & WESTON, *op. cit.*, p. 850
60. 1963 Trade Cases, nr. 70, 600 (S.D.-N.Y.)
61. *cf.* HANDLER, *op. cit.*, p. 1170; BLAKE & PITOFSKY, *op. cit.*, p. 1270
62. 1958 Trade Cases, nr. 68, 941 (E.D.-La), cited in OPPENHEIM & WESTON, *op. cit.*, p. 783
63. *cf.* OPPENHEIM & WESTON, pp. 843, 844
64. *ibid.*, p. 844; also, *cf.* SUPPLEMENT, p. 227
65. *Swift & Co.* v. *U.S.*, 276 US 311, 48 S Ct 311 (1928)

complaint in case of intentional non-compliance.[66]
The use of stipulations has been abolished and been replaced, in 1963, by a new procedure, under which an informal settlement is reached by an assurance of voluntary compliance; the device is 'somewhat similar to the stipulation.'[67]
The basis for the procedure rests on the general function of the Federal Trade Commission to police unfair methods of competition and unfair or deceptive practices. It will be used to dispose of a suspected violation of the antitrust laws by way of this informal non-adjudicatory method, depending upon the severity of the suspected violation, the public interest, the good faith of the parties involved.[68] Because it is an informal disposition, the Federal Trade Commission can, in case of non-compliance with the assurance of voluntary compliance, take steps to compel compliance, utilizing the full range of formal remedies it has at its disposal.
ad (4): The Federal Trade Commission 'Administrative Treatment'
The 'administrative treatment' is a method of dealing with suspected false advertising and other misrepresentation, leading to the closing of a case without public announcement, whereby the party under investigation simply must give the Federal Trade Commission a written assurance that he will abandon the acts or practices in question, without a contest of the charges made against him.[69]
This procedure, which has also been termed the 'assurance of discontinuance'[70] is closely related in its method to the assurance of voluntary compliance referred to above sub (3). Here too, it aims at obtaining an assurance of voluntary compliance, and is thus, 'a device for disposing of an investigation or an adjudicative proceeding on an informal nonadjudicatory basis.'[71]
For the party involved these assurances have the advantage that they only amount to a halting of the practices, without an admission that the challenged practices are illegal.[72] This means that in case of non-compliance and subsequent adjudicative proceedings, he will have all the opportunities to defend himself against the allegations. This procedure has been termed 'much more flexible than either the formerly used stipulation procedure or the consent order procedure.'[73]

66. *cf.* OPPENHEIM & WESTON, *op. cit.*, p. 856, who note that 'By 1954 the Commission had executed over 8400 stipulations.'
67. *cf.* SUPPLEMENT, p. 242. The new procedure is based on the revised *Procedures and Rules of Practice, Federal Trade Commission,* which became effective August 1, 1963. We have not found statistical data as to the frequency of use of the assurance of voluntary compliance.
68. *cf.* OPPENHEIM & WESTON, *op. cit.*, pp. 854, 856
69. *ibid.*, p. 856
70. *cf.* WILCOX, *op. cit.*, p. 120. In fact, today they are treated as practically identical; *cf.* SUPPLEMENT, p. 243
71. *cf.* SUPPLEMENT, p. 243
72. *ibid.*, p. 243
73. *ibid.*, p. 243

ad (5): The Federal Trade Commission Consent Order

Although since 1967 the Federal Trade Commission Consent Order follows a procedure similar to the one followed by the Department of Justice in its Judgment and Consent Decree procedure,[74] there are still differences. The Federal Trade Commission Consent Order is based on the following principles:

(a) it eliminates the requirement that the consent settlement contain findings of fact or a statement of the alleged unlawful practices;
(b) it permits disposition of a case by consent at any stage of the proceeding;
(c) it allows settlement of a case as to some or all of the issues or respondents;
(d) it authorizes hearing examiners to accept or reject stipulations containing proposed consent orders, with acceptane subject to Commission review and with rejection subject to appeal to the Commission.[75]

On the part of the respondents, the measure requires:
(a) that the Federal Trade Commission has jurisdiction;
(b) that the complaint (issued by the Commission) may be used in construing the terms of the order;
(c) that the order shall have the same force as if entered after a full hearing;
(d) that the order may be modified or set aside in the same manner as other orders;
(e) that the entry of findings of fact and conclusions of law, as well as further procedural steps before the hearing examiner or the Commission, be waived;
(f) that any court test of the order's validity be waived.[76]

Consequently, violation of the consent order will have the same impact as a violation of an order entered after litigation.[77]

ad (6): The Cease and Desist Order

In addition to the above mentioned steps the Federal Trade Commission can take in order to to achieve compliance with the antitrust laws, it has one formal action at its disposal, the so-called cease-and-desist order. Cease-and-desist orders

74. *cf.* OPPENHEIM & WESTON, *op. cit.*, p. 856; SUPPLEMENT, p. 243
75. *cf. Att'y Gen. Report*, p. 371. The Report notes that the appeal may be taken only if the Trial Staff joins with respondents in seeking review.
76. *ibid.*, p. 371. OPPENHEIM & WESTON, *op. cit.*, p. 856, point out that, 'Since 1961 the Commission has followed the practice of permitting the entry of a consent order only at the initiation of a proceeding (unless application of the Rule is waived in a particular instance).'
Furthermore, since 1967, if an agreement is reached, the order will be placed on the 'public record for a period of 30 days for comments by interested persons. If facts are brought to the Commission's attention imdicating that the proposed order is "inappropriate, improper or inadequate", the Commission may withdraw its consent.'; *cf.* SUPPLEMENT, p. 243
77. *cf.* OPPENHEIM & WESTON, *op. cit.*, p. 856

can be issued either under the *Clayton Act*, or under sec. 5 of the *Federal Trade Commission Act.*[78]

As WILCOX correctly observes, the order 'is purely negative in character,' because it can only issue the order with regard to a practice that is in itself illegal; in other words, the order will only inform parties what they may not do, while there is no provision made for what positive steps are to be taken to correct wrong practices that have been committed in the past.[79]

The cease-and-desist order can be issued either by consent or after a hearing. A review is possible by the federal courts, *in casu*, the Federal Courts of Appeals. The authority to issue cease and desist orders is based on the power of the Federal Trade Commission to prevent and restrain unlawful trade practices. However, because the order 'is confined to a particular offense by a particular offender in a particular case,'[80] a different person committing the same offense can continue to do so until a cease-and-desist order, pertaining specifically to him, has been issued.[81]

ad (7): Advance Clearance by the Federal Trade Commission

The Federal Trade Commission provides an opportunity to businessmen to know in advance whether there will be any antitrust problems in such matters as mergers, trade association activities, pricing policies, allowances, labeling, advertising policies. In those cases the businessman may ask for an advisory opinion of the Federal Trade Commission with regard to the particular activity contemplated; these advisory opinions are published in a digest, hypothetical in form, without making reference to the persons or businesses involved.[82] It needs no elaboration that the advisory opinion is limited to the facts of the activities as the parties submit them.[83]

The Federal Trade Commission may revoke or rescind an advisory opinion; in that case the requesting party must be notified in order to give him an opportunity to change his activities in the light of the rescission of the advisory opinion, and thus, avoid adjudicative proceedings.[84]

Foreign business enterprises having a limited clientele in the United States, and contemplating a merger or other activities in order to obtain a firmer and more substantial foothold on the American market, might do well to avail themselves of the possibility to obtain an advisory opinion from the Federal Trade Commis-

78. For the differences between the two actions, *cf. Att'y Gen. Report*, p. 372; OPPENHEIM & WESTON, *op. cit.*, pp. 855, 856.
79. *cf.* WILCOX, *op. cit.*, pp. 120, 121.
80. *cf.* WILCOX, *op. cit.*, p. 121.
81. While it is still too early to indicate whether a definite reversal of this view has come about, recent decisions of the United States Supreme Court seem to give the Federal Trade Commission considerably broader and farther reaching power; *cf.* SUPPLEMENT, pp. 262, 263
82. *cf.* SUPPLEMENT, p. 241; no statistics as to the use of this procedure are given
83. *cf.* OPPENHEIM & WESTON, *op. cit.*, pp. 441, 442 and 841, *seq.*
84. *cf.* SUPPLEMENT, p. 241

sion before they run afoul of the antitrust laws. Of course, this would only apply if the contemplated activities, merger or otherwise, would be undertaken solely with the American market in mind. We would think it inconceivable that a merger which would come about say, because of changed economic conditions within the European Economic Community needs an advisory opinion of the Federal Trade Commission. It is only when activities are contemplated with the American market in mind that foreign businessmen should consider the advance clearance (advisory opinion) procedure of the Federal Trade Commission.

ad (8): The Federal Trade Commission Trade Practice Conference

So far we have concerned ourselves with the regulatory remedies as they relate to the practices of the individual or of the business enterprise. We now turn our attention to an other aspect of regulation, the so-called trade practice conference, which has been used by the Federal Trade Commission since 1918, although without formal authority. Under the procedure as applied by the Federal Trade Commission, rules are drafted and submitted to the members of a certain industry, to be adopted in subsequent conferences between these members and representatives of the Federal Trade Commission. Conference rules may be designed 'to prohibit unfair competitive practices, to control false and misleading advertising, and to promote nondeceptive description or labeling of industry products.'[85] By 1957, trade practice rules had been developed and adopted for as many as 161 different industries.[86]

In more recent years the Federal Trade Commission, particularly through its Bureau of Industry Guidance, has increasingly utilized an industrywide approach to 'inform businessmen and their legal advisors of its views with respect to specific business practices.'[87] To that effect the Bureau of Industry Guidance is subdivided in several divisions.[88]

(a) the Trade Practice Conference Division, which works out the 'Trade Practice Rules', to provide guidance for compliance with statutory requirements. These trade practice rules are also called 'industry guides'; thus, we find guides concerning the tire industry, or other industries, but also, guides on guaranty claims, or deceptive pricing. These guides do not have the effect of law; the purpose is 'to eliminate by voluntary action, trade practices which violate the law . . .'[89]

(b) the Trade Regulation Rules Division, which promulgates rules in which the illegality of certain acts or practices are set forth. These trade regulation rules come about only after extensive public hearings, open to participation by all interested parties.[90]

85. *cf. Att'y Gen. Report*, p. 369
86. *cf.* WILCOX, *op. cit.*, p. 119
87. *cf.* SUPPLEMENT, p. 240
88. *cf.* BLAKE & PITOFSKY, *op. cit.*, p. 1321
89. SUPPLEMENT, p. 240
90. SUPPLEMENT, pp. 240, 241

The difference between 'trade practice rules' and 'trade regulation rules' is that in case of violation of the former the Federal Trade Commission will have to show that its views of what is lawful and unlawful are correct. On the other hand, in the opinion of the Federal Trade Commission, the trade regulation rules are '. . .accompanied by and based upon determinations of fact made in accordance with statutory rule making procedures . . .' There have been no court decisions, however, to determine whether, indeed, the Federal Trade Commission has the right to apply its trade regulation rules in the adjudicative stage.[91] We perceive the difference to be that the 'trade practice rules' are a *preventive* method to avoid possible violations of the law by way of voluntary cooperation, while the 'trade regulation rules" come about because certain practices have been found to be violative of the law and should be stopped; the latter are therefore, rather *corrective*. Both have in common that no formal proceedings have been instigated, and that future violations of the law are presumably avoided.

One may wonder why we have included the Federal Trade Commission Trade Practice Conference in a discussion of the regulatory jurisdictional aspects of antitrust enforcement. Our reason for doing so is that inasmuch as the purpose of the Trade Practice Conference is to seek compliance with the promulgated rules (in fact, because non-compliance may lead to prosecution to obtain a compulsory compliance), inclusion is justified.[92]

We suggest that regulation is the very purpose of the trade practice conference, even if it occurs at the quasi-judicial level. Therefore, we may consider the procedure regulatory.

Whether the designation 'remedy' is justified is more questionable. We admit that a remedy is commonly thought of as an individualized action, while here we are dealing with a group-directive that has quasi-legislative characteristics. When we, nevertheless, suggest that the designation 'remedy' is justified we do so on the following grounds:

(a) with regard to the trade regulation rules, we find little difficulty to identify the remedial character, because the Federal Trade Commission issues these rules only on the bases of practices that it has encountered and that it considers in violation of the law;

(b) with regard to the trade practice rules, we suggest that the preventive character also gives the procedure a remedial character.

Our conclusion is that because of the objectives to be achieved we are justified to consider the procedure one of (informal) regulatory jurisdiction.

Both the trade practice rules and the trade regulation rules may affect the

91. *ibid.*, p. 241. Also, see BLAKE & PITOFSKY, *op. cit.*, p. 1321, where the statement is made that, 'these rules do not have the force of law.'

92. Some authors designate this procedure 'industry-wide enforcement', thereby giving it a remedial aspect; *cf.* OPPENHEIM & WESTON, *op. cit.*, p. 857

foreign businessman, and therefore, have an extraterritorial reach.

In order to illustrate the point, we might mention the rules for labeling and advertising in such diverse industries as cotton yard goods, silk, rayon, linen, luggage, watches, watch cases, and radio receiving sets. These industries are by and large located both outside and within the territorial boundaries of the United States. Consequently, any of the foreign located industries desirous of participating with their products on the American market will have to comply with the rules promulgated and set forth by the Federal Trade Commission in the trade practice rules and trade regulation rules; non-compliance may expose violators to subsequent prosecution.

Let us supppose that a foreign manufacturer (or a group of manufacturers) of cosmetic products, eager to find a substantial outlet for these cosmetic products in the United States market, would make certain (untrue) claims in the labeling of their products, or even, succumb to the persuasion of a prominent department store merchandising manager to provide for overgenerous advertising and promotion allowances[93], in contravention of the trade regulation rules: there is little question but that the result might be an extraterritorial reach of the American antitrust laws.

Some Other Procedural Aspects of Antitrust Enforcement

While an exhaustive or even near-exhaustive discussion of the entire spectrum of remedial and other procedural aspects of the antitrust enforcement would go far beyond the scope of our undertaking, we feel it incumbent upon us to at least mention a few items that we have not mentioned heretofore and which should be of importance to foreign defendants. We mention: (1) the plea of *nolo contendere*; (2) the position of the enforcement agencies in the light of recently passed legislation; (3) the cost; (4) the element of time; (5) the discovery procedure. We suggest that each of these aspects might be of concern to the foreign businessman because of the extraterritorial reach of the antitrust laws.

ad (1) The plea of *nolo contendere.*

When a defendant is facing a criminal prosecution, he can plead either not guilty, guilty, or *nolo contendere*. The difference is that if the court finds the defendant guilty, either because of the evidence produced during the trial or because of his own plea of guilty, the defendant may be fined or imprisoned; furthermore, his conviction will be *prima facie* evidence in any subsequent civil action for treble damages. On the other hand, the plea of *nolo contendere* may lead to either a fine or imprisonment, but the sentence may not be used as *prima facie* evidence in a treble damages suit.[94] However, the court must first accept the *nolo conten-*

93. See *R. H. Macy & Co., Inc.* v *F.T.C.*, 326 F2d 445 (1964), cited in SUPPLEMENT, p. 257, where Macy's had solicited contributions of $1,000 apiece from its vendors 'to help defray the advertising and promotional cost of its anniversary celebration.'

94. SUPPLEMENT, p. 222

dere plea; the Antitrust Division of the Department of Justice has the opportunity to oppose the plea. Although the defendant may not use the *nolo* plea to publicly claim that he was not guilty, the advantage to a defendant of a *nolo contendere* plea is the elimination of the use of the sentence as *prima facie* evidence in the civil litigation.

ad (2) The impact of recently legislation.

(a) In 1959 Congress passed the *Finality Act.* This changed considerably the impact of Federal Trade Commission determinations. Until 1959, the Federal Trade Commission had first, to determine that a violation of the antitrust law had occurred, before it could issue a cease-and-desist order. Enforcement of the order needed, furthermore, a court order; in other words, the court too, had to be convinced of the violation of the law. Only thereafter was a defendant in contempt of court if he violated the order. Since 1959 the cease-and-desist order is final upon expiration of sixty days; violation leads then to a civil penalty.[95]

(b) In 1961 the Federal Trade Commission revised its *Rules of Practice*, adopting a 'new central adjudicative concept', according to which a hearing must be held in one place and must continue without interruption until completed. Prior to 1959 long intervals between direct and cross-examinations, as well as between the presentations for the prosecution and the defense were common. The continuous hearing concept has allowed more expeditious proceedings. The saving of time has for the defendant this possible disadvantage that he has less time available to prepare his cross examination, defenses and rebuttals; in order to compensate for that disadvantage, provision has been made for broad pre-hearing discovery procedures.[96]

(c) In 1962 Congress passed the *Antitrust Civil Process Act*, authorizing the Department of Justice to serve a civil investigative demand upon any person, corporation, or other legal entity to produce documents for examination, if the Department of Justice believes that the entity has documents relevant to a civil antitrust examination. However, the courts have interpreted the language of the Act in such a way that the use of civil investigative demands is not permitted if information is asked with regard to activities that may constitute violations in the future; also, the court has allowed a party to advise the court whether the documents under investigation would contain trade secrets or other information that the party wishes to be withheld from its competitors.[97]

In the five years since its enactment, some 888 civil investigative demands have been issued by the Department of Justice under the *Antitrust Civil Process Act.*[98]

95. *cf.* SUPPLEMENT, p. 266
96. *cf.* SUPPLEMENT, pp. 248, 249
97. *cf.* SUPPLEMENT, pp. 218, *seq.*, and the cases there cited.
98. *cf.* SUPPLEMENT, p. 220

Each of the above three developments are of importance to foreign defendants; this is particularly true for the possibility of being served with a civil investigative demand.

ad (3): The cost

While the factor of cost is an important one in any litigation, the expenses of an antitrust suit can be staggering. The proceedings against the Aluminum Company of America were initiated in 1937; it was not until five years later that the District Court held that the company was innocent. Not satisfied with the acquittal, the Government appealed; three years later, in 1945, the Court of Appeals of the Second Circuit found the defendant guilty of violation of the *Sherman Act*; finally, in 1951, the District Court issued the injunction.[99] We do not need to elaborate what this means in terms of cost, both with regard to the citizens' tax money and the individual defendant. In an other case, where a business enterprise successfully contested the action, and found to be not guilty, the costs of its defense were still reputed to have been in excess of $100,000.[100] The exorbitant costs of antitrust litigation will, we submit, weigh proportionately heavier on foreign defendants than on their American counterparts, because:

(a) the dollar exchange rate and its concomitant purchase value in the home market of the foreign defendant are not always equal;

(b) the smaller unit size of the foreign firm as compared with the American firm, may cause any expenditure to result in a greater proportion of the total working capital of the foreign firm.

ad (4): The time element

The experience of the Aluminum Company of America where it took 14 years of litigation before the case had come to rest is a sufficient indication of how long it can take before an antitrust suit has come to an end. Other examples exist.

It is true that due to the revised *Rules of Practice of the Federal Trade Commission* the element of time has been greatly reduced. Nevertheless, the element of time, combined with the uncertainty as to the final outcome, remain important features. It is one thing for a defendant to be able to use 'stalling tactics'; it is quite another thing for a government-initiated action to require so much time (and therefore, cost) of a defendant. It is with regard thereto that we consider the trade practice rules and the trade regulation rules an important element in the struggle against loss of time, particularly for foreign business enterprises.

ad (5): The discovery procedure

The discovery procedure is another important feature of antitrust litigation. In criminal proceedings the federal grand jury can issue a subpoena compelling the production of all relevant documents (*subpoena duces tecum*). In civil proceedings the Government has the choice between seeking voluntary cooperation of

99. *cf.* WILCOX, *op. cit.*, p. 109
100. *ibid.*, p. 111

the respondent, or to proceed under the *Antitrust Civil Process Act* and issue a civil investigative demand.

Because of the revised Rules of Practice, referred to above, the discovery of relevant documents enables the respondent to prepare his case around the facts which the Government wants to discover.

One of the members of the Attorney General's National Committee stated: 'Nothing could be more appropriate than the existence and exercise of this sovereign jurisdiction to compel great corporations, whose activities affect the public interest, to disclose the facts as to their acquisition and use of economic power . . .'[101]; this is the opinion of one member. Others may and do feel differently. The decision of the Court in the *Upjohn* case[102] that a respondent could advise the court whether any of the documents retained by the custodian contained information of importance to competitors is, of course, a safeguard. Particularly outside the United States the discovery procedure may unleash a fear (apart form the emotionality involved) that important trade secrets may thus be revealed.[103] Partly in response to this fear, the courts are careful with *subpoenas duces tecum* with regard to foreign defendants.[104]

Nevertheless, rather strong objections can be expected, caused by fear and suspicion that an order to produce foreign located documents may be abused to disclose closely held company secrets and other information.[105] No official assurance that such fear and suspicion are unfounded can allay the apprehension of foreign businessmen that what the American Government is really after is an inside knowledge of the commercial know-how of foreign competition. Thus, the order to produce foreign located documents will be decried as a 'violation of a nation's sovereignty'.

At a later time we will have an opportunity to return to this aspect of the extraterritorial reach of the American antitrust laws.

101. *cf. Att'y Gen. Report*, p. 348
102. *Upjohn Co.* v *Bernstein*, 1966 Trade Cases, nr. 71, 830 (D.C.), cited in SUPPLEMENT, p. 220
103. We know from personal experience how in a sizeable European firm even wages were considered a company secret, notwithstanding the fact that many outsiders were well acquainted with the wage scale of this firm. Contrary to this experience was our visit to an American enterprise: when we indicated an interest to visit the company's laboratory we were given to understand that if we had been in the same type of business our request would have been granted; a mere curiosity interest was considered a waste of time on either side. Almost anywhere outside the United States, the reaction would have been exactly the opposite.
104. See CHAPTER I, *supra*, pp. 35, *seq.* But in *In re Grand Jury Investigation of the Shipping Industry,* 186 F Supp 298 (1960), the Court specifically asserted the right to require the production of foreign located documents, even though the Court, at the same time, temporarily deferred a decision whether it would actually require production; *cf.* SUPPLEMENT, p. 53
105. This was precisely the fear expressed to the writer by one of the chief executives of one of the larger European shipping enterprises during the investigations of the shipping industry, referred to *supra, n.* 104.

CHAPTER III

THE SPECIAL CHARACTER OF THE AMERICAN ANTITRUST LAWS

General

In the present chapter we should like to finish our descriptive survey of the American antitrust laws.-

In Chapter I we emphasized that the antitrust laws should be approached with the historical and philosophical bases as points of departure, even with regard to the extraterritorial reach of these laws. It is only against that background that one acquires the proper perspective of the various aspects of antitrust enforcement.

Subsequently, we examined the mechanism which is applied in order to implement the enforcement of the antitrust laws. We did so by utilizing the functional approach, i.e., we explored which remedies are available to effectively achieve the alleged objectives of the law. Those remedies are all applicable with respect to the extraterritorial reach.

We submit that the conclusion to which our survey leads is a logical one: any *a priori* attempt to classify the American antitrust laws within one of the existing categories (such as private law, public law, criminal law, administrative law, market regulatory law) is doomed to fail, because the law contains elements of all of these. The above conclusion is of particular importance when the extraterritorial reach of the antitrust laws is considered, because:

(1) the rules pertaining to the extraterritorial reach of private law are different from those which deal with criminal law, or administrative law;

(2) to our knowledge, no satisfactory body of rules has as yet been developed pertaining to the extraterritorial reach of a composite of private, criminal and administrative law;

(3) any comparative study of the antitrust laws of different nations must take this peculiarity into account;

(4) any attempt to arrive at a harmonization of antitrust legislation in the international community of nations must reflect an awareness of this peculiarity.

Concepts and semantics.

Study of a legal system requires a familiarity with the language, ideology and concepts of that system. This is true of one's own system; it applies all the more

if the study of a different system is undertaken.[1]
An example is the use of the word 'jurisprudence': the term may refer to the philosophy, or the science of law (as is the case in the common law countries).[2]
Another example is the use of the term *ius sui generis:* in the civil law this term would refer to a separate area of the law with its own theoretical and philosophical adjuncts. This is understandable because of the desire to achieve doctrinal unity and consistency.
But in the common law the term means only a separate area of the law.[3] Thus, we find in a *dictum* of the Illinois Supreme Court that there has been a definite trend toward judicial treatment of the close corporation as *sui generis.*[4] While nobody will interpret this statement to mean that the Illinois Supreme Court suggested that the close corporation be considered as an area of corporation law with its own jurisprudential attributes, the *dictum* will be understood to mean that the Court indicated that the close corporation had sufficient characteristics of its own to merit consideration as a legal entity of its own kind, subject to judicial consideration in accordance therewith.
Similarly, when we refer to the American antitrust laws as a special area of the law, we might use the term *ius sui generis*, as long as we have made sure that no different meaning would be conveyed from what we have intended.[5]
Again, when referring to the antitrust laws as a separate area of the law, we even should define what we mean with the seemingly rudimentary term 'law'.
Indeed, the literature abounds with attempts to define law; of these, we opt for the descriptive definition, *that what officials do about disputes,*[6] without discarding the equally widely accepted definition of law as *a rule of conduct*.
That there is reason to consider the American antitrust laws as a separate area of the law will hopefully be demonstrated in this chapter. But in order to do so, we should from the very outset keep the functional aspects, and particularly the remedial aspects of these laws in mind.

1. *cf.* YNTEMA, H. A., 'Foreword,', in LAWSON, *op. cit.*, p. xv: '... to inculcate understanding of a legal system, attention should be concentrated... upon its basic structure of ideas.' For more pertinent observations, see LAWSON, *op. cit.*, pp. 66, 79, 88. Also, see DRION, J., STARE DECISIS – HET GEZAG VAN PRECEDENTEN, 's-Gravenhage, 1950, pp. 5, *seq.*
2. *cf.* BLACK'S LAW DICTIONARY, *op. cit.*, p. 992
3. *ibid.*, p. 1602
4. *Galler* v. *Galler,* 32 Ill 2d 16, 16, 203 NE 2d 577 (1965)
5. *cf.* MARSHALL, Ch. J., in *McCulloch* v *Maryland,* 4 Wheat. 316 (1819): 'Such is the character of human language that no word conveys to the mind, in all situations, one single definite idea; and nothing is more common than to use words in a figurative sense. Almost all compositions contain words, which, taken in their rigorous sense, would convey a meaning different from that which is obviously intended.'
6. *cf.* LLEWELLYN, *op. cit.*, pp. 12, *seq.*, 76, *seq.*

The Purpose, Nature and Functions of the Antitrust Laws.

General

In order to explore the suggested special character of the American antitrust laws, we must explore the purpose, nature and functions of these laws.

The purpose of the law will be reflected in its philosophical, or political, or economic bases; in Chapter I we have briefly dealth with that aspect.

We also will have to distinguish between the nature and the functions of the law. It may be the *function* of the law to regulate relationships between parties (as in contract law), or behavior (as in tort law, or criminal law, or fiscal law, or antitrust law). At the same time, the *nature* of contract law is different from tort law, or criminal law, or fiscal law, or antitrust law.

For instance, the nature of contract law can be described as making the sovereign power of the State available to one party in order to enable him to exercise his will over the other party.[7] This power is made available because the American economic system has opted for the free exchange of promises, goods, and services, in favor of other methods for the allocation and distribution of resources; this, in turn, necessitated the creation of a legal machinery to accomplish that purpose.[8]

The implementation of the nature of contract law leads to the *function* of contract law, which can be described as the enforcement of agreements made by parties.

While the nature of contract law may reveal some changes when viewed against the background of its centuries-old development, it is in the area of the function of contract law that we can discern the great changes which have taken place because of the development of our society from an individualistic one to a society where collectivism plays an ever increasing role. In fact, these changes are so great that contract law, traditionally considered as one of the most private of private law, is no longer the sole concern of two parties it once was, but rather, an integrated part of a social institution, which reaches far beyond the interests of the two contracting parties.

It was this recognition that a rational compromise had to be found between individual rights and public welfare which led the United States Supreme Court to state that in contract law 'the fundamental interests of the State are directly affected,' necessitating the finding of a formula to use 'reasonable means to safeguard the economic structure upon which the good of all depends.'[9]

7. *cf.* COHEN, M. R., 'The Basis of Contract', 46 *Harvard Law Review* 553, 591 (1933), where the author suggests that for that reason 'the law of contract may be viewed as a subsidiary branch of public law.'
8. *cf.* KESSLER, F., & SHARP, M. P., CASES AND MATERIALS ON CONTRACTS, Boston, 1953, p. 4.
9. *cf. Home Building and Loan Assn.* v. *Blaisdell,* 290 US 398, 54 S Ct 231 (1934).

It is with this view in mind that the prediction has been made that eventually courts will even come to disregard what the parties agreed upon and instead, determine whether the arrangement was fair to both parties and in harmony with the needs of society.[10]

If this prognosis would come true, we might say that the *nature* of contract law (i.e., making the sovereign power of the State available to one party in order to enable him to exercise his will over the other party) has not substantially changed, yet, the *function* of contract law (i.e., the implementation, through the enforcement of agreements by the courts) will have undergone a radical and fundamental development progress, because contracts would have developed from a two-party arrangement to an undertaking in which, at the implementation stage, the needs of society will be a constant if not paramount factor in the recognition of private persons' interests.

In view of our suggestion that there is reason to consider the American antitrust laws as a special area of the law, we will have to analyze, on a similar basis as we have traced the distinction between the nature and the function of contract law, the nature and the function of these antitrust laws.

The Purpose of the American Antitrust Laws.

In order to do so, we must first, identify the purposes of these laws. On the basis thereof, we might be able to define the nature, and thereafter, analyze the function, i.e., the implementation of the American antitrust laws.

There is ample reason to formulate first, the purpose of the law, because if one consults either the opinions of the judiciary (as expressed in the various decisions), or the literature, one will find a considerable lack of consensus with regard to the objectives to be achieved by the antitrust laws.[11]

This uncertainty may, at least in part, have been caused by the widely observed phenomenon that both the position of the particular enterprise and the behavior of that firm within the business structure[12] have been the objects of attack. Attacks on either behavior (i.e., performance) or position (i.e., structure) will invariably lead to the conclusion that the antitrust laws aim at undesirable performance or structure.

To properly evaluate the purpose of the antitrust legislation one has to examine the political and socio-economic forces which prevailed during the period imme-

10. *cf.* ANDERSON, R. A., 'Law A.D. 2067,' 5 *American Business Law Journal* 249, 258 (1967). It is worthy of note that the Draft of the new Civil Code of The Netherlands (Book 6, Title 5, dealing with the general aspects of Contract Law) has incorporated a provision to that effect; see WIARDA, G. J., 'Drie Typen van Rechtsvinding', in EEN BUNDEL GEDACHTEN, Zwolle, 1963, pp. 130, *seq.*, particularly p. 147.
11. *cf.* MASON, E. S., 'Preface,' in KAYSEN, C., & TURNER, D. F., ANTITRUST POLICY – AN ECONOMIC AND LEGAL ANALYSIS, Cambridge, 1965, p. xii.
12. *ibid.*, p. xiii.

diately preceding the enactment of the *Sherman Act*, as well as the difficulties encountered in the attempts to implement the objectives of the proposed legislation.[13]

In Chapter I we have dealt briefly with some of the philosophical bases which are basic to a proper perspective of the American antitrust laws. We now will focus on the aspects which were the more immediate cause for the first antitrust act. There was popular resentment against the power of railroads, banks, and large industrial firms. This resentment reached substantial proportions after 1880, when the Standard Oil Company, through the trust device, succeeded in obtaining a dominant position in the petroleum refining industry. The trust device was subsequently applied to the formation of the sugar trust, the whiskey trust, the salt trust, the asphalt trust, and many others.[14]

The desire to destroy the power of the trusts inevitably culminated in the antitrust laws, because it was felt that regulation (in the form of specially drafted antitrust legislation, would effectively curb if not nullify the monopolistic positions occupied by the trusts.[15]

Therefore, one can state that, at the time of enactment, the purpose of the antitrust laws was to curb if not destroy the power of the big industrial and commercial combinations, simply (!) by solving the trust problem.[16]

13. We have omitted the discussion of the political and socio-economic aspects when reviewing the historical sources of the American antitrust laws, *supra*, Chapter I, because we felt that it was better to deal only with the *periods* that can be identified when the American antitrust laws are viewed in historical perspective. Furthermore, we were at that time only concerned with the legal antecedents of these laws.
14. For an interesting description, see LETWIN, W. L., 'Congress and the Sherman Antitrust Law 1887-1890,' 23 *University of Chicago Law Review* 221 (1956); also, see THORELLI, *op. cit.;* NEALE, A. D., THE ANTITRUST LAWS OF THE UNITED STATES OF AMERICA, Cambridge, 1960, pp. 23, *seq.*
15. Interesting to note is the emotion-laden terminology used in those years, referring to the Bank of the United States as a 'monster monopoly'; to West Point and Annapolis as 'nurseries of caste'; to the railroads as 'arbitrary, extortionate' institutions; *cf.* LETWIN, *l.c.*, p. 233. Terminology such as mentioned above is not easily associated with the philosophy of a country usually described as capitalistic; it is, rather, what one would expect to hear in a Marxist-oriented country. It is with respect thereto that attention might be asked for an observation made as early as 1835: 'There are at the present time two great nations in the world, which started from different points, but seem to tend towards the same end. I allude to the Russians and the Americans. . . The American struggles against the obstacles which nature opposes to him; the adversaries of the Russian are men. . . The Anglo-American relies upon personal interest to accomplish his ends, and gives free scope to the unguided strength and common sense of the people; the Russian centers all the authority of society in a single arm. The principal instrument of the former is freedom; of the latter, servitude. Their starting-point is different, and their courses are not the same; yet each seems marked out by the will of Heaven to sway the destinies of half the globe,'; TOCQUEVILLE, A. DE, DEMOCRACY IN AMERICA (REEVE, H., transl.), vol. I, 6th ed., Boston, 1876, pp. 558, 559.
16. *cf.* NEALE, *op. cit.*, p. 27. It was through the trust device that the fomula had been found to effectively make combinations permanently cohesive and easily manageable; *cf.* LETWIN, *l.c.*, p. 234.

Of course, additional arguments had to be supplied in support of the primary objective. Searching for convincing language, trusts were denounced as threats to liberty, destroyers of competition, institutions that would victimize consumers and cause unemployment. In order to combat these evils a system was proposed that on the one hand would allow for a limited system of free competition (as recommended by the economists), on the other hand would prohibit illegal monopolies (as recommended by the lawyers).[17] The thinking was that competition and combination would be mutually corrective forces which would prevent the emergence of monopolies. Here, too, the main purpose was to prevent powerful combinations and trusts which would restrain trade and make effective competition illusory.

But while destroying or curbing trusts might have been the moving force in passing the *Sherman Act* of 1890, it would not be sufficient to consider this the moving force for the subsequent enactment of other antitrust legislation and the continuous refinement of judicial application of these laws. Not even phrases such as 'the preservation of the competitive system,' or 'the maintenance of competition in open markets' would be satisfactory to sufficiently state the continuous purpose of the antitrust laws.

It is for that reason that we find today in the literature the suggestion that antitrust policy (and that includes antitrust legislation) purports to achieve several purposes:

(1) promoting desirable economic performance, both by individual firms and by the economy as a whole;
(2) protecting the competitive processes in the market place, by limiting market power;
(3) formulating and enforcing a code of fair competition as a standard of business conduct;
(4) equitably distributing social power, by preventing an undue growth of big business, and by promoting small business.[18]

If we were to define the purposes of the antitrust laws in the light of presentday government policy, we would state that *the purposes of the American antitrust laws are the limitation of undue market power and the maintenance of competition in open markets.*[19]

The Nature of the Antitrust Laws.

Turning our attention subsequently to the *nature* of the antitrust laws along the same lines as we have done earlier for the law of contracts, we submit that we

17. *cf.* LETWIN, *l.c.*, p. 235.
18. *cf.* KAYSEN & TURNER, *op. cit.*, p. 11, *seq.*
19. *cf. Att'y Gen. Report,* p. 1; KAYSEN & TURNER, *op. cit.*, pp. 44 *seq.*; NEALE, *op. cit.*, pp. 419, *seq.*

may define same as *making the sovereign power of the (Federal) government available to affect the structure and the functioning of business in such a way that competition in open markets be maintained.*[20]

In view of the plurality of purposes, it follows that in the exercise of this sovereign power we can detect both a positive and a negative aspect.[21]

While we have limited our definition of the nature of the antitrust laws to the above indicated exercise of power, this does not mean that there would be no other ways in which the exercise of power could be carried out in order to control business.[22] However, these alternatives are no part of the antitrust policy and therefore, do not qualify for consideration in a definition of the nature of the antitrust laws.

The Function of the Antitrust Laws.

Turning to the *function* of the antitrust laws, i.e., the implementation phase, we cannot simply state that the function is to enforce competition, or even to maintain competition. Nor is it sufficient to state that the function of the antitrust laws is to prevent restraint of trade.

Because of the complexity of the antitrust laws, the multiple purposes, and the dual nature (both economic and legal; furthermore, both positive and negative), we submit that *the function of the American antitrust laws is to provide a mechanism to limit undue market power and to encourage competition in open markets.*

In view of the plurality of purposes of the antitrust laws and because of the dual nature thereof, it follows that the mechanism provided to achieve these purposes will, by necessity, reflect this complexity. All of the foregoing would not necessarily make the antitrust laws sufficiently unique to warrant the suggestion that they be considered as a separate area of the law. Nevertheless, if an argument for a suggestion such as here referred to is to be made, it will have to be substantiated on the basis of the nature and the function of these laws.

It is our contention that the nature and function of the American antitrust laws justify our suggestion. We base our arguments with regard to the nature of these

20. NEALE, without singling it out as the *nature* of the antitrust laws, describes same as 'bringing the administration and enforcement of pre-existing law within the domain of executive responsibility. . .'; *op. cit.*, p. 27.
21. *cf.* NEALE, *op. cit.*, p. 29, who finds the positive aspect in the phrase 'maintaining competition,' and the negative aspect in the literal expression 'anti-trust." Also, see Chapter I, *supra*, p. 42.
22. *cf.* NEALE, *op. cit.*, p. 27, who mentions as alternative the interference in the judicial role of deciding what would constitute unlawful restraint of trade. Also, see KAYSEN & TURNER, *op. cit.*, pp. 214, *seq.*, who mention as major alternatives taxation; government procurement; direct aid to small business; import tariffs and a government directed commercial policy.

laws both on the common law historical development in its early period[23] and the legislative history preceding the enactment of the *Sherman Act.*[24] Both of these culminated in the wording of sec. 1 of the *Sherman Act* which declares *contracts, combinations in the form of trusts,* and *conspiracies in restraint of trade* illegal.

The inclusion of contracts and conspiracies in restraint of trade, along with combinations in the form of trusts or otherwise, conveys that the common law views with regard to restraint of trade were also recognized in the newly enacted statutory provisions.

While the destroying or curbing of trusts and similar monopolies clearly had a public law character, the same cannot be said with regard to the contract and tort aspects.

Nor will it do to suggest that these private law and public law aspects of the *Sherman Act* were adopted in order to achieve the purpose which the antitrust laws sought to obtain. To make such a suggestion would be tantamount to ignoring the legislative history of the *Sherman Act.* If anything, the reverse would be true: what the lawyers in the period prior to 1890 had in mind was to bolster the body of common law in such a way that the major purpose of the law, i.e., destroying the trusts, could be achieved.

Thus, the nature of the American antitrust laws, reflects a composite of common law, private law, and public law, not so much in order to obtain the results the legislature was after, but rather, because the law which was in force at the time needed some bolstering-up to make it more adequate to the needs of the time.

Similarly, we find that the *function* of the American antitrust laws reflects this composite origin, as can be easily demonstrated by pointing at the remedial aspects of these laws.[25] Of course, these remedies have as major goal that they achieve the purposes to be served. However, we submit that the remedies did not come about to serve the purposes of the antitrust legislation; rather, we think that the legislature was convinced that the purposes of the antitrust laws were adequately served by the remedies which existed, augmented by the newly introduced ones. Thus, we find that while Congress intended to (continue to) use private self interests as a means for enforcement, it also empowered the Department of Justice to bring both civil and criminal actions; later, the Federal Trade Commission was given the authority to further implement the objectives sought, by encouraging voluntary compliance, or compelling involuntary compliance through administrative procedures; while other regulatory agencies also were enabled to secure law enforcement through a host of miscellaneous sanctions.[26]

23. *cf.* Chapter I, *supra.*
24. *cf.* LETWIN, *l.c.*, pp. 241, *seq.*
25. *cf.* Chapter II, *supra.*
26. *cf.* VAN CISE, Cise, *op. cit.*, pp. 39, 40; also, see NEALE, *op. cit.*

Conclusions

It is on the basis of the above mentioned peculiar characteristics, particularly the functional aspects, that we submit that the American antitrust laws should be considered as a separate area of the law.
Similar arguments have been advanced elsewhere with regard to social-economic legislation.[27]
There is even judical support for our suggestion: in an opinion of the United States Supreme Court we find the following statement pertaining to the *Sherman Act*:

> 'As a charter of freedom, the act has a generality and adaptability comparable to that found to be desirable in constitutional provisions.'[28]

Elsewhere, we find reference made to the *Sherman Act* as 'a basic statute known as a charter of economic freedom.'[29]
The very use of terminology such as *constitutional provisions, basic statute*, and *charter* suggests that we are dealing with something more than a run-of-the-mill statute; we submit that this is based on the special characteristics of the law.[30]

The Consequences.

The Necessity of a Coordinated Unified Body of Law

27. *cf.* MULDER, A., DE HANDHAVING DER SOCIAAL-ECONOMISCHE WETGEVING, 's-Gravenhage, 1949, pp. 22, *seq.*, where social-economic legislation is defined as:
(1) the composite of legal prescriptions, promulgated by the central government or specifically authorized agencies, the purpose of which is to directly or indirectly influence the market place;
(2) the composite of agreements made by private voluntary associations for the purpose of similarly influencing the market place, insofar as these agreements also have been declared applicable to non-members.
Based on this concept of social-economic legislation as a separate area of the law, MULDER submits the desirability to delineate a system of sanctions with its own special characteristics, and to group together, from the entire area of the law, those prescriptions that are conducive to classification within one system of sanctions; *op. cit.*, p. 24. For a German view, see WENGLER, W., 'Laws Concerning Unfair Competition and the Conflict of Laws,' 4 *Am. Journal of Comparative Law* 167 (1955), who uses the terminology *Marktrecht* (in contrast to *Standesrecht*). Particularly, we refer to REHBINDER, *op. cit.*, p. 57, and SCHWARTZ, I. E., *op. cit.*, p. 4, both cited in INTRODUCTION, *supra*.
28. *Appalachian Coals, Inc.* v. *U.S.*, 288 US 344, 53 S Ct 471 (1933)
29. *cf. Att'y Gen. Report*, p. 1
30. *cf.* 1964 *Tokyo Proceedings*, p. 327: 'Anti-trust is a unique phenomenon. . .'. The observation was made with specific reference to the American antitrust laws. Also, see RIEDWEG, *l.c.*, p. 385: 'Restrictive trade laws are special enactments of public law in the field of economic regulation.' Although no mention is made of any specific country to which this statement refers, other than that, 'Until quite recently, there were only a few States with such laws,' we must assume that the United States was included in the statement. On the basis of our historical survey we submit that the statement is incorrect with regard to the United States; see Chapter I, *supra*.

(a) The National Level:

Because there has been no serious attempt to undertake a general review of the entire statutory framework, save for a few suggested revisions proposed by individual authors,[31] there is an absence of official formulation of clear policies. This has resulted in a description of the body of antitrust laws as a 'hodge-podge pattern of uncoordinated regulations and activities that contain a potpourri of procedures for enforcing the substantive laws.'[32]

Yet, because the American antitrust laws cannot be classified within the existing broad categories of law, a coordinated attempt should be made to unify the various antitrust provisions into one comprehensive unified body of law.

While a common law practitioner, who by training and temperament is oriented toward remedies rather than doctrinal consistency may not think that such an undertaking is all that important, we happen to think differently.

On the contrary, we submit that the classification of the antitrust laws as a separate area of the law into one comprehensive unified body of law will have practical implications, also for the practicing lawyer. This is particularly true when the extraterritorial reach of the antitrust laws is taken into consideration, because the old categorizations would no longer apply; new ones will have to worked out.

(b) The Supra-national Level:

In our Introductory chapter we have indicated that problems occur when the extraterritorial reach of the antitrust laws results in enforcement of the national laws with regard to commercial practices committed outside the boundaries of the United States.

These problems occur partly because there is no clear picture to which rules these laws should adhere: are the principles of private law, or public law, or criminal law, or administrative law applicable?

We submit that this special area of the law should have its own rules with regard to making law (i.e., legislative jurisdictional competency) and applying law (i.e. judicial jurisdictional competency).

It is the failure to recognize the special character of the antitrust laws as a special area of the law that has lead the writers on the subject to come out with statements such as:

31. *cf.* OPPENHEIM, S. C., 'Federal Antitrust Legislation: Guideposts to a Revised National Antitrust Policy," 50 *Michigan Law Review* 1139 (1952); McCRACKEN, R. T., 'The Federal Antitrust Laws From the Viewpoint of a Business Lawyer,' *Antitrust Law Symposium* 1953, Chicago, 1953, p. 87; KAYSEN & TURNER, *op. cit.*

32. *cf.* MASSEL, M. S., COMPETITION AND MONOPOLY, Washington, 1962, pp. 2, 42, 80

(1) The principles of private international law are applicable;[33]
(2) The principles of international administrative law are applicable;[34]
(3) The principles of public international law are applicable;[35]
(4) The principles of international criminal law are applicable;[36]
(5) There is no universally recognized legal background to the antitrust laws.[37]

It goes without saying that the jurisdictional competency in matters involving the extraterritotial reach of antitrust enforcement will differ in each of the above instances, depending on the proper categorization.[38]

We submit that this apparent lack of unanimity is caused by the failure to recognize that the antitrust laws should be viewed as a separate area of the law, to which the existing principles of international law cannot be applied. We also submit that a proper categorization can only take place after the fundamental nature of these laws has clearly been established.[39] We suggest that our earlier discussion of the remedial aspects of the American antitrust laws, with their concurrent or alternate availability of civil, criminal, and regulatory remedies, shows that a categorization along the traditional lines of demarcation does not work.[40]

33. *cf.* TIMBERG, S., 'Extraterritorial Jurisdiction under the Sherman Act,' 11 *The Record* 101, 111 (1956); DUBBINK, A., 40 *Mededelingen van de Nederlandse Vereniging voor Internationaal Recht* 7 (1959).
34. *cf.* VAN DER GRINTEN, W. C. L., & BIEGER, K. S., 'Internationale aspecten op het gebied van de economische mededinging," 39 *Mededelingen van de Nederlandse Vereniging voor Internationaal Recht* 6 (1959). Similarly, by inference, WENGLER, *l.c.*, p. 179; at least, this seems to us a necessary consequence of the proposition that the antitrust laws have to be considered as *market regulations.* Also, see BREWSTER, *op. cit.*, p. 287.
35. *cf.* KAHN-FREUND, O., 'English Contracts and American Anti-Trust Law; The Nylon Patent Case,' 18 *Modern Law Review* 65 (1965). Also, see Verzijl, *l.c.*, p. 4
36. *cf.* VERZIJL, J. H. W., 'The Controversy Regarding The So-Called Extraterritorial Effect of the American Antitrust Laws', VIII *Nederlands Tijdschrift voor Internationaal Recht* 3 (1961), p. 4, who refers to this view as the traditional approach; FUGATE, *op. cit.*, p. 21; HAIGHT, G. W., 'International Law and Extra-Territorial Application of the Antitrust Laws, 63 *Yale Law Journal* 639 (1954). Also, see JENNINGS, R. Y., 'The International Law Covering Anti-Trust Jurisdiction', 1964 *Tokyo Proceedings,* pp. 354, *seq.*
37. *cf.* FUGATE, *op. cit.*, p. 55, referring to the 1957 statement of the Special Committee on Antitrust and Foreign Trade of the Association of the Bar of the City of New York. Also, by inference, REYNOLDS, W. B., 'Extraterritorial Application of Federal Antitrust Laws: Delimiting the Reach of Substantive Law Under the Sherman Act,' 20 *Vanderbilt Law Review* 1030, 1050 (1967).
38. *cf.* RIEDWEG, *l.c.*, at p. 403
39. Thus, we find that REHBINDER, after having observed that one does well to remember that both public law and private law elements are involved, concludeds that doubt exists where exactly the antitrust laws belong. 'Dazu fehlt es bis heute nicht nur an völkerrechtlichen Präjudizien, sondern auch bereits an einer tragfähigen internrechtlichen dogmatischen Grundlage.'; *op. cit.*, p. 58
40. 'We must realize that taken in the aggregate, they [i.e., the common law statutes pertaining to restrictive practices] have effect as (1) criminal enactments, (2) regulatory measures, and (3) statutes creating civil rights sounding in tort, with attending remedies'; see 'Impact of Antitrust Laws on Foreign Trade', *American Bar Association,* 1953, p. 78

Thus, after having recognized that the *Sherman Act* is commonly regarded as a criminal statute, the *Clayton Act* simultaneously penal, regulatory and civil, and the *Wilson Tariff Act* criminal, the Committee on International Trade Regulation of the American Bar Association comes to the conclusion that the concurrent existence of a number of statutory provisions, which are in part declaratory of the common law and in part explicit in themselves, results (when considered in the aggregate) in the concurrent existence of penal, regulatory and civil elements.[41] This conclusion gives the appearance of a 'patchwork' approach that could be avoided by molding the antitrust laws into one separate area of the law. Even authors with less doctrinaire fixations, who have occupied themselves with the extraterritorial reach of the antitrust laws, have found it necessary to deal alternately, with the civil, criminal, and administrative aspects of antitrust enforcement.[42]

We concede that as long as the present uncertainty with regard to the nature of the antitrust laws continues this is the only realistic approach.

Some illustrations of antitrust enforcements

Judicial opinions reflect that the current method of antitrust enforcement is a problem area. To substantiate our statement we refer to the following cases:

(1) *U.S.* v. *Scophony Corp. of America*[43], holding that a foreign patent company could be brought under the jurisdiction of the court by serving process on the American subsidiary. Although the District Court held that the parent company had not been 'found' in the jurisdiction, the United States Supreme Court reversed the District Court.
With this case as authority, any foreign corporation having a business interest in the United States, could be subject to the *in personam* jurisdiction of the American judicial or quasi-judicial enforcement agencies.

(2) *U.S.* v. *Imperial Chemical Industries, Ltd.*[44], ordering a British corporation to reconvey to its American grantor the patent licenses it had received, and which it had assigned on an exclusive basis to another British corporation, according to British law. The American court order had its sequel in a British court, where the court granted an injunction, so that I.C.I. was

41. *ibid.*, pp. 79, 80

42. *cf.* SCHWARTZ, I. E., *op. cit.*, pp. 165, *seq.*, who recognizes that, 'über den Anwendungsbereich des Gesetzes auf internationale Wettbewerbsbeschränkungen erhebliche Unklarheiten und Meinungsverschiedenheiten bestehen.' 'Uberhaupt trägt die Unterscheidung zwischen privatem und öffentlichem Recht auf einem Grenzgebiet wie dem des Kartellrechts wesentlich dazu bei, die Abgrenzung des internationalen Anwendungsbereichs des Gesetzes – man ist versucht zu sagen unnötig – zu komplizieren.' Also, see REHBINDER, *op. cit.*, p. 38, who uses the term 'rechtliche Zwischenstellung'; he admits that international antitrust law has taken the position of a 'Sachgebiet', that 'in der Hand einiger Spezialisten ein Eigenleben führe.'

43. 333 US 795, 68 S Ct 855 (1948). For a synopsis of the case, see Chapter I, *supra*, p. 32

44. 105 F Supp 215 (1952)

enjoined from complying with the American decree,[45] thus technically exposing it to contempt of court proceedings.

(3) *U.S.* v. *Deutsches Kalisyndikat Gesellschaft*[46], enjoining a French corporation to violate the American antitrust laws, even though the French Ambassador had remonstrated that the French corporation was protected by sovereign immunity (the French government owned the majority of the capital stock).

(4) *U.S.* v. *General Electric Co.*[47], causing the Ambassador of The Netherlands to protest a provision in the decree as proposed by the Attorney General, according to which representatives of the Department of Justice would come to The Netherlands to examine the books, records, and affairs of the N.V. Philips Gloeilampenfabrieken, N.V., a Dutch corporation.

(5) *U.S.* v. *Watchmakers of Switzerland Information Center, Inc.*[48], whereby an American court, in effect, interfered with arrangements made by Swiss watchmanufacturers in Switzerland. On the basis of this case a distinction has since been made between what conduct a foreign government authorizes and what it requires, implying that authorized conduct is no defense. The Swiss defendants were ordered to amend their Collective Convention.

(6) *In re Grand Jury Investigation of the Shipping Industry*[49], in which the Court refused to quash subpoenas for the production of foreign located documents, including those of the foreign defendants. That the court deferred a decision as to whether it would actually require the production of the documents does not deter from the attitude of the court that it considered itself competent to compel foreign defendants to produce foreign located documents.

(7) *U.S.* v. *Singer Mfg Co.*,[50] where cross-licensing between an American, an Italian, and a Swiss corporation was held to be illegal, because the parties shared a common purpose to suppress competition from Japan. The facts of this case could convey that American antitrust enforcement would interfere with foreign agreements if the effect thereof would be a substantially lessening of competition, thus making policy decisions of foreign corporations subject to scrutiny by American enforcement agencies.

45. *British Nylon Spinners, Ltd.* v. *Imperial Chemical Industries, Ltd.*, Ch. 19 (1953) (C.A. 1952)
46. 31 F2d 199 (1929) (S.D.-N.Y.). For the reasoning of the Court, see BREWSTER, *op. cit.*, p. 61
47. 115 F Supp 835 (1953) (D.-N.J.); for a discussion of the problems, see BREWSTER, *op. cit.*, p. 46
48. 1963 Trade Cases, nr. 70, 600 (S.D.-N.Y. 1962), *order modified,* 1965 Trade Cases, nr. 71, 352. For a more extensive discussion of the case, see SUPPLEMENT, pp. 42, *seq.* Also, see Chapter I, *supra,* pp. 33, *seq.*
49. 186 F Supp 298 (1960) (D.-D.C.)
50. 374 US 174, 83 S Ct 1773 (1963). For a discussion of the case, see SUPPLEMENT, pp. 56, *seq.*

(8) *U.S.* v. *Jos. Schlitz Brewing Co.*,[51] where the acquisition by an American corporation of a controlling interest in a foreign corporation was held to be a 'substantial lessening of actual and potential competition in the United States.' If one compares the facts ot this case with those of the preceding one, and one considers the effects of the policy decisions with the American market in mind, it will be clear that the doubt expressed above is not entirely without foundation.

(9) *U.S.* v. *R. P. Oldham Co.*,[52] where an exclusive import agreement was attacked, even though by Japanese law this agreement was perfectly legal. The facts of this case reveal that five American importers of wire nails had agreed with Japanese manufacturers and exporters that no other American importer could be supplied by those sources. Wire nails may not need extensive promotion campaigns, but let us substitute, say cigars or perfumes for wire nails, would the same view not be unfair to the foreign manufacturer? We say so, because it is hard to imagine that any importer will be eager to promote an imported product if he cannot be sure of an exclusive arrangement. Even if the initiative would lie with the importer, we still wonder about the implications of the decision.

(10) *Pacific Seafarers, Inc.* v. *Pacific Far East Line, Inc.*[53], where the Court dealt with an alleged conspiracy between two shipping conferences to monopolize trade between two foreign ports, without any involvement of importation into or exportation from the United States. The Court held that the *Sherman Act* would apply, because the case pertained to the economic activity of Americans. That the case has some far reaching implications for Americans abroad needs no elaboration.

The problems we have alluded to are not just problems of theoretical categorization of the antitrust laws, they are also problems dealing with the sovereignty of foreign nations and foreign defendants, problems dealing with managerial decisions of foreign located enterprises, problems dealing with the jurisdiction *in personam* over foreign defendants.

Conclusions.

Summarizing our findings we submit that postponement to recognize the entire area of antitrust enforcement as a separate area of the law unnecessarily complicates matters, particularly with regard to the legislative and judicial extraterritorial reach of the law.

51. 253 F Supp 129 (1965), *aff'd per curiam,* 385 US 37, 87 S Ct 240 (1966)
52. 152 F Supp 818 (1957) (N.D.-Cal)
53. 404 F 2d 804 (1968), *certiorari denied,* US, 89 S Ct 872 (1969). An extensive discussion of the extraterritorial aspects of the case can be found in 1 *Case Western Res. J. of Int'l Law* 132 (1969), at pp. 138, *seq.* The commentator states: 'Impetus for an expansive reading of the foreign commerce clause of the Sherman Act is likely to flow from the increasing balance of payments problem.'

On the positive side we mention that a recognition would facilitate the development of special jurisdictional rules, adaptable to the peculiar exigencies of transnational commercial activities and national sensitivities.

The Implementation

Unification of Legislation

(a) At the National Level:

We have already indicated that the functional aspects of the antitrust laws make it highly desirable if not necessary to draft legislation which would contain, in one single code, the various antitrust provisions. Because of its broad composition, the American Law Institute[54] would be a logical choice for drafting such a general Antitrust Code.

The desirability of a complete overhaul of the antitrust laws has been proposed by a number of authors at various times. Generally, these proposals are based either on the number of separate laws presently existing, or on the desirability to coordinate and harmonize these laws with the entire body of government regulation of the American economy, including the foreign aid and military assistance programs of the United States; or because the present laws do not sufficiently convey the purposes and policies which the antitrust laws purport to achieve.[55]

We submit the following shortcomings of the present antitrust laws as substantiation:

(1) With regard to the substantive law:
   (a) the provisions are spread over too great a variety of enactments;[56]
   (b) forbidden practices are covered in different provisions; for instance:
      (1) refusals to deal may be reached by the *Sherman Act*, the *Clayton Act*, the *Federal Trade Commission Act*;
      (2) exclusive territorial arrangements and tying clauses may be reached under the *Sherman Act* and the *Clayton Act* (section 3);

54. 'The American Law Institute is an organization of judges, practitioners and law teachers, formed 'to promote the clarification and simplification of the law and its better adaptation to social needs, to secure the better administration of justice, and to encourage and carry on scholarly and scientific legal work'. The Institute is particularly known for its 'Restatements'; the law has been 'restated' in such diverse fields as Contracts, Torts, Foreign Relations; *cf.* SHARTEL, B., OUR LEGAL SYSTEM AND HOW IT OPERATES, Ann Arbor, 1951, pp. 393, *seq.*, and the literature there cited.

55. *cf.* OPPENHEIM, S. C., 'Federal Antitrust Legislation: Guideposts to a Revised National Antitrust Policy', 50 *Mich. Law Review* 1139 (1952); BREWSTER, *op. cit.*, pp. 4, *seq.;* MASSEL, *op. cit.*, pp. 317, *seq.;* KAYSEN & TURNER, *op. cit.*, pp. 44, *seq.;* NOTE in 1 *Case West. Res. J. of Int'l Law* 312 (1969); SUPPLEMENT, pp. 60, *seq.*

56. *cf.* Chapter I, *supra*, p. 26, *n.* 37

(3) price discrimination may be reached under the *Sherman Act* and the *Robinson-Patman Act* (i.e., section 2 of the *Clayton Act*);[57]

(c) the statutory provisions are not in harmony with one another and thus, raise 'legal puzzles'; this is particularly the case with regard to the philosophy underlying the *Sherman Act* and the *Clayton Act* and the provisions of the *Robinson-Patman Act* (which is section 2 of the *Clayton Act*);[58]

(d) the language of the provisions lacks clarity, thus making for uncertainty as to what is permitted and what is forbidden; this is particularly true with regard to the provisions of the *Robinson-Patman Act.*[59]

(2) With regard to the principle of fairness:

(a) while theoretically price differentials are allowed if they can be justified on the basis of savings in the cost of doing business, yet, 'attempts to invoke the cost justification have involved mammoth expenditure of costly expert effort', with the result that 'only the most prosperous and patient business firms' could afford to become entangled in lawsuits.[60]

(b) the requirement of mathematical exactitude in cost justification imposes excessive demands on the business community;[61]

(c) the provisions of the *Webb-Pomerene Act* exempt from the antitrust laws 'associations entered into for the sole purpose of engaging in export trade and actually engaged solely in such export trade.' The rationale for the exemption is 'to help American firms compete in foreign markets with more powerful rivals as well as bargain on equal footing with European buying cartels.'[62] However, where foreign exporters would band together in order to compete with the more powerful American rivals on the American market, no such exemption will be available; yet, often the foreign combination may need more protection because of lack of resources to successfully participate in the American marketing process.

(3) With regard to organizational aspects:

(a) the non-separation of prosecuting and adjudicatory activities within the Federal Trade Commission;[63]

57. *cf. Att'y Gen. Report*, p. 4
58. *ibid.*, p. 131
59. *cf. ibid.*, pp. 130, 172; SUPPLEMENT, p. 155
60. *Att'y Gen. Report*, pp. 172, 173
61. *ibid.*, p. 174
62. *ibid.*, p. 109
63. *ibid.*, p. 176, singling out the activities of the accounting staff

(b) the possibility of concurrent enforcement proceedings by the enforcement agencies;[64]

(c) the adjudicatory activities of the Federal Trade Commission. It seems to us that the dangers of entrusting adjudication to an arm of the executive branch of government is not imaginary. We are aware of the legislative history of the *Federal Trade Commission Act*, permitting enforcement of the *Sherman Act* both by the Department of Justice and by the administrative process of the Federal Trade Commission.[65] In our opinion the functions of each should be limited to the investigative and advisory aspects of antitrust enforcement, while adjudication should be limited to the courts. We do not quarral with the conclusion of the Attorney General's National Committee, i.e., to reject either the abolition of the Federal Trade Commission's antitrust function, or the transfer of all antitrust matters from the Department of Justice to the Federal Trade Commission.[66] Our disagreement is with the adjudicatory activities of an executive agency; we prefer to have the activities limited to the investigative or advisory aspects.

A complete overhaul and unification of the antitrust laws into one comprehensive code could help to eliminate the currently existing confusion between the civil, the regulatory, and the criminal jurisdictional aspects of antitrust enforcement, and the concomitant conflicts resulting from the delimitation of these various aspects in transnational relationships.[67] It could also greatly reduce the above indicated shortcomings of the antitrust laws as they exist today.

(b) At the Supra-National Level:

The need for unification of the antitrust laws becomes particularly relevant when the extraterritorial reach is taken into consideration. To show the relationships between the extraterritorial reach of the antitrust laws and transnational business activities we point at some recent developments, to wit:

(1) the increase of American private investments abroad;[68]

(2) the increase of foreign investments in the United States;[69]

(3) the increase of foreign participation in international commerce;[70]

64. SUPPLEMENT, p. 272. Mention should be made, however, of the statement: 'When either agency proposes to conduct an investigation it notifies the other, specifying the purpose, scope and probable charges. . . If there is an overlap, further liaison is carried out in order to minimize duplication.' The possibility of duplication is therefore, not excluded, only 'minimized'.
65. *cf. Att'y Gen. Report*, p. 375
66. *ibid.*, p. 375
67. *cf.* REYNOLDS, *l.c.*
68. see INTRODUCTION, *supra*, p. 1
69. Particularly for Germany's share, see *Time*, February 9, 1970, p. 52 (European edition)
70. For Japan's and Germany's share, see *Time*, January 5, 1970 (European edition)

(4) the widely recognized interests of the developing nations of the world in a further liberalization of world trade; this coincides entirely with the declared policy of the United States to encourage private initiative and competition in the free world.[71]

It would, indeed, be counter to the interests of free competition in open markets, on a global scale, to allow a division of world markets to occur, either through horizontal or through vertical arrangements.[72] These practices will only lead to restrictive trade practices legislation. But in that case, fairness requires that because of this increased commercial activity (actual and potential) the antitrust provisions be clearly formulated and easily accessible to the foreign businessman. As far as the United States is concerned, for that reason alone, a comprehensive and unified overhaul of the existing antitrust laws would be desirable. A clear and comprehensive American codification might even set the stage to spur other nations to follow suit and hopefully, achieve unity of purpose an worldwide scale.

A unified codification would furthermore, provide an opportunity to explore new approaches to a special judicial machinery to be established, such as giving recognition to the needs of a judiciary to which not only law-oriented members would be appointed, but also members with a specialization in the fields of marketing and economics, so that equal or weighted consideration can be given to the legal, the marketing and the economic aspects of competition.[73] This, in turn, would reinforce in a demonstrable manner that the functional aspects of the antitrust laws need special consideration, legislatively and judicially.

A unified Antitrust Code could also pave the way for harmonization of national laws with the antitrust legislation of other nations, and for harmonization of national views of economic legislation with the internationally accepted or acceptable rules and concepts of legislative and judicial jurisdiction. We readily admit the difficulty of this suggestion in view of the objectives which the various antitrust laws purport to achieve.[74]

Finally, a codification such as here suggested could conceivably set the stage for further amplification pertaining to supra-national tribunals dealing with transnational aspects of national antitrust laws.

That there is a need to harmonize the various national antitrust laws because of possible conflict situations can be quantitatively substantiated by the statement that as of 1964 twenty-four nations had enacted legislation dealing with restric-

71. *cf. Att'y Gen. Report,* p. 93
72. A similar view can be found in the opinion of the European Court of Justice in *Consten-Grundig* v. *Commission of the E.E.C.*, see Chapter I, *supra*, p. 42
73. *cf.* MASSEL, *op. cit.*, p. 323
74. Furthermore, the American antitrust laws rely to a large degree on a process of regulation by private parties; elsewhere, the regulation is primarily in the hands of the government. The reason for this distinction can be found in the historical development bases of the American antitrust laws (see Chapter I, *supra*)

tive trade practices, some of these just statutes on the books, others actual instruments of governmental policy.[75]

More important than the quantitative aspects, however, are the qualitative differences which exist between these various antitrust laws. Even Canada's *Combines Investigation Act*, which probably comes closest to the United States antitrust laws, still differs markedly from the latter, particularly when the enforcement aspects are taken into consideration.[76]

As reason for the differences between the attitudes of Americans and Europeans toward concentration of power we frequently find statements that United States policy reflects a hostility against massive concentration of power, be it in the private or the public sector of society.[77]

On the other hand, in Europe concentration of power is usually accepted, as long as no abuse of power occurs. The reasons for this difference have alternately been explained either on the basis of the historical and cultural backgrounds of the European nations;[78] or on the grounds that any limitation on the freedom of contract is regarded with greater concern in Europe than in America; or on the argument that in smaller countries (such as we find in Europe) there is more compulsion to conform to moral traditions, while government is more based on political consensus than in a country the size of the United States; or even on the existence of ideologically divided political parties in a parliamentary system, so that the political decisions do not result from compromise but rather from rivaling ideas and attitudes.[79]

These historical, cultural, and political differences also affect the extent to which the national laws are applied to activities occurring outside the territorial boundaries of the enforcing country, albeit with variations among these various nations.[80]

In a world in which the movement of commerce across national boundaries is an accepted activity, it will not need much imagination to see that there is, indeed, a need to deal with problems which result from diverse national regulations. The first step toward the solution of problems of this order would probably be

75. *cf.* EDWARDS, C. D., TRADE REGULATIONS OVERSEAS, New York, 1966 (hereinafter referred to as EDWARDS, TRADE REGULATIONS); *idem*, CONTROL OF CARTELS AND MONOPOLIES, New York, 1967 (hereinafter referred to as EDWARDS, CONTROL OF CARTELS); RIEDWEG, *l.c.*, 1964 *Tokyo Proceedings*, pp. 385, *seq.;* BREWSTER, *op.cit.*, and the literature there cited; HANDLER, *op. cit.*, p. 1201, and the sources there cited; SCHWARTZ, L. B., *op. cit.*, pp. 14, *seq.*, and the literature there cited; OPPENHEIM & WESTON, *op. cit.*, pp. 776, 777, and 813, *seq.*, and the literature there cited.
76. *cf.* NEALE, *op. cit.*, p. 1.
77. *cf.* NEALE, *op. cit.*, p. 23; LETWIN, *l.c.;* THORELLI, *op. cit.;* EDWARDS, CONTROL OF CARTELS, *op. cit.*, p. 16.
78. *cf.* EDWARDS, CONTROL OF CARTELS, *op. cit.*, pp. 16, *seq.*
79. *cf.* ibid., *p. 22, 23.*
80. *cf. ibid.*, p. 30, *seq.* Also, see RIEDWEG, *l.c.*, pp. 385, *seq.*, and the 'Summary of Restrictive Trade Legislation'; *ibid.*, pp. 417, *seq.*

international consultation leading to the harmonization of these different regulations.[81]

There is no question but what this will cause difficulties. There are in the first place, different concepts with regard to the extent to which national laws can be applied to foreign nationals or to conduct abroad.[82]

More difficult to solve is the harmonization of the different objectives which the various antitrust laws purport to achieve; particularly when these objectives aim at such different goals as: destroying or curbing trusts and combinations; allowing the citizen a maximum choice for the allocation of his resources; promoting better economic performace through the encouragement of competition; keeping prices down; maintaining stability in a nation's economic system.[83]

However difficult as these obstacles may be, they are worth surmounting in a world in which international and political cooperation are not just mere concepts, but goals to be aspired to. We therefore, wholeheartedly support the attempts to arrive at a harmonization of the various national laws and to adopt a common standard with regard to the approach to the regulation of trans-national business practices.[84]

At the same time, recognition has to be given to the fact that a unified national legislation is an almost necessary prerequisite for such harmonization. We therefore, submit that *a unified national antitrust legislation, leading to a comprehensive antitrust code, is a first necessary step to further implementation of national and international regulation.*

Establishment of a Special Antitrust Judiciary

(a) At the National Level:

We have earlier intimated that recognition of the antitrust laws as a separate area of the law might pave the way for the creation of special courts, equipped to deal with the peculiar exigencies of the problems of antitrust enforcement.

What we are suggesting is that special antitrust courts be established, similar to the bankruptcy courts,[85] to be attached to the Federal District Courts. Establish-

81. *cf.* OLIVER, C. T., 'The Harmonization of Laws and the Development of Principles for the Resolution of Conflicts of Enforcement Jurisdiction as to Transnational Monopolistic and Restrictive Trade Practices,' 1964 *Tokyo Proceedings,* pp. 544, *seq.*
82. *cf.* EDWARDS, CONTROL OF CARTELS, *op. cit.,* p. 30.
83. *cf.* LETWIN, *l.c.,;* KAYSEN & TURNER, *op. cit.,* pp. 45, *seq.;* EDWARDS, CONTROL OF CARTELS, *op. cit.,* pp. 32, *seq.*
84. For a proposed method, see OLIVER, *l.c.,* pp. 546, *seq.*
85. Section 2 of the *Bankruptcy Act* invests the Courts of Bankruptcy with jurisdiction at law and in equity, to deal with all matters related to bankruptcy; they may 'arraign, try, and punish persons' for violations of the Bankruptcy Act (section 2(a)(4)), and 'enforce obedience by persons to all lawful orders, by fine or imprisonment or fine and imprisonment' (section 2(a)(13)); *cf.* HANNA, J., & MACLACHLAN, J. A., THE BANKRUPTCY ACT, Brooklyn, 1958, pp. 7, *seq.*

ment of these courts would maintain the concept of federal jurisdiction, but a jurisdiction exercised by special courts made up by qualified experts in the field of antitrust.

We suggest that these courts consist both of members of the legal profession and members whose academic and professional specializations are in the fields of marketing and economics. This will better assure that antitrust enforcement deals with legal, marketing and economic aspects.[86]

The subject matter jurisdiction for these courts would be for all matters civil, criminal, and regulatory (administrative). Appeals could conceivably be taken to a special appellate court, which we shall for convenience sake designate as the Court of Antitrust Appeals. This would not be too serious a deviation from the existing pattern of appellate jurisdiction in the United States: for precedent we could point to the Court of Military Appeals and to the Court of Customs and Patent Appeals.[87]

We admit that the suggestion for the appointment of judges better attuned to the peculiar exigencies of the cases submitted to their adjudication is always a tempting proposition. At the same time, when carried to the extreme, this would lead to judges specialized in airplane accidents, or automobile hazards, or construction engineering, to mention a few fields where expertise is important. We submit that the situation is different in antitrust litigation.

We mention as arguments in favor of a special judiciary for antitrust cases:

(1) Antitrust courts could hear cases with panels of three judges instead of the traditional one-judge courts as we find them in other instances of original jurisdiction. A three-panel court as proposed by us would consist of one law-trained member and two members respectively trained in marketing and economics. Judgments would then better reflect the various aspects that need consideration and analysis, such as the marketing and economic effects of competition (or the suppression thereof).[88]

(2) Appointments of judges to the federal bench occur not infrequently on a political patronage basis; expert knowledge of antitrust legislation is rarely if ever a determining factor. While there are fortunately a number of judges who have shown a thorough understanding of the antitrust laws, the mere appointment of a judge to the federal bench does not guarantee that he is adequately prepared to deal with the complexities that often mark antitrust cases.

86. *cf.* MASSEL, *op. cit.*, p. 11, who also includes other social sciences in the complex area of antitrust, to wit, political science, psychology, sociology, accounting and statistics.

87. For a pictorial chart of the appellate organization of the American federal court system, see BERMAN & GREINER, *op. cit.*, p. 142.

88. This would also conceivably preclude the apprehension that a court would hand down a decision 'in a perplexing opinion whose rationale is not clear'; *cf. Att'y Gen. Report*, p. 141

3) Many antitrust cases require extensive hearings, thus taking up a considerable amount of time. Freeing the judges from hearing antitrust cases would allow for expediting other litigation in the already overtaxed courts, while antitrust cases would only be heard by antitrust courts.

(4) A special antitrust court could remove all adjudicatory activities from the Federal Trade Commission and would put adjudication where it properly belongs: in the courts. This would at the same time enable the Federal Trade Commission to investigate possible antitrust violations, and give advise to the business community.

(5) The proposed special antitrust judiciary would still maintain the United States Supreme Court as the highest Court of the land, thus preserving the present judicial system of the United States, but making those modifications as required by the needs of modern society. Constitutional issues would then still be submitted to the Court that is the highest interpreter of the Constitution. For antitrust cases at the domestic level an organizational structure as here proposed would therefore, not only be conceivable, but in our opinion even desirable.

The question that may be raised is: will these courts have sufficient work to do to keep them fully occupied? During the years 1955-1968 (the period of special interest to the writers of the SUPPLEMENT) some 800 cases were listed as having been decided by the courts;[89] that is an average of almost 70 cases per year. This is only a rough count, and pertains only to the cases listed by the authors of the SUPPLEMENT. Furthermore, most of the private antitrust suits were not cited; for these, the following figures are given:

(a) for the period 1956-1960: 1163 private suits (more than 200 per year);

(b) for the period 1961-1965: 3598 private suits (more than 700 per year; however, 1948 of these cases pertained to the electrical price fixing conspiracy. If we deduct those, a number of 1650 private suits remains, i.e., an average of about 330 suits per year).[90]

On the basis of these quantitative aspects alone we feel justified in maintaining that the special antitrust courts would have sufficient work to do to keep them occupied.[91]

(b) At the Supra-National Level:

An entirely different question which we will have to answer is how the above

89. SUPPLEMENT, pp. 349, *seq.*

90. *ibid.*, p. 274

91. This is particularly the case in view of the fact that many antitrust suits, because of their complexity, take months if not years of trial time and time to write the opinions and/or decrees. Also one should keep in mind that for all consent orders the prior approval of the court is required; therefore, the number of investigations ending in a consent decree should in all fairness be added to the number of cases decided by the courts.

proposed system would function with regard to the transnational aspects of restraint of trade. Two different situations will have to be considered:

(1) The domestic level.

At the domestic level, the judges can be expected to be conversant with and attuned to the legal and the business problems involved, both from the national and the transnational points of view. It is of course, particularly with respect to the generally accepted and recognized principles of international (antitrust) law that we may insist that the judges apply these principles. This holds true both at the trial level and the appellate levels.

Even then it may happen that an appeal taken to the Court of Antitrust Appeals will be decided in a manner to which a foreign defendant, or his national government, objects on the grounds that the economy, or the sovereignty of the foreign State will be adversely affected, contrary to the rules of international law.

In such a case a review by the United States Supreme Court might seem of little value to the foreign government, particularly if the Supreme Court would only consider the proceedings in the courts below on the basis of the proper application of the law, and not on the basis of the merits of the case. This depends on the wording of the law. If the law contains clearly written rules with regard to transnational aspects of restraint of trade, it would seem highly improbable that the Supreme Court (or even the courts below) would ignore these rules.[92]

(2) The supra-national level.

The possibility exists that the interpretation of the law by the American domestic courts would lead to an unacceptable result as far as the foreign government is concerned.

To solve problems of this nature provisions need to be made for the review by a supra-national tribunal of cases with trans-national aspects. For convenience sake we shall designate this supra-national tribunal International Antitrust Court. Such a tribunal could conceivably be attached to the International Court of Justice. Another possibility would be to establish an independent Supra-National High Authority for Antitrust Matters, part of which could be a Supra-National Antitrust Court.

A third possibility could be the creation of an International Court of Arbitration for Antitrust Matters. While the organization of the above suggested tribunals may differ slightly in its practical day-to-day work, these differences will not

92. These rules would have to be worked out in consultation between the various governments, conceivably utilizing the machinery of the United Nations. While they would have to recognize certain generally recognized and accepted principles of international law, they would also have to recognize certain generally accepted principles of marketing and economics. As such, these rules would constitute an entirely new field of special international antitrust law.

have great impact, since the objectives remain the same.[93]

We submit that a supra-national tribunal such as suggested by us would not severely jeopardize the sovereignty of the nations affected, because law and economics rather than political considerations would be the major concern of these tribunals.

Furthermore, while these supra-national institutions would review national adjudication on the basis of internationally accepted rules of law and economics, still, they would have to be guided to a certain extent by the ratiocination of the antitrust courts at the national level. To that extent, these courts might even be considered as an extension of the national courts into the trans-national sphere. Conversely, these supra-national tribunals might provide proper guidance to national courts in those cases where trans-national problems of antitrust are submitted to the antitrust courts at the national level. To that extent, a proper interaction would result between the international and the national legal order of the nations of the world.[94]

Of course, emotional outbursts can be expected if these supra-national tribunals would find that the national antitrust court had violated the accepted rules of international law. These outbursts will simply have to be countered by the statement that no international cooperation can effectively come about unless even the powerful nations of the world stand ready to have their judicial findings be tested against generally accepted rules or principles. Furthermore, international tribunals have at times reviewed cases which had been decided by national courts, including cases decided by the United States Supreme Court.[95]

Also, the creation of one more international court in addition to the existing ones does not disturb us; as matters stand today, there are several international tribunals dealing with a variety of rather heterogeneous subject matter.[96]

A creation such as here suggested would not only be a vehicle to settle disputes. It would also significantly contribute to the further growth of international law, because it would develop and formulate new principles and rules of international antitrust law; that this is necessary will be shown later in this study.

Furthermore, a tribunal as here alluded to would be of importance with regard to the presently emerging extraterritorial reach of the antitrust law of the Euro-

93. 'International arbitration and judical settlement are virtually identical procedures'; *cf.* KAPLAN, M. A. & KATZENBACH, N. de B., THE POLITICAL FOUNDATIONS OF INTERNATIONAL LAW, New York, 1961, p. 275.

94. '. . . the international legal order is largely achieved through the medium of internal law'; *cf.* JESSUP, P. C., THE USE OF INTERNATIONAL LAW, Ann Arbor, 1959, p. 63

95. 'Although to some it is still a source of astonishment, it is a commonplace that international tribunals have reviewed cases decided even by the Supreme Court of the United States, have found that this high tribunal incorrectly applied international law. . .'; *cf. ibid.*, pp. 63, 64.

96. *cf. ibid.*, p. 102, and the literature there cited. It should be observed that Arbitral Tribunals and Mixed Commissions are included in the list because they basically perform a judicial function; *cf.* KAPLANN & KATZENBACH, *op. cit.*, p. 275

pean Economic Community,[97] and thus, provide proper guidance with regard to the norms set there. Finally, the tribunal would be an aid to the courts in the emerging and developing nations of the world, in that it could provide guidance with the formulation of principles pertaining to the extraterritorial reach of restrictive trade legislation in those countries. Thus, the principles of international law would increasingly reflect the position that it contains the norms and notions of all nations of the world, rather than the domain of European countries who developed principles to regulate the international relations among themselves.[98]

There is an added reason for the establishment of an International Antitrust Court. The case for a unilateral application of national law enforcement exclusively by national courts has certainly not been made. On the contrary, this form of adjudication has even provoked the accusation that the (American) national courts were guilty of judicial aggression.[99]

It just might be possible that a case for antitrust enforcement at the supranational level could be made if the addmittedly slower process of adjudication in accordance with the accepted principles of international law were undertaken in a spirit of cooperative effort.[100]

We do not underestimate the problems that will confront a Supra-national Antitrust Court, particularly because of the conflicting regulatory policies which prevail in the various countries.[101] It is our conviction however, that the effort is worth the trouble because of the advantages we anticipate to be derived from it. As early as 1946 the establishment of an international tribunal dealing with antitrust problems was proposed.[102] However, where that suggestion was made for the purpose to determine whether an international cartel would or would not be in conflict with international law, we submit that our proposal would purport to review the decisions of national courts on the basis of the internationally accepted rules of law and economics, against the background of what is necessary to maintain the harmony in the community of nations.

Thus, a body of rules of law to which national governments would submit would

97. For an illustration we refer to the *Aniline* Case, see INTRODUCTION, *supra*, p. 11, and Chapter IV, *infra*, p. 106.
98. *cf.* KAPLAN & KATZENBACH, *op. cit.*, pp. v, vi
99. *cf.* *The Record, l.c.*, pp. 121, *n.* 36, and 137; BREWSTER, *op. cit.*, p. 50
100. *cf.* JESSUP, *op. cit.*, p. 154. For the United States, it would necessitate repealing the so-called *Connally Amendment,* because it would be improper to pay lip service to the idea of submitting controversies of a trans-national character to the jurisdiction of a Supra-National Court of Justice while reserving the right to determine which disputes are essentially within a nation's domestic jurisdiction; *cf.* JESSUP, *op. cit.*, 50; KAPLAN & KATZENBACH, *op. cit.*, p. 282
101. *cf.* TRAUTMAN, D., 'A Study of the International Environment: The International Reach of American Regulatory Legislation Other Than the Sherman Act', in BREWSTER, *op. cit.*, pp. 309, 310
102. *cf.* MACASSEY, L., 'Controlling Cartels Under the Rule of Law,' 31 *Grotius Society-Problems in Public and Private International Law* 232, 244 (1946).

gradually emerge.[103] in which the special character of the antitrust laws, as a separate area of the law, would find recognition.[104]

103. *cf.* RESTATEMENT OF THE LAW (SECOND), FOREIGN RELATIONS LAW OF THE UNITED STATES, 1965, p. 1.

104. We find support for this suggestion by statements in the literature recognizing on the one hand that the extraterritorial reach of the antitrust laws has created a special area of international law (*cf.* REHBINDER, *op. cit.*, p. 29); while elsewhere we read that we should not ask whether there is a positive principle of international law which regulates the extraterritorial legislative and judical jurisdiction, but only whether there is a principle that collides with the assertion of such jurisdiction (*cf.* SCHWARTZ, I. E., *op. cit.*, pp. 245, 246). It seems to us that once the special character of the antitrust laws has been recognized (as both SCHWARTZ, I. E., *op. cit.*, p. 4, and REHBINDER, *op. cit.*, p. 57, seem to do), then, the need to formulate positive rules for this special area of the law follows as a necessary sequel.

CHAPTER IV

THE EXTRATERRITORIAL REACH OF THE AMERICAN ANTITRUST LAWS JURISDICTIONAL ASPECTS

General

The use of the term 'jurisdiction' may cause confusion if no further indication is given to what aspect of jurisdiction the reference is made. In its most general aspect, the term jurisdiction 'embraces every kind of judicial action.'[1]
Yet it is commonly understood that the term connotes three different aspects:[2]
(a) jurisdiction over the person;
(b) jurisdiction over the subject matter;
(c) jurisdiction with regard to the territory where the case is adjudged.
Small wonder that the concept has been described as 'at once too elemental and too ambigious to be defined.'[3]
Yet no matter from what angle one views jurisdiction, in all instances the term connotes power, i.e., the power to render a binding decision.[4]
When dealing with the extraterritorial reach of law enforcement, we are without any doubt referring to power, i.e., the power of a State to render a binding decision, even with regard to persons not under its allegiance.
But the use of power must find its justification either on a legal basis (under normal circumstances), or on an extra-legal basis (under unusual circumstances, such as in an emergency). Not to accept this basic principle as a point of departure would, in the absence of an emergency situation, only expose a nation to the charge of illegal use of power. This means that if an International Court of Justice would review those acts, it might find them counter to what is generally considered acceptable under international law.
Therefore, powerful nationas might have to impose upon themselves a policy of restraint in cases of extraterritorial jurisdictional reach, lest the result would be a use of power beyond the internationally accepted standards. Extra-legal use of power may be resorted to only in those cases where the national survival (politically or economically) would be at stake.[5] Both the legislature and the judiciary

1. *cf.* BLACK'S LAW DICTIONARY, 4th ed., St. Paul, 1951, p. 991.
2. *ibid.*
3. FOSTER, R. S., in ENCYCLOPEDIA OF THE SOCIAL SCIENCES, Vol. VII, New York, 1959, p. 471.
4. *cf.* GOODRICH, H. F., HANDBOOK OF THE CONFLICT OF LAWS, 3rd ed., St. Paul, 1949, p. 166.
5. *cf.* BREWSTER, *op. cit.*, pp. 286, 287.

have to be guided by this principle of jurisdictional limitation. These limitations upon the power to render a binding decision become particularly important when foreign conduct or foreign defendants are involved.

The right to determine what shall constitute legally reprehensible conduct

One of the more important questions to answer is: who has the right to determine what conduct outside the borders of a given nation shall violate the norms of that nation? When phrased more aggressively, the question would read: does a State have the right to take judicial cognizance of conduct outside its borders, to the effect that, when such conduct violates the norms of that State, the persons guilty of such conduct could be prosecuted? We will, in answering this question, overlook the aspect of mere power to assume jurisdiction. Rather, we will consider the question from the angle of power based on legal authority.

The authority to determine what is reprehensible is generally considered the prerogative of the State that has to maintain the social order in that given area; this would entail that the State also may set the norms that will be enforced.[6]

In order to avoid misunderstanding, we should emphasize that we are, at this point, not concerned with the question *who may prosecute* a violation of the norm. We will deal with that aspect of legal enforcement later.

All we are concerned with at present is the question *who may determine* what conduct outside the borders of a given nation shall be a violation of the norms, both with regard to conduct committed by nationals of the State that claims the right to enforcement, or by foreign nationals.

On the basis our previous statement we suggest that it is the State whose social order is threatened that has (or should have) the right to determine what conduct shall be considered reprehensible, because harmful to its orderly community process.

The above statement is in keeping with the views expressed in the literature that:

> '... la détermination des infractions est essentiellement une règle d'ordre public que dépend uniquement de la souveraineté de chaque Etat.'[7]

If we analyze this statement, we find that each sovereign nation has the right to maintain its *ordre public;* further, that in the implementation of the maintenance of its *ordre public,* a State has (to have) the right to determine what conduct shall be violative thereof and therefore, reprehensible.

The problem with these general phrases is that as long as the State making the rules is reasonable there will be little commotion in the international commu-

6. *cf.* MULDER, A., 'De extra-territoriale werking van het strafrecht' in 51 *Mededelingen van de Nederlandse Vereniging voor Internationaal Recht*, 14, (1964).
7. DONNEDIEU DE VABRES, H., LES PRINCIPES MODERNES DU DROIT PÉNAL INTERNATIONAL, Paris, 1928, pp. 32, 33.

nity of nations. But the situation may become different if a State makes rules which no other civilized State would consider making. Yet if such a State would shield itself behind its sovereign right to maintain its national *ordre public*, it would be difficult to raise theoretical objections against those rules.

The problem can become still more thorny if among the civilized nations of the world an honest difference of viewpoint occurs with regard to the regulation of each State's national economic system. This happens to be the case when we are dealing with antitrust enforcement: the United States views cartels as odorous, while in other countries cartels are either favorably considered, or only limitedly disapproved.[8]

It does not need much imagination to realize that this diversity of views might easily lead to a conflict situation, because whatever right one State assumes is almost inevitably in conflict with the legal sphere of another State.[9]

Thus we find with regard to international cartels the following statement:

> 'Seul le gouvernement peut déterminer si la politique d'un cartel est compatible ou non avec la politique économique. Dans le même ordre d'idées on pourrait dire qu'au niveau international aussi, un organe devrait être chargé du contrôle, qui a aussi qualité pour intervenir dans les principaux problèmes de coopération économique internationale. Selon cette conception une surveillance internationale des cartels internationaux n'a de sens que dans la mesure oú on peut parler d'une politique économique internationale commune qui ne doit pas être traversée par des cartels.'[10]

The author clearly recognizes the problems which a national regulation will cause when viewed against the international consequences of such a one-sided regulation. In order to solve these problems he suggests two alternate solutions:

(1) '. . . on met l'accent sur la réglementation nationale. Dans ce cas il sera nécessaire de tâcher de réaliser par la voie internationale une répartition de compétence. . .'

(2) '. . . on part de la fonction internationale de cartels internationaux. . . La solution la plus radicale est celle qu'offre la Communauté Européenne du Charbon et de l'Acier. . .' 'On peut aller moins loin encore et prevoir seulement une possibilité de coordination internationale de la *formation d'une opinion*, tout en laissant la compétence définitive quant aux mesures à prendre entièrement aux pays nationaux. C'est cette voie que le Conseil

8. *cf.* KRONSTEIN, H. 'Conflicts Resulting From The Extraterritorial Effects Of The Antitrust Legislation of Different Countries,' in XXth CENTURY COMPARATIVE AND CONFLICTS LAW, Leiden, 1961, p. 432. Also, see KAPLAN & KATZENBACH, *op. cit.*, pp. 185, *seq.*
9. *cf.* EHRENZWEIG, A. A., A TREATISE ON THE CONFLICT OF LAWS, St. Paul, 1962, p. 3, who describes the conflict as a struggle between a unitarian and a pluralistic tendency.
10. VERLOREN VAN THEMAAT, P., 'Les Cartels Internationaux devant les Législations Nationales d'un Point de Vue Juridique,' in 3 *Sociaal Economische Wetgeving*, 18 (1955).

Economique et Social de L'ONU a choisie, en s'inspirant de la Charte de la Havane.'[11]

The author seems to opt for the latter solution (the one proposed in the draft of the United Nations treaty); even then, he mentions a few unsolved problem areas:

(1) '. . . si selon une opinion internationale coordonnée les activités d'un cartel ne sont pas nuisibles, il n'y a aucune garantie que les pays nationaux ne prennent quand-même pas de mesures contre le cartel. . .'

(2) '. . . le traité n'offre en effet aucune certitude qu'après qu'il a été décidé au niveau international, que les activités du cartel sont nuisibles, des mesures contre ce cartel seront prises. . .'[12]

In other words, there is no certainty that national governments will not take steps of their own even if international opinion would consider the activities of the cartel not harmful, neither is it certain that steps will be undertaken even if international opinion would consider the activities of the cartel harmful.

All this brings us right back to the main question we are trying to answer: who has the right to determine what is reprehensible or objectionable?

In our attempt to answer that question we consider it advisable to follow the often made distinction between judicial and legislative jurisdiction, even though, unfortunately, this distinction has not always been kept in mind, either by the lawyers or by the courts.[13]

There is reason for making the distinction. While normative determination of reprehensible conduct is largely a prerogative of legislative jurisdiction, this is not absolutely or always the case. For instance, the extensive interpretation of legislative determinations in a Penal Code can (and often does) result in new normative determinations.[14] Particularly in the common law countries, much normative law which elsewhere is solely promulgated by the legislature may be announced by the judiciary or even by the quasi-judicial authorities of the executive branch of government.[15]

Particularly because the term 'jurisdiction' connotes power; furthermore, be-

11. *ibid.*, pp. 22, 23
12. *ibid.*, pp. 24, 25
13. *cf.* OLIVER, C. T., 'The Range of Effect of the Anti-Trust Laws of the United States,' in 1964 *Tokyo Proceedings,* 511, 517: 'The difference between judicial and legislative jurisdiction is not disregarded in the United States, although in some of the anti-trust cases it is probable that the attorneys involved did not differentiate between the two problems, with the result that the courts did not either, in those particular cases.'
14. As an example we mention the decision of the Netherlands Supreme Court that electricity is a good of which the lawful owner can be deprived; *cf.* H. R., May 23, 1921, *Nederlandse Jurisprudentie* 1921, p. 564. This decision resulted in the norm that one who unlawfully converted electricity to his own use would be guilty of larcency. (*Public Prosecutor* v. *A.M.M.*).
15. As illustration of the latter we might mention the rule-making authority of the Federal Trade Commission, to which we have alluded in Chapters I and II.

cause this power can be exercised by the legislature and by the judiciary; and finally, because this power may be used legally (under normal circumstances), extra-legally (in situations of urgency or emergency), or illegally (i.e., without any justification), an expression such as 'The problem of anti-trust is a problem of the use of power. . .'[16] does not convey when the power is used properly or improperly (or even illegally).

While not stated specifically, we must assume that the statement here referred to pertains to the judicial jurisdiction; we say so in view of the following observations of the 'Rapporteur' RIEDWEG:

> 'Some U.S. commentators take the position that international law has no application in this area. They say a State does have *jurisdiction* so *to apply* its restrictive trade legislation. . .'[17]
>
> 'It does not seem appropriate to assume that international law contains no meaningful limitations on the exercise of a State's *jurisdiction to apply* its restrictive trade legislation to the conduct of aliens. It seems more fitting for international lawyers to turn first to the existing principles of international law to see whether in fact such principles contain meaningful restrictions on the exercise of a State's power.'[18]
>
> '. . . there is no agreement among States that *one may apply its law* to economic conduct in another.[19]

Inasmuch as in each of the above quotations only reference is made to *applying law* and not to *making law* we take it that judicial and not legislative jurisdiction was the issue. At the same time, it should be recognized that, in general, a law can be applied only after the law has been made. Consequently, it seems to us that the pivotal point is the time that the law is made. Once the law is made, the judiciary will have an opportunity to examine the merits of the law against the background of international law.

We concede that presently the examination of the law against the principles of international law depends largely upon the pertinent national requirements. In countries such as Germany[20] or The Netherlands [21] the supremacy of international law has been recognized by the provision that the legislature or the judiciary are restricted in the exercise of their jurisdiction by the principles of

16. *cf.* 1964 *Tokyo Proceedings*, p. 305.
17. *ibid.*, p. 305. (Italics supplied.)
18. *ibid.*, p. 306. (Italics supplied.)
19. *ibid.*, p. 308. (Italics supplied.)
20. *cf.* REHBINDER, *op. cit.*, pp. 30, 31: 'Artikel 25 des Grundgesetzes bestimmt den Vorrang der allgemeinen Regeln des Völkerrechtes vor dem Bundesrechte.'
21. Art. 13a Wet Alg. Bepalingen, as amended by the Act of April 26, 1917: 'De regtsmagt van den regter en de uitvoerbaarheid van regterlijke vonnissen en van authentieke akten worden beperkt door de uitzonderingen in het volkenregt erkend.' (The jurisdiction of the judiciary and the authority to carry out judicial decisions and officially certified documents are restricted by the principles recognized in international law)

international law. We are not aware of any such an provision in, say the legislative provisions of the United States.

At the same time we submit that even where judicial jurisdiction is restricted by the principles of international law States seem to have little difficulty to justify, under one formula or another, their competency to apply law, even if other States do not like what is being done.[22]

When it comes to the legislative jurisdiction of a State, i.e., its competence to make or prescribe laws, we find that States consider themselves competent to prescribe laws as a protection against acts which would seriously impair the orderly community process of that State.[23]

That means that even in States that subscribe to the principle of the supremacy of international law, a formula is often found to justify what is being done (either judicially or legislatively), so that the practice cannot be branded as violative of the principles of international law. In its generality we do not find this objectionable: why should a State disregard behavior that would thwart its efforts to establish and maintain what it considers a viable community process? The problem, however, is not where the practive begins, but where it should stop. For instance, does a State that considers the free enterprise system (i.e., free competition in open markets) the viable system for its community process have the right to compel a State with a different point of view to submit to its politico-economic views, if the latter wants to participate in the domestic trade of the former? If so, what would be left of the sovereignty of States? At the same time, what if the results of the politico-economic community process of the non-free-enterprise State would thwart the community process of the free-enterprise State?

We suggest that the line should be drawn there where the vital community processes of a State are threatened, or potentially threatened.

Consequently, we submit that as a preliminary answer to our question: Who shall have the right to determine whether conduct outside the boundaries of a given State constitutes legally reprehensible conduct? we may state:

> *The right to determine whether certain conduct constitutes a legally reprehensible practice is the prerogative of the State whose vital community processes are thereby affected.*

Although we have earlier referred both to the judicial and the legislative jurisdic-

22. *cf.* 1964 *Tokyo Proceedings,* p. 329: 'With respect to the first kind of competence, that of *applying* law, it does not yet appear that international law imposes much, if any, limitation upon the discretion of States.' Also, see JESSUP, Ph.C., TRANSNATIONAL LAW, New Haven, 1956, p. 71: 'When a State wishes to find and punish the "whodunit" it follows strange fictional clues. . .'
23. *cf.* 1964 *Tokyo Proceedings,* p. 330: 'The most fundamental policy underlying all the principles for allocation of competence among States is, then, that each State is authorised to make – and, when it has effective control, to apply – law for events, even when occurring beyond its territorial boundaries, which substantially affect its own community process.'

tional perspectives, we have limited our answer to the legislative jurisdictional aspects of the extraterritorial reach. We therefore, should consider the judicial jurisdictional aspects of extraterritorial law enforcement separately.

The right to adjudicate legally reprehensible conduct

When discussing the judicial jurisdictional aspects of extraterritorial antitrust enforcement, several questions need to be answered. We mention the following: which jurisdiction is competent to apply the law? Under which circumstances can this competency be exercised?

While we have earlier stated that both legislative and judicial jurisdiction are typically the prerogative of the State that makes a claim to maintaining the social order in the specific area, there is no reason why this prerogative should be exclusive when dealing with judicial jurisdiction. In a world of close cooperation and similar views with regard to law enforcement it would be quite conceivable that a violation committed in one State would be adjudicated in another State.[24] Thus, it would be possible that more than one jurisdiction would have judicial jurisdiction. We consider this still extraterritorial reach, because the exercise of judicial jurisdiction would result from the violation of a law of another State.

With regard to the question: Under which circumstances can judicial jurisdiction be exercised? we find different views. Sometimes the view is presented that one of the prerequisites of the extraterritorial reach of national laws is that the conduct be reprehensible both in the prosecuting State and in the State where the conduct took place.[25] There is reason to believe, however, that judicial authorities do not always act in conformity with this prerequisite element of judicial jurisdictional competency.

To substantiate the latter statement, we point to a case adjudicated in The Netherlands:[26]

> A woman of Belgian nationality and domiciled in Belgium, was accused of having acted (in Belgium) as an accessory to offences committed by Netherlands subjects against the Dutch Currency Decree of 1945. The Special Police Court of Breda convicted the woman, thereby rejecting her contention that she was not subject to Dutch criminal law. The Court of

24. *cf.* MULDER, *l.c.*, p. 14: 'It is however in no way necessary that the State itself makes its force felt under all circumstances. If a person who disturbs the peace is a citizen of another State, and that other State, too, would reprehend the behavior if it had occurred within its own territory, then, it could be useful, in fact better, that the law enforcement be carried out in that very country. This is not so much a matter of principle but rather of expediency.'
25. *cf. ibid.*, p. 14
26. *Public Prosecutor* v. *L.*, 48 *Int'l Law Rep.* 206, 1951, Ned. Jr. 1952, n. 42. The case is cited in KATZ, M, & BREWSTER, K. Jr., THE LAW OF INTERNATIONAL TRANSACTIONS AND RELATIONS, Brooklyn, 1960, p. 667.

Appeals at 's Hertogenbosch upheld the conviction. The Supreme Court of The Netherlands held that the woman was rightly convicted; in its opinion the Court stated that the provisions of the Dutch Emergency Decree on Currency Restrictions were not only directed against Netherlands subjects, who committed currency offences in a foreign country, but also against foreign nationals abroad who were accessories to such offences. This was apparently sufficient to bring the woman under the reach of the law.

Interesting is the comment by POMPE in *Nederlandse Jurisprudentie,* following the case, stating that application of a criminal sanction with regard to conduct committed abroad by foreigners is tantamount to treading dangerous ground.[27] But this treading of dangerous ground is caused by the pertinent legislative provisions. We submit that the comment should first, have drawn attention to the distinction between the judicial and the legislative jurisdictional competency, if necessary accompanied by the recognition that a State should be entitled to enact those laws that it feels important to the proper maintenance of its vital community processes.

An approach as here suggested would still enable the legislature to discharge itself of its duties as it sees fit in the best interests of the nation, even if there are limitations, imposed by the generally recognized principles of international law (or even expediency). This would shift the proper burden to the judicial branch. We mention as problem areas for the (Dutch) judiciary:

(1) the requirement that the judge is bound to adjudicate in accordance with the (Dutch) law, without liberty to examine the intrinsic value or the fairness of the law:[28]

(2) the requirement that the exercise of judicial power and the authority to carry out judicial decisions and officially certified documents are restricted by the general principles of international law.[29]

Thus, the judicial branch of government must discharge itself of its duties in conformity with the law (as given by the lawmaker), making an exception only where the principles of international law, or similar very exceptional circumstances, require a different solution.[30] Whether on the basis of the above made distinction the (Dutch) law was wrong, or whether the prosecutor or the judge were in error, we need not say; either one could be the case.

We have earlier stated that the determination of what is reprehensible is basically a rule of public policy (*ordre public*), which uniquely depends on the sovereign-

27. *cf. Ned. Jur.* 1952, n. 42, p. 123.
28. Art. 11 Wet Alg. Bepalingen
29. Art. 13a Wet Alg. Bepalingen
30. *cf.* LANGEMEYER, G. E., 'Le Principe de Territorialité," in LE DROIT PENAL INTERNATIONAL, Leiden, 1965

ty of each State.[31] It is equally true, however, that while the determination of reprehensible behavior is a lawful exercise of the police power of the sovereign State,[32] the legislature in the exercise of its law-making authority will have its eye fixed on the public policy of the State and the objectives to be achieved by the particular legislation.

The reason why a State should be empowered to enforce antitrust legislation is that only the State whose community process will be affected can determine whether its economic policy needs prescriptions (or protection) with regard to antitrust regulation.[33] That this principle also holds where foreign enterprises or foreign nationals are involved can be justified on the grounds that anyone who wants to engage in commercial dealings in another country must take into account the norms that prevail in that other country.[34] There is nothing unreasonable in the requirement that a (foreign) merchant who wants to do business within the United States must do so within the legal framework of the United States. In other words, anyone who acts in contravention of the laws prevailing in another country must by necessity accept the consequences of his behavior. There is ample reason to support the above requirement. It may be reasonably expected that the businessman, prior to his entry into the market – either at the domestic level or in the international sphere – will acquaint himself with all the tools and data necessary to successfully participate in the market. These tools and data entail, of course, managerial skill. But they also encompass a thorough

31. We use the term *public policy* as a translation for *ordre public* for the following reasons: (a) it better reflects the doctrine underlying the term; *cf.* DELAUME, G. R., AMERICAN-FRENCH PRIVATE INTERNATIONAL LAW, New York, 1961, p. 83: 'The doctrine of public policy . . . is a rough approximation of *ordre public* . . .' For a different view, see KATZENBACH, N. de B., 'Conflicts on an Unruly Horse: Reciprocal Claims and Tolerances in Interstate and International Law," 65 *Yale Law Journal* 1087, 1088, *n.* 9 (1956), and the literature there cited; (b) the various American legal dictionaries do not define the term *public order,* while they do attempt to define the term *public policy;* (c) the term *public order* does not convey an American legal concept, other than the use of the police power by a State; it is not used when referring to the Constitutional limits of the law-making authorities; (d) the term *public order* in American law is an element of the police power of the State, while the term *public policy* is a widely known concept in the American legal doctrine, even though the courts intentionally have been loath to define it with accuracy, so that the use of the concept would be flexible enough to be adapted to changed conditions; (e) even where the language of the law refers to 'morality, public order and the general welfare', we are, in effect, dealing with the public policy of the State.
32. *supra*, p. 94.
33. *cf.* VERLOREN VAN THEMAAT, *supra*, p. 95.
34. *cf.* MULDER, *l.c.*, p. 26. For a similar opinion, see KRONSTEIN, H., 'The Nationality of International Enterprises,' 52 *Columbia Law Review* 983, 998 (1952): '. . . American Courts can reasonably demand that even outside the jurisdiction of the United States the corporate owner and central business enterprise so act that the American part of the total organization can fulfill its purpose in the American economic order without disruptive effect. If the foreigners believe they cannot comply with such demands, they have the alternative of withdrawing from the American scene.'

familiarity with the typical characteristics of the particular market under consideration, such as the channels of distribution, the methods of pricing (including the legality of retail price maintenance), and the government regulation of business.

It is with regard to the last mentioned item, the government regulation of business, that the businessman is expected to conduct his enterprise within the legal framework of the given market. If he fails to do so, he can be reproached of being grossly negligent if not derelict in his managerial duties.

This gross negligence, which some courts may treat as 'willful and wanton negligence,' may expose the entrepreneur to legal action at the hands of the governmental law enforcement agencies.

For persons with a criminal law specialization, this approach to the topic at hand is not too surprising: criminal lawyers are used to such concepts as 'intentional,' '*dolus eventualis,*' 'wanton negligence,' all taking into consideration the level of consciousness of the acting person.[35]

It seems to us that based on the above observations the possibility of a prosecution based on 'wanton negligence' would fit into this because of the imputed consciousness of the acting person.

The need for treaties

As far as the Netherlands is concerned part of the problem seems to be created by the fact that there are no treaties regulating the relations between States in matters of antitrust enforcement.[36] Because the subject matter deals with international law and consequently, has to be regulated either by the general rules of international law or by treaty provisions (which is customarily considered one of the constituent elements of the total field of international law)[37], the absence of a treaty is a valid reason for concern.

It is with a view to avoid the international complications that otherwise might be expected that the United States has concluded a number of bilateral treaties, agreeing to regulate problems of competition by mutual consultation.[38] We have earlier mentioned the major provisions of such a treaty.[39] However, inasmuch as the States only agree to consult with regard to harmful practices and to take those steps which are deemed appropriate to eliminate the harmful effects, there

35. For an interesting background description and analysis of these concepts, see BEMMELEN, J. M. VAN, ONS STRAFRECHT, Part I, 2nd ed., Haarlem, 1965, pp. 72, *seq.*
36. *cf.* ELLIS, J. J. A., 'De extraterritoriale werking van het nationale strafrecht,' 51 *Mededelingen van de Nederlandse Vereniging voor Internationaal Recht* 29 (1964)
37. *cf.* OPPENHEIM, L., INTERNATIONAL LAW, 8th ed., (LAUTERPACHT), Vol. I, p. 25, New York, 1963
38. *cf.* ELLIS, *l.c.*, p. 30
39. *cf.* Chapter I, *supra*, p. 29, *n.* 51

is a lack of regulation of the extent to which the law enforcement power of a State can reach outside its national boundaries.[40] Thus, the treaties do not impinge upon the legislative jurisdictional competency of a State, but assure consultation with regard to judicial jurisdiction in case of conflict situations. This appears to us a satisfactory method: a mechanism to avoid conflicts through mutual consultation has been provided, without putting limits to the legislative jurisdictional competency of each of the contracting States.

The question that is not answered is: what happens if the mutual consultation procedure does not provide satisfactory results in the eyes of the enforcement seeking State? Can such a State, after having first attempted a solution by way of consultation, proceed with steps aimed at enforcement? Would such an attitude be in conformity with the generally recognized and accepted principles of international law?

DONNEDIEU DE VABRES, in addressing himself to the judicial jurisdictional competency of France, rejects the idea of a prosecution of foreigners for offences committed abroad, with two exceptions:

(1) a 'légitime défense', in the nature of a 'réflexe', for threats to the security, or the 'crédit' of the State;[41]

(2) a 'compétence réelle', in view of the national interests, irrespective of the laws of the place of the conduct.[42]

If the above view would be the internationally accepted one, then, all one has to do is to either substitute 'disruption of the economic order' for some of the conditions, or add such a provision to the listed items and achieve legitimacy of the extraterritorial judicial reach. This would fit nicely into the existing 'protection principle' as known in international law. But allowing the matter of judicial jurisdictional competency to be guided by the protection principle has the inherent danger that nobody can properly state whether a State properly asserts that it enforces a rule because it wants to protect its community interests. Protection should only be allowed in instances where the *vital* community processes are threatened. And even there, we feel that there should be some restriction as to what may legitimately be called a vital community process. Absent such a determination, we do not see why it would be proper to assert extraterritorial judicial jurisdiction for offences committed against the security or the credit of a State, but improper (or doubtful) for commercial practices that thwart the politico-economic system of a State.

We think that there are better ways to solve the jurisdictional problems related

40. *cf.* ELLIS, *l.c.*, p. 30

41. DONNEDIEU DE VABRES, H., TRAITE DE DROIT CRIMINEL ET DE LEGISLATION PENALE COMPAREE, 3ieme ed., Paris, 1947, p. 958

42. *ibid.*, p. 961: '. . . elle s'exerce sans aucune considération des lois du pays où l'infraction a été commise.' For France, this 'compétence réelle' would exist on the basis of art. 7 of the French Code of Criminal Procedure

to the extraterritorial reach of the antitrust laws; later we hope to indicate what they are.

Suffice it at this time to formulate our views with regard to the jurisdictional reach:

> *'The right to adjudicate reprehensible conduct committed outside the territorial boundaries of a State is the sovereign prerogative of the State whose vital community interests and processes are threatened, subject to the limitations imposed by the general rules of international law or by treaty law.*

The subject of the law enforcement

So far we have considered the legislative and the judicial jurisdictional competency. The question which still needs to be answered is: who shall be the subject of this law enforcement?[43] We submit that there are three possible subjects of law enforcement:

(1) natural persons; these can be categorized as nationals and foreign persons;
(2) legal entities (i.e., corporations, partnerships, voluntary associations, foundations, etc.); these too, can be categorized as respectively, domestic and foreign entities;
(3) government owned or controlled corporations, again categorized as domestic and foreign.

The jurisdiction *in personam* over natural persons.

The wording of the American antitrust laws leave little doubt that natural persons are subject to the enforcement of the antitrust laws. The only requirements that need to be satisfied are that they are found and that process has properly been served. This, in turn, depends on whether they conduct substantial business in the jurisdiction, or happen to be there. As far as the law is concerned, no distinction is made between nationals and foreign persons.

The jurisdiction *in personam* over legal entities.

The *Sherman Act* and the *Clayton Act* state explicitly that 'corporations and associations existing under or authorized by the laws of either the United States, the laws of any of the Territories, the laws of any State, or the laws of any foreign country' are included in the word 'person, or persons, whereever used' in the acts.[44] Furthermore, the *Federal Trade Commission Act* makes 'any person, partnership, or corporation' subject to the authority of the Federal Trade Com-

43. The preceding observations pertained to the jurisdiction over the subject matter, while presently we are directing our attention to the jurisdiction *in personam* (i.e., over the subject); hence the title-heading of this section.
44. Section 8 *Sherman Act;* section 1 *Clayton Act*

mission.[45] That corporations could become defendants in (criminal) antitrust actions seems worthy of some special discussion, particularly because in a number of countries the view is widely held that only natural persons can be held accountable for having committed a criminal act.[46]

In the Netherlands the possibility of criminal prosecution of juristic persons received special attention at the 1966 annual meeting of the *Nederlandse Juristen Vereniging*, the national association of members of the legal profession. The question to which the 'rapporteurs' had to address themselves was: 'Should the Penal Code contain provisions regarding the perpetratorship and the criminal responsibility of other than natural persons?'[47]

In addressing himself to the above question, KIST answered in the affirmative,[48] albeit with reservations with regard to public enterprises, either at the national, the provincial, or the municipal level.[49]

HULSMAN, while also answering the question in the affirmative,[50] emphasized that an affirmative answer necessitated a solution to the companion question as to what stand to take with regard to the natural person who acted within the scope of his organizational authority, where the juristic person itself would be the subject of the imposition of a criminal sanction.[51] In posing this problem, he rejected the idea that the natural person in a situation as here suggested should be free from all prosecution.[52]

He recommended an amendment of the Dutch Penal Code in such a way that it would be possible to incorporate provisions which would lead to a criminal prosecution of the actual perpetrators of the reprehended conduct, be they either the natural person,[53] or the corporate entity.[54] At the same time he felt it incumbent upon him to point out that it would be proper, from a social-paedagogic point of view, to promote understanding for the view that there is no inflexible rule which requires to find a scapegoat for each and every undesired occurrence.[55]

With regard to the position of the corporation and/or the corporate executives in criminal antitrust prosecutions in the United States, we specifically single out

45. References thereto can be found all through the Act: Section 5(c); section 12 (a); section 14(a)
46. *cf.* MULDER, *l.c.*, p. 8, and the literature there cited
47. *cf.*, HANDELINGEN DER NEDERLANDSE JURISTEN VERENIGING 1966, I, Tweede Stuk, Zwolle, 1966.
48. *l.c.*, p. 49
49. *l.c.*, p. 67
50. *l.c.*, p. 141
51. *l.c.*, p. 79
52. *l.c.*, p. 80
53. *l.c.*, p. 155
54. *l.c.*, p. 156
55. *l.c.*, p. 92

the *Electrical Equipment* cases,[56] and see what can be learned from these widely publicized cases.

In the *Electrical Equipment* cases 29 electrical equipment manufacturers, including such giants as General Electric and Westinghouse, were punished with fines totaling $1,787,000, while seven corporate executives were sentenced to prison for conspiring to violate the antitrust laws against price fixing.

Judge GANEY, of the United States District Court for the Eastern Disctrict of Pennsylvania, made it a point to observe that both the conduct of the corporate *and* the individual defendants had threatened the survival of the free-enterprise system.

The then Attorney General KENNEDY publicly stated that he concurred with Judge GANEY'S decision to send high-ranking corporate executives to jail, together with 'crooks, gangsters, pimps and prostitutes,' because, 'These conspiracies undoubtedly defrauded the United States government, and therefore the American taxpayer, out of millions of dollars.'[57]

In other words, we find that the American judiciary does not evidence great inhibition to hold natural persons responsible for criminal conduct committed within the sphere of the corporate entity.

Thus, it seems fair to state that in the present state of the law juristic persons will have to face the consequences of their criminal behavior, while natural persons acting within their corporate authority also will be held accountable.

In the various continental legal systems juristic persons can be subjected to so-called 'administrative sanctions' such as the closing of the enterprise, or the revocation of permits, or fines (as, e.g., in Western Germany for the violation of cartel provisions).[58] Furthermore, we find that according to Article 15 of Regulation No. 17,[59] implementing Articles 85 and 86 of the Treaty of Rome,[60] the Commission of the E.E.C. is empowered to impose heavy fines on business enterprises either for supplying false or misleading information, or for infringements of the provisions of the Treaty. In fact, on July 24, 1969 the Commission assessed penalties ranging from 40,000 to 50,000 units to ten different corporations, to wit, one British, one French, one Italian, three Swiss, and four German corporations. Basis for the assessment of penalties was an allegedly collusive increase in the price of aniline pigments.[61]

56. For an interesting and detailed discussion of these cases, see SMITH, R. A., 'The Incredible Electrical Conspiracy,' *Fortune* Magazine, April, 1961, pp. 132, *seq.*, and May, 1961, pp. 161, *seq.*
57. *cf.* KENNEDY, R. F., 'This Case is a Reflection on All of Us,' *Life* Magazine, February 24, 1961, pp. 30, 31.
58. *cf.* MULDER, *l.c.*, p. 9
59. *cf. Board of Trade Journal,* March 9, 1962; for the official French text, see 13 *Journal Officiel des Communautés Européennes* 204 (1962)
60. Treaty of Rome of March 25, 1957, establishing the European Economic Community
61. *cf.* 12 *Publikatieblad van de Europese Gemeenschappen* of August 7, 1969, nr. L-195/11 (69/243/EEG); the case is commonly referred to as the *Aniline* case

In other words, the concept (and practice) of exposing corporate entities to penal prosecution has also been accepted in the Common Market countries.[62]

The American view with regard to juristic persons is probably best expressed in the often repeated statement by Chief Justice MARSHALL in *Dartmouth College* v. *Woodward*:[63]

> 'A corporation is an artificial being, invisible, intangible, and existing only in contemplation of law. Being the mere creature of law, it possesses only those properties which the charter of its creation confers upon it, either expressly or as incidental to its very existence. These are such as are supposed best calculated to effect the object for which it was created. Among the most important are immortality, and, if the expression may be allowed, individuality, properties by which a perpetual succession of many persons are considered as the same, so that they may act as a single individual.'

The view that a corporation possesses individuality, leads to the concomitant result that the 'person,' be it a natural or an artificial one, can be held responsible for criminal behavior.

At the same time it ought to be kept in mind that one of the requisites to punishability is that the actor was aware of what he was doing. This requirement is usually referred to as the requisite of criminal intent or guilty knowledge. This has led WAITE[64] to the statement:

> 'Some logical difficulty has been encountered by the courts through the premise that because a corporation has no physical body it cannot be guilty of the physical acts essential to punishability, nor, since it has no mind, can it entertain the mental attitude essential.'[65]

To this and similar arguments, SMITH AND ROBERSON have humorously answered:

> 'As a juristic fiction, a corporation is theoretically immortal. It may not

62. We use the term 'penal prosecution' notwithstanding the specific provision in Article 15, paragraph 4, of Regulation 17 stating that the decisions of the Commission shall not be of a criminal nature (*n'auront pas un caractère pénal*). Our reasoning is that fines of five thousand units of account (for false or misleading information) or one million units of account (for infringements) clearly denote a penal character, both in terms of the reasons for which the fine will be imposed, and the amount of the fine. That no 'criminal record' will come about does not obviate the fact the the fines are the result of normative violations (and aimed at punishment).

63. 4 Wheat (US) 518, 4 L. Ed. 629 (1819).
While so far we have frequently used the term 'juristic persons,' it might be opportune at this time to point out that in the United States the term 'legal entities' is used as being synonymous with 'juristic person.' We therefore, will feel free to use these terms alternately.

64. *cf.,* WAITE, J. B., THE CRIMINAL LAW AND ITS ENFORCEMENT, Chicago, 1947, pp. 223. '. . . the basic proposition of the criminal law is that there is no convictability in the absence of some punishability of mind.'

65. *ibid.,* p. 418.

> have a soul to save, but the absence of a soul in its incorporal body does not noticeably inhibit or prevent the welfare and safety of the community and the State. Corporations do not go to heaven because no business is transacted there. Corporations are amenable to the criminal law for violations of which they may be indicted and punished.'[66]

Thus, WAITE simply states 'courts have sufficiently disregarded logical difficulties so that they do hold corporations criminally liable for many types of offenses.'[67] It therefore should come as no surprise that in a case where the defendant corporation had been found guilty of grand larceny, and subsequently argued 'that a corporation cannot commit the crime of larceny as it is impossible for a corporation as such to have intent to steal or misappropriate property,' the New York Court of Appeals in its well-documented opinion tersely stated:

> 'We think this question has been fairly well settled to the contrary.'[68]

While a corporation, or any other legal entity, may be held criminally liable for violation of the criminal law, it does not follow that the same punishment can be meted out to artificial beings as to natural persons. One cannot sentence a corporation to the electric chair, or imprison it. But punishment can be inflicted in other ways, the imposing of a fine being the most readily identifiable one. Thus, we find in the Criminal Code of 1961 for the State of Illinois, in Title 1, article 1, section 7, paragraph (h) that, 'upon conviction, a fine may be imposed upon a corporation. . .'[69]

Apart from the above, when dealing with antitrust enforcement we find that Sec. 8 of the *Sherman Act* specifically states:

> 'That the word "person" or "persons," wherever used in this act shall be deemed to include corporations and associations existing under or authorized by the laws of either the United States, the laws of any of the Territories, the laws of any State, *or the laws of any foreign country.*'[70]

Therefore, a United States Court, dealing with a violation of the American antitrust laws, can only view a legal entity in accordance with its own notions as explicitly stated in the particular Act.

The jurisdiction *in personam* over Foundations.

While the *Sherman Act* only refers to 'corporations and associations,' we feel confident in expressing the opinion that legal entities which could not be entire-

66. SMITH, L. Y. & ROBERSON, G. G., BUSINESS LAW, UCC EDITION, 2nd ed., St. Paul, 1966, p. 799.
67. *cf.* WAITE, *op. cit.*, p. 418, and the literature there cited. Also, see American Law Institute, *Model Penal Code*, Tentative Draft no. 4, 1955, sec. 2.07, Liability of Corporations, Unincorporated Associations and Persons Acting, or Under Duty to Act, in Their Behalf.
68. *People* v. *Canadian Fur Trappers Corporation*, 248 NY 159, 161 NE 455 (1928).
69. Illinois Criminal Code of 1961, H.B. No. 342, approved July 28, 1961, effective January 1, 1962, incorporated in Chapter 38 of *Illinois Revised Statutes* 1961.
70. Sec. 8 of the *Sherman Act* of July 2, 1890, as amended by the Act of August 17, 1937, and the Act of July 7, 1955. (Italics supplied).

ly considered either a corporation or an association (such as the 'stichting,' as encountered in the Netherlands legal system) still would come under the reach of the Act. We base this opinion on the case *Henry Chauncey* v. *Republic of Chile (The Alsop Claim)*,[71] from which we infer that the decisive issue is whether the entity is 'a juridical person distinct from the members individually.'

Not adhering to the above view seems to us untenable in the light of American antitrust enforcement.

The jurisdiction *in personam* over Government owned or controlled corporations.

Even where a foreign government would become a partner of a (foreign) trading company, the American courts would not recognize the immunity from suit just because a foreign sovereign is involved. As early as 1824 Chief Justice MARSHALL stated:

> 'When a government becomes a partner in any trading company, it divests itself, so far as concerns the transactions of that company, of its sovereign character, and takes that of a private citizen.'[72]

That this opinion maintained its authority in the courts may be illustrated with the case *U.S.* v. *Deutsches Kalisyndikat Gesellschaft.*[73]

In this suit against the Deutsches Kalisyndikat Gesellschaft, the Société Commerciale des Potasses d'Alsace, and others, the French Ambassador (on behalf of his government) intervened with the objection that the Société Commerciale des Potasses d'Alsace was not amenable to the service of process, because the French corporation was created and controlled by the Republic of France; therefore, a suit against the French company was in fact an action against the French government.

The District Court for the Southern District of New York made the following observations:

1. The law under which the French corporation was incorporated, as well as its certificate of incorporation, provide that it may be sued.
2. The French law, like the law of the United States, regards a corporation as an entity distinct from its stockholders. Therefore, a suit against a corporation is not a suit against a government, merely because it has been incorporated by direction of the government, and is used as a governmental agent, and its stock is owned solely by the government.
3. Neither principle nor precedent requires that the immunity, which, as a matter of comity, is extended to a foreign sovereign and his ambassador,

71. *United States – Chile Claims Commission* (1901), Appendix to *Case of the United States Relating to The Alsop Claim before his Majesty George V* (1910), vol. 2, p. 558 cited in KATZ & BREWSTER, *op. cit.*, p. 290.
72. *Bank of United States* v. *Planters' Bank of Georgia,* 9 Wheat 904 (1824), cited in FUGATE, *op. cit.*, p. 74.
73. 31 F 2d 199 (SDNY), (1929), cited in FUGATE, *op. cit.*, p. 74; KATZ & BREWSTER, *op. cit.*, p. 372; BREWSTER, *op. cit.*, pp. 23, 45, 61, 71.

should be extended to a foreign corporation merely because some of its stock is held by a foreign state, or because it is carrying on a commercial pursuit, which the foreign government regards as governmental or public.

Therefore, the court denied the motion to dismiss the process of service against the Société Commerciale des Potasses d'Alsace.

Yet, in 1952 the Federal District Court for the District of Columbia granted sovereign immunity to the Anglo-Iranian Oil Company, Ltd., a British company with headquarters in London, and in which the British government had a capital investment of approximately 35% of the total capital, although it dominated the ownership of the 'ordinary shares,' which control the voting rights and, thus, the company.[74]

Of course, the Court compared the situation of the Anglo-Iranian Oil Company with that of the Société Commerciale des Potasses d'Alsace, thereby noting the following distinctive features in favor of granting sovereign immunity to the British corporation:

1. The Anglo-Iranian came into being as the result of an agreement between the Anglo-Persian Oil Company, Ltd. and the British Government in the year 1914.
2. The British government acquired its interest in the company to insure a proper supply of petroleum, crude oil and other products for the British fleet.
3. One of Great Britain's contentions before the Permanent International Court of Justice in 1951 (dealing with the Iranian Oil disputes) had been that the agreement of 1933 between Iran and the Anglo-Iranian Oil Company was in effect a treaty or convention between *two sovereign states* (thus providing jurisdictional competency for the Permanent International Court of Justice).

On the basis of the above the District Court found that the Anglo-Iranian Oil Company was *indistinguishable from the government of Great Britain.*

It seems fair to draw the following conclusion from the above court rulings:

While an American court will grant sovereign immunity to a foreign corporation which is primarily a government run organization, organized primarily for the purpose to serve governmental needs, no such immunity will be granted to foreign corporations whose ways of doing business and purposes are primarily of an everyday commercial nature, merely because the foreign government is the dominant stockholder.

This view corresponds with and finds support in the May 12, 1952, 'Letter of the acting Legal Adviser of the State Department to the U.S. Attorney General concerning Sovereign Immunity of Foreign Governments,'[75] from which the following statements are quoted:

74. *In re Investigation of World Arrangements,* 13 FRD 280 (1952) (D.D.C.).
75. 26 *Dep't. State Bull.* 984 (1952), cited in KATZ & BREWSTER, *op. cit.,* p. 305.

'A study of the law of foreign immunity reveals the existence of two conflicting concepts of sovereign immunity, each widely held and firmly established. According to the classical or absolute theory of sovereign immunity, a sovereign cannot, without his consent, be made a respondent in the courts of another sovereign. According to the newer or restrictive theory of sovereign immunity, the immunity of the sovereign is recognized with regard to sovereign or public acts (*jure imperii*) of a State, but not with respect to private acts (*jure gestionis*). . .

'. . . with the possible exception of the United Kingdom little support has been found except on the part of the Soviet Union and its satellites for continued full acceptance of the absolute theory of sovereign immunity. They are evidences that British authorities are aware of its deficiencies and ready for a change. . .

'. . . the Department feels that the widespread and increasing practice on the part of the governments of engaging in commercial activities makes necessary a practice which will enable persons doing business with them to have their rights determined in the courts. For these reasons it will hereafter be the Department's policy to follow the restrictive theory of sovereign immunity in the consideration of requests of foreign governments for a grant of sovereign immunity.'

CHAPTER V

THE EXTRATERRITORIAL REACH OF THE AMERICAN ANTITRUST LAWS REMEDIAL ASPECTS

General: The Scope of the Problem

In this chapter we will focus on the problems of foreign business enterprises caused by their participation in the American market, in so as far as these problems relate to American antitrust enforcement.

The questions we will have to answer are:

(1) To what extent do the antitrust laws apply equally to American and foreign businessmen? Is this true, both from the legislative and the judicial jurisdictional angles? Is this justified, when viewed against the principles of international law?

(2) To what extent do transnational commercial activities and practices require a discriminatory modification of antitrust enforcement, both with regard to legislative and judicial jurisdictional competency?
Is such modification of the domestic method of antitrust enforcement based on the principles of international law, or expediency, or both?
Is this a satisfactory solution?

(3) Do the above raised questions require to make a distinction with respect to the remedy which is invoked?
Is it appropriate to make a distinction based on whether the remedies invoked have a civil, a criminal, or a regulatory (administrative) character?
Is such a distinction based on the principles of international law, or expediency, or both?
Is this a satisfactory solution?

(4) Is the distinction between the jurisdiction *in personam* and the jurisdiction over the subject matter of special importance to the extraterritorial reach of the antitrust laws?
Is this distinction based on the principles of international law, or expediency, or both?
Is this a satisfactory solution?

(5) Would the problems that may occur because of antitrust enforcement be better solved if the antitrust laws were to be recognized as a separate area of the law? If so, why?

It is far from us to pretend that we have ready answers to all of the questions we raised. We have stated them because they point to the problem areas. Furthermore, in order to determine 'where we stand, and where we should go' we

should, at least, try to find some answers to some of the questions. Some of the topics have been discussed in other chapters, and will therefore, not be dealt with again.
Nor do we feel it necessary to answer the questions in the same order as they are listed, or separately. Some of the questions might well be answered in one section.

The Present Form and Extent of the Extraterritorial Reach.

We have in previous chapters shown that antitrust enforcement has at least three entirely separate aspects:
(1) the general aspect, i.e., that the antitrust laws encompass both positive (i.e., the encouragement of free competition in open markets) and negative (i.e., the prevention of excessive concentration of economic power in private hands) elements;
(2) the functional (remedial) aspect, i.e., the availability of a multiplicity of remedial actions in order to achieve the desired objectives, encompassing civil, criminal, and regulatory (administrative) remedies;
(3) the jurisdictional aspect, i.e., that courts must be convinced that they have both jurisdiction over the subject matter and jurisdiction *in personam* (over the subject), before they can exercise their adjudicatory function.

Each of these aspects has its own consequential implications where the extra-territorial reach of antitrust enforcement is concerned.
Although we admit that the first mentioned aspect is an all-pervasive one, it does not lend itself to an extensive discussion at this time: that would carry us beyond the scope of our undertaking.[1]
With regard to the other mentioned aspects, we submit that they have so many intertwining contact points that it seems best to treat them as a unified whole. Thus, when considering the jurisdictional aspects, we will in each instance review the remedies invoked, with the jurisdictional angle in mind.

Jurisdiction in Personam

For a court to assert judicial jurisdiction it must first, have jurisdiction over the person of the defendant.[2] This requirement is satisfied if process has properly been served. We have earlier indicated what the requirements are for proper

1. It would, among other things, require a politico-economic study of international economics and commerce, as well as a philosophical discussion of the 'ways-of-life' in the international community of nations.
2. *cf.* SCHWARTZ, I. E., *op. cit.*, pp. 154, 155: 'Fehlt es an der personal jurisdiction, kann demnach trotz wegen Inlandsauswirkungen der Wettbewerbsbeschränkung zu bejahender jurisdiction over the subject matter keine Sachentscheidung gefällt werden."

service of process, and how the courts interpret the wording of the antitrust laws with respect thereto, i.e., whether the defendant was properly *found.*[3]

It makes little difference whether process is served in anticipation of a civil, a criminal, or a regulatory (administrative) remedy, because in either case the only question with which the court can occupy itself is: 'Has process properly been served on this defendant?' This holds true for natural persons and legal entities alike.

Furthermore, for a court to have jurisdiction over the person there must be proper *venue*. With regard to the jurisdiction *in personam* involving a foreign defendant, we mention as illustration *Hoffman Motors Corp.* v. *Alfa Romeo S.p.A.*[4]

> Hoffman Motors Corporation, a New York automobile dealer, had been a franchised dealer for automobiles manufactured by Alfa Romeo, S.p.A., an Italian automobile manufacturer. Subsequently, the automobile dealer brought an action against the automobile manufacturer, a.o. under the *Robinson-Patman Act*[5]
>
> The District Court found that the Italian manufacturer had transacted business in New York, and that the suit arose out of those transactions. This was considered sufficient to establish venue.[6]
>
> Process was served by registered letter at the corporation's Italian headquarters and by personal service on the corporation's general manager in Italy, by a court designated Italian attorney. The District Court held that this was proper service of process under the so-called New York long-arm statute. The court rejected the argument that process could only be served in the United States; the court's reasoning was based on the view that an alien may be sued in any district *from which* process may be served.[7]
>
> Finding that venue and service of process were proper, the court accepted jurisdiction *in personam*[8]

With regard to legal entities, the courts hold that process can be served through an agent of the foreign entity. Thus, in the *Alcoa* case[9] the court was satisfied

3. *cf.* Chapter. . ., *supra*, pp. 31, *seq.*, and the cases there cited
4. 244 F Supp 70 (1965) (S.D.-N.Y.), cited in SUPPLEMENT, pp. 42 and 44
5. The *Robinson-Patman Act* declares it unlawful to discriminate in price (including advertising allowances and commissions) between purchasers for reasons other than savings in the cost of doing business. Consequently, offering different conditions to different automobile dealers is a violation of the *Robinson-Patman Act.*
6. Venue is proper if it is established that the judical district in which the proceedings are brought is one in which the defendant was *found or transacts business; cf.* SUPPLEMENT, p. 40. The test is the practical, everydag business or commercial concept of doing or carrying on business of any substantial character.
7. *cf.* SUPPLEMENT, p. 42, and the cases there cited
8. With regard to subject matter jurisdiction, the court held the corporate executives subject to treble damage liability; *cf.* OPPENHEIM & WESTON, *op. cit.*, p. 869
9. *U.S.* v. *Aluminum Co. of America,* 148 F 2d 416 (1945)

that it had jurisdiction over Aluminium, Ltd., a Canadian company, by a showing that process had properly been served through the American parent company. Similarly, in the *Swiss Watchmakers* case[10] process had been served on the jointly owned American subsidiary, the Watchmakers of Switzerland Information Center; on this basis, the court held that it had jurisdiction over the Swiss defendants FH and Ebauches.

Jurisdiction over the Subject Matter

In addition to having jurisdiction over the person (based both on venue and service of process) a court must also determine whether it has jurisdiction over the subject matter, i.e., whether it is competent to adjudicate and resolve the particular kind of claim before it.[11] This means that a defendant has two grounds on which to base his claim that the particular court lacks power to render a binding decision (the lack of jurisdiction over the person, and the lack of jurisdiction over the subject matter).[12]

This emphasis on the distinction between personal and subject matter jurisdiction is of particular importance to the extraterritorial reach of the antitrust laws.[13]

10. *U.S.* v. *Watchmakers of Switzerland Information Center, Inc.*, 133 F Supp 40 (1955), *reargument refused*, 134 F Supp 710 (1955) (S.D.-N.Y.)
11. *cf.* STEINER, H. J., & VAGTS, D. F., TRANSNATIONAL LEGAL PROBLEMS, Mineola, 1968, p. 642, who put subject matter jurisdiction first, venue and notice thereafter. Also, see BREWSTER, K., Jr., ANTITRUST AND AMERICAN BUSINESS ABROAD, New York, 1958, p. 299, who warns against a confusion between personal and 'substantive' jurisdiction. Also, see SCHWARTZ, I. E., *op. cit.*, p. 154: 'Begrifflich unterscheidet das amerikanische Recht zwischen *personal jurisdiction* (jurisdiction in personam), die nicht dem deutschen Begriff Gerichtsbarkeit, sondern dem Begriff der verfahrensrechtlichen internationalen Zuständigkeit über den Beklagten entspricht, und *jurisdiction over the subject matter* oder materiellrechtlicher internationaler Zuständigkeit im Sinne von Anwendbarkeit des materiellen Rechts.'
12. *cf.* CHEATHAM, E. E., GRISWOLD, E. N., REESE, W. L. M., ROSENBERG, M., CASES AND MATERIALS ON CONFLICT OF LAWS, 5th ed., Brooklyn, 1964, p. 92. Also, see VON MEHREN, A. T., & TRAUTMAN, D. T., 'Jurisdiction to Adjudicate: A Suggested Analysis', 79 *Harvard Law Review* 1121, 1134 (1966): 'To the extent that the common law approached jurisdiction to adjudicate in terms of personal service on the defendant within the territory of the judicial system, notice did not emerge as a separate problem. The asserted basis of jurisdiction served as a double function, both establishing the propriety of exercising jurisdiction and notifying the defendant of the proceedings.'
    Also, see TRAUTMAN, D., 'A Study of the International Environment: The International Reach of American Regulatory Legislation Other Than the Sherman Act," in BREWSTER, *op. cit.*, p. 312: 'The subject matter involved may also play a part in defining our jurisdictional reach.'
13. *cf.* SUPPLEMENT, p. 40. Also, see OLIVER, C. T., 'The Range of Effect of the Anti-Trust Laws of the United States,' 1964 *Tokyo Proceedings*, at pp. 514, 515: '. . . the anti-trust laws have been applied to action outside the territory of the United States, provided that (i) the actors are properly, under American constitutional principles, before an American court and (ii) the activity complained of (either by the United States or a private suitor claiming under the anti-trust laws) can be shown to have had an intended economic effect upon imports or exports.'

It is with regard to the jurisdiction over the subject matter that the remedial aspects of the antitrust laws become relevant, because it makes a difference whether a civil, a criminal, or a regulatory (administrative) remedy is invoked. At least, this is true with regard to foreign defendants and/or foreign conduct. For that reason we will separately discuss the extraterritorial reach pertaining to respectively, the civil, the criminal, and the regulatory (administrative) remedies.

(a) Civil remedies resulting in extraterritorial reach

As illustration we have selected *Steele* v. *Bulova Watch Co.* [14]

The Bulova Watch Company, a New York corporation, sued for injunctive and monetary relief, because it claimed that a mr. Steele, a resident of San Antonio, Texas, conducted a watch business in Mexico City, Mexico, where he stamped the name 'Bulova' on watches there assembled and sold.[15]

This, according to the Bulova Watch Company, he could not do, because the trademark 'Bulova' was properly registered under the laws of the United States for the designation of the watches produced and nationally advertised and sold by the Bulova Watch Company. (Some of the watches were offered for sale in the United States, by third parties.)

In his defense, Mr. Steele challenged the jurisdiction of the Federal District court over the subject matter of the suit.

The court dismissed the suit on the ground that it lacked jurisdiction: in the court's opinion Mr. Steele had committed no illegal acts within the United States.

In a 2-1 split decision, the Federal Court of Appeals reversed the decision. It is interesting to note that the dissenting judge felt that the district court was without jurisdiction to enjoin Mr. Steele's conduct, because that conduct related to 'acts done and trade carried on under full authority of Mexican law, and were confined to and affected only that Nation's internal commerce.'

In addressing itself to the question whether a U.S. Court had jurisdiction, the

14. 344 US 280, 73 S Ct 252 (1952). Use of this case is justified, because the *Lanham Act* (which formed the basis for the lawsuit) is customarily considered within the group of antitrust laws, because the act purports to protect persons against unfair competition. We have alluded thereto in Chapter I, *supra*, p. 42. Also, see SCHWARTZ, I. E., *op. cit.*, p. 234, who refers to the case under the heading 'Die neuere amerikanische Entwicklung.'

15. Sec. 32, paragraph (1) of the *Lanham Act* of July 5, 1946, states: 'Any person who shall, in commerce, (a) use, without the consent of the registrant, any reproduction, counterfeit, copy, or colorable imitation or any registered mark in connection with the sale, offering for sale, or advertising of any goods or services on or in connection with which such use is likely to cause confusion or mistake or to deceive purchasers as to the source or origin of such goods or services . . . shall be liable to a civil action by the registrant. . .'

U.S. Supreme Court noted that sec. 45 of the *Lanham Act* specifically states that it is the intent of the act to regulate commerce 'within the control of Congress.'[16]

In reviewing the case, the U.S. Supreme Court stated:

> 'This court has often stated that the legislation of Congress will not extend beyond the boundaries of the United States unless a contrary legislative intent appears.'

Then, asserting the principle whereby a law may have extraterritorial effect, the Court, citing previous decisions, claimed:

> '. . .the United States is not debarred by any rule of international law from governing the conduct of its citizens upon the high seas or even in foreign countries when the rights of other nations or their nationals are not infringed. With respect to such exercise of authority there is no question of international law, but solely of the purport of the municipal law which establishes the duty of the citizen in relation to his own government.'[17]

The Court, then, stated that a person cannot evade 'the thrust of the laws of the United States in a privileged sanctuary beyond our borders,' by so simple a device as moving across the borders and commit there an act that would be illegal within those borders. Then, claiming that there was no interference with the sovereignty of another nation, the Court held that a U.S. Court 'may command persons properly before it to cease or perform acts outside its territorial jurisdiction.'[18]

What is important in the above cited case is that the U.S. judiciary not only claims the right, but actually exercises jurisdiction over acts committed abroad,

16. Sec. 45, last paragraph, states: 'The intent of this Act is to regulate commerce within the control of Congress by making actionable the deceptive and misleading use of marks in such commerce; to protect registered marks in such commerce; to protect registered marks used in commerce from interference by State, or territorial legislation; to protect persons engaged in such commerce against unfair competition; to prevent frauds and deception in such commerce by the use of reproductions, copies, counterfeits, or colorable imitations of registered marks; and to provide rights and remedies stipulated by treaties and conventions respecting trademarks, trade names, and unfair competition entered into between the United States and foreign nations.'
17. *cf.* OPPENHEIM, L., *op. cit.*, p. 330, stating: 'The Law of Nations does not prevent a State from exercising jurisdiction, within its own territory, over its subjects travelling or residing abroad, since they remain under its personal supremacy.' While the U.S. Supreme Court cited OPPENHEIM'S opinion on the subject, it is open to question whether the reference is entirely correct. OPPENHEIM deals with this topic in his chapter on jurisdiction. When reviewing the entire context, it should be observed that on the basis of what precedes and what follows, there is room for the argument that the author was referring to criminal, confiscatory and similar jurisdiction only. Even his reference in n. 4, p. 328, to the extra-territorial effect of the American antitrust laws, does not convince us of anything to the contrary.
18. In this respect, it is noteworthy that in the (dissenting) opinion of Mr. Justice REED we can find the statement that 'Congress has the power to control acts of our citizens throughout the world. . .' This would limit the assertion of jurisdiction to conduct abroad *by Americans.*

thereby giving its laws extraterritorial effect. This jurisdiction is asserted in a civil suit between two private parties.[19]

(b) *Criminal remedies resulting in extraterritorial reach*

As illustratition we have selected *U.S.* v. *Aluminum Co. of America.*[20]

> The Aluminum Company of America (Alcoa), an American corporation, and Aluminium Limited, a Canadian company (a wholly owned subsidiary of Alcoa) were charged with having entered into an unlawful conspiracy in restraint of interstate and foreign commerce, particularly in the manufacture and sale of 'virgin' aluminum ingot.
>
> From the facts of the case it appears that a Swiss corporation had been created (the 'Alliance'), in pursuance of an agreement, the signatories to which were two German corporations, a French, a Swiss, a British corporation, and 'Limited.' The original agreement, or 'cartel,' provided for the formation of a corporation in Switzerland, which would issue shares, to be taken up by the signatories.
>
> This corporation was from time to time to fix a quota of production for each share, and each shareholder was to be limited to the quantity measured by the number of shares it held. Later, the system of unconditional quotas was substituted for a system of royalties: if a shareholder exceeded his quota, he was to pay a royalty; these royalties the 'Alliance' divided among the shareholders in proportion to their shares.

The question before the court was whether the above agreements violated sec. 1 of the *Sherman Act*, which declares every contract, or conspiracy, in restraint of trade or commerce among the several States, or with foreign nations, illegal, and which declares the person who makes such a contract, or enters into such a conspiracy, guilty of a misdemeanor, and subjects him to a punishment of either a fine, or imprisonment, or both.

In its opinion, the Court stated:

> 'The answer does not depend upon whether we shall recognize as a source of liability a liability imposed by another state. On the contrary we are concerned whether Congress chose to attach liability to the conduct outside the United States of persons not in allegiance to it.'
>
> '. . .it is settled law . . . that any state may impose liabilities, even upon persons not within its allegiance, for conduct outside its borders that has consequences within its borders which the state reprehends; and these liabilities other states will ordinarily recognize.'

19. However, we should also keep in mind that although the acts complained of occurred in Mexico, both parties to the suit were U.S. citizens.
20. 148 F2d 416 (1945). Much like the preceding case, the Court considered what (legally, according to foreign laws) occurs abroad. It is in that sense that the case has extraterritorial effect. Also, a Canadian company was made a party defendant; process had been served on Aluminium Limited through the American parent company.

Then comes the analysis, on the basis of which in the opinion of the Court the assertion of jurisdiction depends:

> 'Two situations are possible. There may be agreements made beyond our borders not intended to affect imports, which do affect them, or which affect exports. Almost any limitation of the supply of goods in Europe, for example, or in South America, may have repercussions in the United States if there is trade between the two. Yet when one considers the international complications likely to arise from an effort in this country to treat such agreements as unlawful, it is safe to assume that Congress certainly did not intend the Act to cover them.
>
> Such agreements may on the other hand intend to include imports into the United States, and yet it may appear that they have had no effect upon them . . .
>
> . . .we shall assume that the Act does not cover agreements, even though intended to affect imports or exports, unless its performance is shown actually to have had some effect upon them.'

That means that the United States courts will consider themselves competent to adjudicate a case where the following two elements are shown to be present:

(1) there must be an intent to affect either imports into, or exports from the United States;

(2) the performance must have had some effect.

Although the trial court had found that the agreement did not materially affect the foreign trade or commerce of the United States, the Court of Appeals did not accept this finding.

The end result was that the Court found the agreement to be in violation of sec. 1 of the *Sherman Act.*

In another case, involving a number of foreign firms, the federal District Court of the Southern District of New York found no difficulty in accepting jurisdiction.[21]

> In this case, the dominant procedures of titanium compounds had divided the world market into exclusive territories for each of the participants; this was in part accomplished by an elaborate system of cross-licensing agreements. The cross-licensing amounted to a patenting of the process for producing titanium oxide in the country of the inventor and in other countries having patent systems; subsequently, each of the patentees licensed his process exclusively to dominant producers in any given country, in exchange for a similar reciprocal license. Occasionally provision was made for joint exploitation of patent rights in a country without a strong producer of its own, by means of a corporation whose stock was owned by several of the licensors.

21. *U.S.* v. *National Lead Co.,* 63 F. Supp. 513 (1945), *aff'd* 332 US 319, 67 S Ct 1634 (1947).

In his opinion District Judge RIFKIND stated:

> 'In detail, the elapsed quarter century is crowded with negotiations, conferences, correspondence and agreements. The men who participated in these were all articulate, literate and . . . recorded what they saw, heard, said and thought with Boswellian fidelity. When the story is seen as a whole, there is no blinking the fact that there is no free commerce in titanium . . .
>
> 'It was more difficult for the independent outsider to enter this business than for the camel to make its proverbial passage through the eye of a needle.'
>
> 'No citation of authority is any longer necessary to support the proposition that a combination of competitors, which by agreement divides the world into exclusive trade areas, and suppresses all competition among the members of the combination, offends the Sherman Act.'

Of course, the argument that the Court would be without jurisdiction to consider conduct abroad on the part of foreign corporations, relating to the commerce of foreign nations, was duly advanced.

While the opinion states, first, that this aspect did not constitute the gravamen of the complaint, the following passage is of interest with respect to our consideration of the extra-territorial reach:

> 'The absence of . . . foreign associates will, of course, place a practical limitation upon the scope of the court's decree; it does not prevent the court from finding a violation as the facts warrant, and from restraining those within the reach of its mandate from continuing a conspiracy in defiance of the Sherman Act.'

Summarizing the above, we can state that the American judiciary finds it not difficult to restrain parties to violate the antitrust laws, as long as they are, in the opinion of the court, within its mandate.

(c) *Regulatory remedies resulting in extraterritorial reach*

To illustrate how regulatory remedies may result in extraterritorial reach we have selected the *I.C.I.* case.[22]

> duPont, an American corporation, and Imperial Chemical Industries, Ltd., a British corporation, were charged (and subsequently adjudged guilty) with violation of sec. 1 of the *Sherman Act* by a succession of agreements dividing world territories in connection with a continuing interchange of patented and unpatented technological information and by the formation

22. *U.S.* v. *Imperial Chemical Industries*, 100 F Supp 504 (1951) (S.D.N.Y.). Having found that duPont and Imperial Industries, Ltd., had violated sec. 1 of the *Sherman Act*, the second phase, more important to our study, was settled in 105 F Supp 215 (1952) (S.D.N.Y.). We will particularly deal with the latter phase of the case. For an abridged version, *cf.* KATZ, and BREWSTER, *op. cit.*, pp. 592, *seq.*

of joint ventures in Canada and various South American countries. One of the pooled-patented products was a synthetic product, nylon.

During the period that these patents were in the hands of I.C.I. an exclusive license had been granted to the British Nylon Spinners, a British corporation, 50% of whose stock was owned by I.C.I. This was entirely valid according to English law.

To prove its case, the U.S. Government applied for an order requiring I.C.I. to produce foreign located documents. While the Court concluded that there should be production of the designated papers in New York City, I.C.I, proposed that the examination be undertaken in Great Britain. The Court thereupon directed the Government to examine the files there. The Government, subsequent thereto, selected documents, which were produced, either in the original, or by photostatic copies, in New York. 'The discovery was accomplished with no difficulty whatever due to the cooperation of counsel for both sides.'[23]

In his opinion, District Judge RYAN stated:

> '. . .acting on the basis of our jurisdiction *in personam*, we are merely directing ICI to refrain from asserting rights which it may have in Britain . . .'
>
> 'It is not an intrusion on the authority of a foreign sovereign for this court to direct that steps be taken to remove the harmful effects on the trade of the United States.'

The judge, then, decreed that I.C.I. should reconvey its patents to duPont; furthermore, I.C.I. was forbidden to make any disposition of foreign patents, unless it required an agreement in writing to hold its license subject to the rights of American manufacturers of these nylon products to freely import and sell their products in Great Britain.[24]

The Legal Bases of the Extraterritorial Reach

General: The guidelines by which courts are guided.

While the preceding cases may have shown that there exists, in effect, an extraterritorial reach of the antitrust laws, this does not necessarily mean that the assertion of jurisdiction over persons or conduct abroad is justified when viewed against the background of the generally recognized and accepted principles of international law. In fact, the *Alcoa* case, the *ICI* case, the *Swiss Watchmakers*

23. *cf.* EMMERGLICH, L. J., 'Antitrust Jurisdiction and the Production of Documents Abroad,' in 11 *The Record* of the Association of the Bar of the City of New York 122, 124 (1956).
24. For a discussion of these aspects of the case, *cf. American Bar Association,* Section on International and Comparative Law, Chicago, 1953, pp. 84, *seq.*

case have all been attacked as being in violation of the principles of international law.[25]

It therefore, behooves us to determine by what guidelines a court is (or ought to be) guided when it adjudicates an antitrust case with transnational dimensions, particularly pertaining to foreign defendants or conduct abroad.

The above statement needs some clarification. When we refer to the guidelines by which a court is guided, we allude to the rules which the court accepts as applicable when it adjudicates a case. These rules can be based on domestic law, international law, or expediency.

On the other hand, when we refer to the guidelines by which a court ought to be guided, we allude to one of two different possibilities:

(1) the rules which a court ought to follow because of precedent (as long as the precedent is not specifically overruled);

(2) the rules which a court ought to follow (regardless of precedent) because of a superior rule of international law.

At this time we will only deal with the guidelines which a court follows because of its own notions of justice, based on judicial precedent. We will not (yet) deal with the guidelines which a court ought to follow because of a superior rule of international law. Once we have determined by what guidelines a court considers itself bound, we will be able to examine these groundrules against the background of international law.

Notwithstanding our effort to distinguish between the two, it might appear at times that we have overlooked our self-set limitation. To a certain extent many people confuse all too often the distinction between the *is* and the *ought* by talking about the two in one breath; we do not consider ourselves beyond that verdict. But it is also true that the courts have not always been clear on the subject when a case was submitted to their adjudication. Nevertheless, we hope to indicate, on the basis of what can be abstracted from the judicial decisions, that there are differences, depending on whether we are dealing with civil, criminal, or regulatory remedies. We furthermore, hope to demonstrate that, where the decisions are not entirely clear on the point, greater clarity could have been achieved if the courts had been consciously aware of these differences. In fact, we submit that much of the present confusion with regard to the extraterritorial reach of American antitrust enforcement could be eliminated, if a consistent approach were maintained, both by the courts and in the literature.

To a certain extent the confusion is caused by the desire on the part of authors

25. *cf.* SCHWARTZ, I. E., *op. cit.*, p. 245: 'Die erörterte amerikanische Rechtsprechung hat verschiedene völkerrechtliche Fragen aufgeworfen. . .' Also, see REHBINDER, *op. cit.*, p. 49: 'Seit 1954 haben eine Reihe von amerikanischen und europäischen Autoren völkerrechtliche Bedenken gegen die extraterritoriale Anwendung des amerikanischen Antitrustrechtes geltend gemacht. Die Kritik richtete sich dabei in erster Linie gegen die verfolgung ausländischer Unternehmen im ALCOA-Fall, im Glühlampen-Fall und im ICI-Fall.'

to classify the antitrust laws into one of the existing classifications, be it private international law, international administrative law, international criminal law, a special branch of public international law, or market regulatory law.[26] That such attempts are doomed to fail has been elaborately discussed in Chapter III; we need not repeat it here.

The remedies as determinative factors.

We reiterate that one should not lose sight of the principle that any categorization is predicated on the remedy asked for. Thus, an action directed at an agreement in restraint of trade does not indicate at all which remedial action is invoked to counter the alleged violation.[27] In other words, it is only after legal proceedings have been instigated that we can determine whether we are dealing with a civil complaint (be it by one private party against the other, or by the United States Government against a private party), or a criminal prosecution, or a regulatory proceeding, or a preliminary investigation on the part of the Antitrust Division of the Department of Justice to produce documents in order to determine whether (and if so, which) legal proceedings shall be instituted.

All of the above becomes even more relevant when we consider the legal justification of the jurisdictional reach in cases with international dimensions.[28] It is not so much a question whether a systematic approach can be developed, but rather, that present attempts to categorize the extraterritorial reach of the American antitrust laws must necessarily be made within the context of the remedial aspects and the exercise of jurisdiction flowing therefrom.[29] In adhering to this principle we shall subsequently, analyze the assertion of extraterritorial jurisdiction in the light of the remedial aspects.

(a) *Civil Remedies*

As example to demonstrate on what basis the courts will assert or reject the assertion of extraterritorial jurisdiction we have selected two cases, one

26. *cf.* VERZIJL, *l.c.,* pp. 3, *seq.;* TIMBERG, S., 'Extraterritorial Jurisdiction under the Sherman Act,' 11 *The Record* 101, 111 (1956); WENGLER, *l.c.*, p. 179.
27. A similar approach is taken by SCHWARTZ, I. E., *op. cit.*, and REHBINDER, *op. cit.*
28. *cf.* BREWSTER, *op. cit.*, p. 286: 'Legal authorities themselves cannot be expected to yield a pat formula since international law is not that definite or authoritative. . .'
29. Failure to do this would lead to the same observation as made by SCHWARTZ, I. E., *op. cit.*, p. 154: 'Bemerkenswert ist zunächst, dasz das Antitrustrecht der Vereinigten Staaten *keine je nach der Verfahrensart verschiedenen Regeln* für die verfahrensrechtliche internationale Zuständigkeit der Bundesgerichte und der Bundesantitrustbehörden kennt. Vielmehr richtet sich ihre internationale Zuständigkeit. . . nach den gleichen Rechtsgrundsätzen.' There are, of course, procedural differences between civil and criminal procedures; these differences are in turn, predicated on the remedial aspects of the proceedings. At the same time, it is true that American judges do not differentiate between cases involving domestic and foreign defendants with regard to the subject matter, as long as the requirements of the jurisdiction *in personam* have been satisfied.

> representing the view cited as authority from 1909 until 1969, and one probably advancing a modern view of the courts, decided in 1969.
> *American Banana Co.* v. *United Fruit Co.*[30] has long been cited as authority to show that the American antitrust laws adhere strictly to the *territoriality* principle.[31]
> The facts of the case are the following: when the American Banana Company (an American corporation) tried to operate a railway and a banana plantation in competition with the United Fruit Company (also an American corporation), Costa Rican soldiers, at the instigation of the United Fruit Company, seized a part of the plantation. Attempts to halt the interference failed. Subsequently, the American Banana Company brought an action in the United States federal courts against the United Fruit Company, asking for treble damages.[32]
> This means that the action was a tort action, i.e., a civil action.[33]
> Having classified the action as sounding in tort, the only logical conclusion any court could arrive at was to decide the case in accordance with the principles of tort in the Conflict of Laws . . . which was exactly what the Court did.

We therefore, must take exception to the statement by TIMBERG that mr. Justice HOLMES was suffering of legal schizophrenia.[34] On the contrary, we consider the reasoning a correct one.

As far as we are concerned, the Supreme Court denied recovery because no tort had been committed, even though one American corporation claimed to have been restrained in its trade of the banana trade by another American corporation. We feel all the more justified in our assertion because TIMBERG based his statement on mr. Justice HOLMES'S reasoning in the *Banana* case as contrasted with the latter's reasoning in an entirely different case of a conspiracy to obtain money by fraudulent practices leading to a criminal prosecution.

Nevertheless, a problem remains. This is caused by the provision that 'any person who shall be injured in his business . . . by anything forbidden in the antitrust laws may sue therefor,'[35] coupled with the provision that 'Every contract . . . in restraint of trade or commerce . . . is . . . illegal.'[36]

30. 213 US 347, 29 S Ct 511 (1909)
31. *cf.* BREWSTER, *op. cit.*, p. 67
32. The action was based on Section 7 of the *Sherman Act;* this section was repealed by the Act of July 7, 1955, and has been superseded by Section 4 of the *Clayton Act.*
33. We substantiate this by quoting mr. Justice HOLMES, who delivered the opinion of the Court, stating: '. . . *the acts . . were not torts* by the law of the place and therefore not torts at all.' Also, see BREWSTER, *op. cit.*, p. 68: '. . . the action was one in which *a private plaintiff sought damages.'* (Italics supplied)
34. *cf.* TIMBERG, *l.c.*, p. 103: 'Is there a persuasive legal distinction between the two situations, or was Justice Holmes a legal schizophrenic on this subject? I think the latter to be the case. . .'
35. Section 4 *Clayton Act*
36. Section 1 *Sherman Act*

Now let us consider one of the well-known principles in the Conflict of Laws, to wit, that the validity of a contract is determined by the law of the place where the contract was made,[37] unless the parties have specifically designated a specific law to be applicable to the contract.[38]

Thus, a contract perfectly valid according to the place where the contract was made, and to which the parties, within the acceptable limitations, declare a certain law to be applicable, might still be sued by an American party who has been injured in his business by the contractual arrangement.

Under the principle as enunciated in the *Banana* case the foreign conduct would be unassailable. The American law does not have a provision which specifically regulates which law shall prevail in such a case; this is different from the regulation elsewhere.[39]

Recently, a change seems to have come about. In *Pacific Seafarers, Inc.* v. *Pacific Far East Line, Inc.*[40] the court stated: '. . .the test which determines whether the United States law is applicable must focus on the nexus between the parties and their practices and the United States . . .'

This is clearly a departure from the principle as laid down in the *Banana* case, because the actions of the defendants in the *Seafarers* case were not so very different from the actions of the defendant in the *Banana* case. To be sure, there were no soldiers involved; neither did a foreign government lend its support to the alleged illegal practices. But there are striking similarities. What had happened in the *Seafarers* case was that the defendants (American-flag ship owners) had

37. This traditional rule is no longer the prevailing one; *cf.* RESTATEMENT OF THE LAW, SECOND, CONFLICT OF LAWS, Proposed Official Draft, Part II (1968).
§ 188. (1) The rights and duties of the parties with respect to an issue in contract are determined by the local law of the state which, as to that issue, has the most significant relationship to the transaction and the parties under the principles stated in § 86.
(2) In the absence of an effective choice of law by the parties (see § 187), the contracts to be taken into account in applying the principles of § 86 to determine the law applicable to an issue include:
(a) the place of contracting,
(b) the place of negotiation of the contract,
(c) the place of performance,
(d) the location of the subject matter of the contract, and
(e) the domicil, residence, nationality, place of incorporation and place of business of the parties.

38. This so-called 'autonomy of the parties' is limited only by the requirement that the selected law have a 'connexion with the facts of the case;' *cf.* RABEL, E., THE CONFLICT OF LAWS, Vol. I, 2nd ed., Ann. Arbor, 1958, pp. 47, *seq.*

39. *cf.* REHBINDER, *op. cit.*, p. 280: 'Die allgemeine Regel des deutschen internationalen Privatrechtes von der Maszgeblichkeit der Parteiautonomie wird dadurch ausgeschaltet. . .' Similarly, SCHWARTZ, I. E., *op. cit.*, p. 176, and particularly, p. 178, citing RABEL, *op. cit.*

40. 404 F 2d 804 (1968), *cert. denied,* US, 89 S Ct 872 (1969).

driven the plaintiffs (also American-flag ship owners) out of the business of carrying cargo (fertilizer and cement) between South-East-Asian ports. They had been able to do this by lowering their prices in such a way that the South-Vietnamese importers only made use of the defendants' ships. Thus, by practices outside the borders of the United States (practices which were not wrong according to the law of the place) the trade of one American corporation had been restrained by another American corporation.

Nevertheless, the federal Court of Appeals accepted jurisdiction over the case, because of some nexus with the United States.

Because there were no foreign defendants involved in the *Seafarers* case, we have no way of knowing what the court's attitude would have been if there had been a foreign defendant. We suggest that under the modern view of the *Seafarers* case a civil remedy would be available, as long as there is a *nexus* between what is being done and the United States.

(b) *Criminal Remedies*

The application of criminal remedies in antitrust cases involving foreign defendants or foreign conduct presents different problems.

In *Continental Ore Co.* v. *Union Carbide & Carbon Corp.*[41] a unanimous Supreme Court stated that 'a conspiracy to monopolize or restrain the domestic or foreign commerce of the United States is not outside the reach of the Sherman Act just because part of the conduct complained of occurs in foreign countries.'

The Attorney General's Committee stated that 'conspiracies between foreign competitors alone should come within the Sherman Act only where they are intended to, and actually do, result in substantial anticompetitive effects on our foreign commerce.'[42] Thus, the location of the forbidden conduct was not considered important.[43] Intention and effect are clearly the yardsticks to be used. This was the principle enunciated in the *Alcoa* case, and this was the principle which lead to the decision in the *Swiss Watchmakers* case. The application of criminal laws to conduct abroad is always a matter which requires great prudence; this is even more so with regard to the extraterritorial reach of antitrust enforcement. Several arguments have been advanced against the extraterritorial reach of the antitrust laws:

(1) other nations do not consider violations of the *Sherman Act* a generally recognized crime;

(2) the antitrust limitations are not clearly delineated;

41. 370 US 690, 82 S Ct 1440 (1962). While the case was a private litigation, the above referred to *dictum* is sufficiently broad to be used here, too. For the facts of the case, see Chapter VI, p. 138

42. *Att'y Gen. Report*, p. 76

43. *cf.* SUPPLEMENT, p. 46

(3) the freedom granted by foreign governments to their corporations would be abridged.[44]

The simplest solution to the problems connected with the extraterritorial reach of criminal antitrust prosecutions would be to require that a court is bound to be guided by the rules of International Criminal Law, if such a body of law exists.

The difficulty is that as yet no single satisfactory body of law has been developed that can qualify as internationally recognized and accepted. To be sure, a number of 'principles' have been formulated, all providing some legal justification for the assertion of criminal jurisdiction (the territorial principle; the principle of objective territoriality; the principle of subjective territoriallity; the protection principle; the universality principle). The net outcome has been that if one principle does not produce the desired outcome another will, so that the final objective, the prosecution of the offender, can be achieved with some semblance of legal justification. To us, this seems pure opportunism covered by the cloak of legality.

With regard to the extraterritorial reach in criminal antitrust enforcement the *Alcoa* case is commonly used to illustrate the limitations which the courts (ought to) impose upon themselves. But in that case we find no theoretical elaboration of principles of international law other than the statement that 'it is settled law . . . that any state may impose liabilities . . . for conduct outside its borders,' amplified by the assertion that 'these liabilities other states will ordinarily recognize.'

The leading judicial authority with regard to the extraterritorial reach of criminal prosecution is the opinion expressed in the *Case of the ss Lotus*[45], where the statement was made that international law does not prohibit a State from exercising jurisdiction in its own territory, in respect of any case which relates to acts which have taken place abroad. The only limitation imposed is that a State 'should not overstep the limits which international law places upon its jurisdiction; within these limits, its title to exercise jurisdiction rests in its own sovereignty.'

When dealing with International Criminal Law, we usually find some reference to the *Case of the ss. Lotus,*[46] particularly to the statement:

'Now the first and foremost restriction imposed by international law upon

44. *cf.* 1 *Case West. Res. J. of Int'l Law* 132, 144, *seq.* (1969)
45. P.C.I.J., Ser. A., No. 10 (1927). Even the dissenting opinion of Justice LODER (the Court split evenly, 6-6, the President casting the deciding vote) allowed for jurisdiction over offences committed abroad by foreigners, 'in so far as they are directed against its security or credit.' Why the exception should stop there, and could not be extended to offences directed against the accepted economic system of a State, is not clear to us.
46. This holds true also for studies dealing with the extraterritorial reach of the antitrust laws; *cf.* SCHWARTZ, I. E., *op. cit.*, p. 246; REHBINDER, *op. cit.*, pp. 53, 54.

a State is that – failing the existence of a permissive rule to the contrary – it may not exercise its power in any form in the territory of another State.'

But any reading of the *Lotus* case demonstrates unequivocally the paramount problem the Court is grappling with, following from its own admission, that 'all that can be required of a State is that it should not overstep the limits which international law places upon its jurisdiction . . .'[47] This requires a clear and universally acceptable definition of what this international law consists of, and what these rules are. . .

All we can therefore state at this time is that in the assertion of extraterritorial criminal jurisdiction in antitrust cases courts should adhere to the rules of International Criminal Law . . . if such a body of law exists.

(c) *Regulatory Remedies*

Much like the application of criminal remedies, does the extraterritorial regulatory antitrust enforcement present problems.

As an illustration we have selected the *I.C.I.* case.[48] The facts of the case have been stated earlier;[49] they need not be repeated. Once the court had satisfied itself that it had jurisdiction *in personam*, it only considered the adverse effects on the foreign trade or commerce of the United States: because of the agreement between duPont and I.C.I., it had been possible for I.C.I. to franchise, on an exclusive basis, British Nylon Spinners, a British Corporation. This, in turn, resulted in the exclusion of American nylon stocking manufacturers from the British market. The court, having its eye fixed on the American nylon stocking manufacturers, ordered I.C.I. to reconvey to duPont the patent rights it had received, thereby disregarding the arrangement I.C.I. had entered into with British Nylon Spinners (an arrangement perfectly legal according to British law). This case does not stand by itself; similar problems occurred in other cases

47. A few paragraphs previous to the citation, the Court defines international law as something that governs the relations between independent States, 'as expressed in conventions or by usages.' Would this allude to the necessity to re-establish, in a modernized version, the medieval system of ascertaining 'the law' or 'the usage' by a *turbe* or a body of *witan?* An almost compelling reason for this suggestion would be found in the dissenting opinion of Justice LODER, stating that international law 'is for the most part unwritten,' inasmuch as it rests primarily 'on a general consensus of opinion.'
Apart from the problem presented by the difficulty of finding representative samples, we cannot imagine that any court anywhere in the world would seriously consider ordering a public opinion poll to ascertain the general consensus of opinion. Yet, leaving the determination thereof up to the Courts does not sufficiently guarantee the correct expression of the 'general consensus of opinion,' either.
48. *U.S.* v. *Imperial Chemical Industries*, 100 F Supp 504 (1951) (S.D.-N.Y.), 105 F Supp 215 (1952)
49. *cf. supra*, pp. 8, 120

involving extraterritorial reach of antitrust enforcement.[50]

The problem is in part caused by the absence of an organized body of law that could qualify as International Administrative Law. In the absence of such a body of law or any Treaties between Contracting States, the attempts by a prosecuting State to enforce its laws by regulatory jurisdiction lack a clearly defined legal basis.

In order to properly appreciate the problems related to the extraterritorial regulatory jurisdiction in antitrust cases we need first, to understand that regulatory jurisdiction refers to the power to prescribe rules by which commerce is to be governed.[51]

Furthermore, we should keep in mind that the remedies pertaining to this regulatory jurisdiction are of a peculiar nature.[52]

Even so, we submit that almost anyone would find it extremely difficult to condone a situation in which an American governmental agency would order a foreign enterprise to divest itself of property, securities, or other assets. But what the federal District Court of New York ordered the (British) corporation Imperial Chemical Industries to do was not so radically different: it ordered I.C.I. to reconvey to duPont the patent-licenses it had received. One might even go further than that: what the District Court in effect ordered was that British Nylon Spinners should, at the direction of an American court, divest itself of its assets (the exclusive franchise to manufacture nylon stockings in the United Kingdom). This is all the more peculiar because British Nylon Spinners was not even a party defendant before the court.

In view of the above we must consider FUGATE'S statement that American courts 'have not purported to exercise *extraterritorial* jurisdiction, but only jurisdiction over acts which operate within United States territory,'[53] a euphemistic one.

Of course, the act of Imperial Chemical Industries to grant British Nylon Spinners an exclusive franchise 'operated within the United States,' because it prevented American nylon stocking manufacturers to import their products into the United Kingdom. But at the same time, the act only operated *indirectly* in the United States.

Part of the problem may be caused by the wording of Article I, section 8, clause 3, of the Constitution of the United States, granting the Congress of the United States the power 'to regulate commerce with foreign nations.'

As early as 1824, Chief Justice MARSHALL stated: 'No sort of trade can be

50. As illustration we mention *U.S.* v *General Electric Co. et al.*, 82 F Supp 753 (1949) (D-N.J.), involving the Dutch corporation N.V. Philips Gloeilampenfabrieken; *U.S.* v *Watchmakers of Switzerland Information Center, Inc.*, 1963 Trade Cases, nr. 70, 600 (S.D.-N.Y.), involving a group of Swiss watchmanufacturers.
51. *cf. supra*, p. 48, *n.* 14
52. *cf. supra*, pp. 54, *seq.*
53. FUGATE, *op. cit.*, p. 20

carried on between this country and any other, to which this power does not extend.'[54]

While FUGATE has pointed out that international comity imposes, in practice, restrictions,[55] we submit that comity alone should not be the dominant factor, for the simple reason that the very concept of comity conveys to the mind something less than law.

It is, however, interesting to note that foreign governments, concerned about prosecution of their nationals for violation of the American antitrust laws, have 'merely called attention to the usual rules of international comity and have not disputed the jurisdiction over foreign companies with respect to United States commerce.'[56]

It seems desirable that a better foundation be considered for the assumption of regulatory jurisdiction where foreign defendants are involved.

Elsewhere too, the lack of a satisfactory legal basis for the assertion of regulatory jurisdiction has been recognized.[57]

Consequently, one can state the extraterritorial reach of regulatory jurisdiction is limited by the applicable rules of International Administrative Law; however the statement has little meaning so long as no uniformly accepted definition of what this law consists of has been formulated.

The Implications of a New Categorization of the Antitrust Laws.

At the beginning of this chapter we have raised the question whether the problems connected with the extraterritorial reach of the antitrust laws would be better solved if these laws were recognized as a separate area of the law. Having raised the question we feel it incumbent upon us to at least partially answer the question.

In a general way we should like to answer the question in the affirmative. That ultimately the judgements and the (amended) court decrees have resulted in an official acquiescence on the part of foreign defendants of governments does not take away the original shock and sensitivity to national sovereignty that the judicial assertion of jurisdiction caused.[58] These amended decrees at best show hind-

54. *Gibbons* v. *Ogden*, 9 Wheat. 1, 194 (1824)
55. FUGATE, *op. cit.*, p. 29
56. *ibid.*, p. 46
57. *cf.* SCHWARTZ, I. E., *op. cit.*, p. 268 stating that '... das Völkerrecht ... keine allgemeine Regel enthält, die die Anwendung des objektiven Territorialitätsprinzips im Verwaltungsrecht ausschlösse oder einschränkte...' Similarly, REHBINDER, *op. cit.*, p. 332: 'Über die verfahrensrechtliche internationale Zuständigkeit entscheidet nicht eine Kollisionsnorm des internationalen Verfahrensrecht...'
58. *cf.* 'Comity and the Oil Companies', 165 *Economist* 556 (1952), where the United States was accused of 'unwarranted extraterritorial assertion of American jurisdiction.' For a reaction to the *Swiss Watchmakers* case, see 1964 *Tokyo Proceedings*, p. 377, where the charge was made that 'the prosecution violates international law.'

sight wisdom, may be merely expediency. What we have been able to observe is more or less 'patchwork', not a unified approach to the entire problem of anti-trust enforcement. No real grappling with the legal problems (which we admit to be knotty) is evidenced.

Conclusions

Answering some of the questions raised by us specifically, we submit:

(1) With regard to the equal application of the antitrust laws to American and foreign businessmen:
   (a) legislatively, no distiction is made between nationals and foreigners; the law applies to all. This is understandable, because it is the American (foreign) trade and commerce that is being protected from restraint. Furthermore, if a distinction were made between the conduct of nationals and foreigners, it would be easy for nationals to adopt a foreign nationality; we think particularly of corporations who could transfer their headquarters elsewhere and thus, acquire a new nationality for the legal entity.[59]
   (b) judicially, no distiction is made with regard to the jurisdiction *in personam*: as long as the requirements of venue and service of process have properly been met, the courts will accept jurisdiction. This was demonstrated with regard to the Italian corporation Alfa Romeo, S.p.A.,[60] and the Canadian company Aluminium, Ltd.[61]
   With regard to the jurisdiction over the subject matter, it seems that for the courts to accept jurisdiction over the subject matter there must be some *nexus* with the United States. This was demonstrated in the *Seafarers* case,[62] where the court specifically stated that 'the test which determines whether the United States law is applicable must focus on the nexus . . .'

(2) With regard to the possible requirement that transnational commercial activities and practices may require a modification of the methods of antitrust enforcement:
   (a) legislatively: for the reasons indicated above, sub (1) (a), we do not see that a discriminatory modification of antitrust enforcement pertaining to foreign nationals or foreign conduct would solve the problems of antitrust enforcement for the United States. Consequently, we do not visualize any practical or other benefit to be derived from such effort.

59. For a description of the magnitude of the problem, see KRONSTEIN, H., 'The Nationality of International Enterprises,' 52 *Col. Law Review* 983 (1952)
60. *cf. Hoffman Motors Corp.* v. *Alfa Romeo, S.p.A.*, 244 F Supp 70 (1965) (S.D.-N.Y.)
61. *cf. U.S.* v. *Aluminum Co. of America*, 148 F 2d 416 (1945)
62. *Pacific Seafarers, Inc.* v. *Pacific Far East Line, Inc.*, 404 F 2d 804 (1968)

(b) judicially: we submit that the courts should display greater circumspection in cases involving foreign defendants and/or foreign conduct.

(1) With regard to the jurisdiction *in personam*, the need for more rigid guidelines was clearly demonstrated in the *Hoffman Motors* case.[63] The problem is partly due to the conflict between Section 1391 (d) of the *Judicial Code*, which subjects aliens to suit *in any district*, and the provisions of the *Clayton Act,* which subject a defendant to suit in the district where he is found or transact business.[64] It seems to us that out of fairness to foreign defendants in antitrust suits the requirement of the *Judicial Code* should be disregarded. Furthermore, we submit that the requirement that the defendant be *found* should be modified by the addition of the words *in the United States*: to *find* a defendant in Italy through a court-designated Italian attorney seems to us a troublesome matter. Long-arm statutes may be proper for United States residents, but aliens should not be subjected to it.

(2) With regard to the jurisdiction over the subject matter, we submit that the requirement of mere *nexus* is not satisfactory: a *nexus* can always be found (if there were no *nexus*, there would in all probability not even be an American plaintiff). Instead, it seems to us that the requirement for the assertion of jurisdiction over the subject matter should be that there is *a demonstrable restraint of the foreign trade or commerce of the United States*. As an example we refer to the *Seafarers* case[65] and the *Swiss Watchmakers* case[66]: in the former, the demonstrable restraint of the foreign trade of the United States was absent, in the latter it was present.

(3) With regard to the remedial aspects of antitrust enforcement:
It seems to us that the functional aspects of antitrust enforcement are so overriding that a distinction in jurisdictional competency based on the remedies which are invoked is not tenable. This would lose sight of the objectives of antitrust enforcement (encouragement of competition in open markets, and the prevention of excessive concentration of economic power in private hands).

63. *Hoffman Motors Corp.* v. *Alfa Romeo, S.p.A.*, 244 F Supp 70 (1965)
64. *cf.* SUPPLEMENT, p. 42, where the statement is made: '. . . the relationships between the Judicial Code and Clayton Act venue provisions for aliens are not yet clear.'
65. *Pacific Seafarers, Inc.* v. *Pacific Far East Line, Inc.*, 404 F 2d 804 (1968)
66. *U.S.* v. *Watchmakers of Switzerland Information Center, Inc.*, 1963 Trade Cases, nr. 70, 600 (1962)

(4) With regard to the suggestion that the entire area of antitrust enforcement be considered as a special area of the law:
We submit that this would particularly solve the problems related to the extraterritorial reach of the antitrust laws, both legislatively (the foreign businessman will better be guided by provisions in one comprehensive code) and judicially (the functional aspects will acquire greater emphasis; this will be particularly true if special Antitrust Courts, national and supranational, are established).

Because the available remedies in antitrust enforcement must be seen against the entire framework of the antitrust laws, i.e., its functional aspects, we submit that the determination of the legality of the extraterritorial jurisdiction on the basis of the existing classification into international private, criminal and administrative law is in the long run an untenable proposition.

A categorization as proposed by us will, of course, not change the procedural requirements of the jurisdiction *in personam*; we consider the present requirements for venue and service of process adequate, provided that defendants must be *found* in the United States. They merely perform the formal assurance that the proper court has jurisdiction over the defendant.[67]

With regard to the jurisdiction over the subject matter the situation would be different.

TRAUTMAN has correctly stated that, 'The subject matter involved may also play a part in defining our jurisdictional reach.' Thus, criminal legislation and economic regulation have different jurisdictional rules.[68]

What we propose is that special jurisdictional rules be devised which would apply to the entire field of antitrust enforcement as a whole, without regard to the remedy which is invoked. This can be done only if the entire body of antitrust law is recognized as a separate area of the law. The test for jurisdictional competency then, becomes a matter for further regulation. In its generality we suggest that it ought to be the impact of the practices that will determine whether the assertion of jurisdiction is justified or not. In the next chapter we will deal with that aspect specifically.

67. *cf.* TRAUTMAN, *l.c.*, at p. 312
68. *ibid.*, pp. 326 and 336

CHAPTER VI

THE EXTRATERRITORIAL REACH OF THE AMERICAN ANTITRUST LAWS INTERNATIONAL LAW ASPECTS

While in the foregoing chapters we have repeatedly referred to the extraterritorial reach of the American antitrust laws, we consider it incumbent upon us to analyze in some detail some of the juridically salient aspects that accompany the observed phenomenon of the United States Government reaching out beyond its territorial boundaries in its antitrust enforcement. We have seen that this 'reaching out' can take several forms, to wit, by way of legislative jurisdiction (remedies available both to private litigants and the government), judicial jurisdiction (by way of civil actions and criminal actions), or regulatory jurisdiction (by way of regulatory, i.e., administrative procedures).

There are several aspects connected with the extraterritorial reach of the antitrust laws which entail theoretical-juridical problems; of these we mention:

(1) the concept of *locus delicti;*

(2) the concept of territoriality;

(3) the extent of the concept of extra-territoriality;

(4) the juridical principles invoked to justify a prosecution of persons for practices committed outside the territorial boundaries of a nation, i.e., the relationship between the assertion of jurisdiction and international law.

The Concept of Locus Delicti

General

We adopt as our major premise that a wrong is a wrong only in relation to time and place.[1] Of these, we address ourselves only to the element of place. This brings us to our major question: what is the proper place of the wrong?

Much has been written about the *place of the wrong,* both with regard to civil wrongs (torts) and public offences (crimes). MULDER has correctly pointed out that some of the major questions which need an answer deal with the question as to the criterion that will be applied in order to determine where a certain conduct took place.[2]

1. Traffic violations are a typical example: driving on the left side of the road is a wrong in some places, while elsewhere driving on the right side of the road would be a wrong.
2. MULDER, *l.c.*, p. 24

With regard to torts the localization of the place of the wrong has two different and almost equally important aspects:

(a) the place of the wrong determines whether an action for tort will be sustained. The *Banana* case[3] which we have discussed in our preceding chapter serves as a good illustration in point.

(b) the place of the wrong determines the measure of damages; this is of particular significance if the measure of damages differs substantially in the various jurisdictions. For instance, suppose that courts in State 'A' generally award $100,000 for damages resulting in the permanent disability of a person, courts in State 'B' $30,000, and courts in State 'C' $15,000. It will need little imagination to suggest that the plaintiff will try to show that the wrong occurred in State 'A'; the defendant that the wrong occurred in State 'C'; while probably neither of the parties will make an attempt to show that the wrong occurred in State 'B', even though parts of the alleged wrong may have occurred in each of the three States.[4]

The above illustrations are sufficient indication that the localization of the place of the wrong in torts with so-called multiple contact points are of importance both to the plaintiff and the defendant. In antitrust cases the importance is accentuated because of the possibility of a plaintiff being awarded treble damages.[5]

The importance of the localization of the wrong holds also true for public offences, regardless of whether they result in criminal prosecution or administrative proceedings. This is based on the prevailing view that the criminal (and administrative) law enforcement by a State is limited to its territorial boundaries. Thus, a State can only prosecute and punish persons (or take administrative steps against them) for behavior within its territory.

SARKAR has stated that 'the *locus delicti* will be at least a significant, and perhaps the most significant, contact with the crime.'[6] MULDER mentions the example of the person standing on one side of the border firing a shot at someone standing across the border, thereby seriously injuring that person.[7] We might build on that example by adding: suppose that the injured person is taken by helicopter to a third country and that he succumbs in that third country. The question now is whether the wrong was committed in country 'A' (where the shot was fired), in country 'B' (where the victim was seriously injured), or in country 'C' (where the victim died).[8]

3. *American Banana Co.* v. *United Fruit Co.*, 213 US 347, 29 S Ct 511 (1909)
4. *cf. Slater* v. *Mexican Nat. R. Co.*, 194 US 120, 24 S Ct 481 (1904)
5. Section 4 *Clayton Act*
6. SARKAR, L., 'The Proper Law of Crime in International Law', in MUELLER, G. O. W., & WISE, E. H., Edit., INTERNATIONAL CRIMINAL LAW, London, 1965, p. 52
7. *l.c.*, p. 24
8. The same question would be important for the measure of damages in a tort action.

The Netherlands Supreme Court faced a question of this nature as far back as 1915: a man standing on Dutch territory pulled a horse standing on German territory by way of a rope tied around the horse's neck across the Dutch-German border. The Supreme Court held that the place where the instrumentality worked (i.e., the rope around the horse's neck by means of which the man could pull it across the border) qualified as the place of the wrong.[9]

With regard to the regulatory jurisdiction the localization of the place of the wrong is important because, regardless whether the procedure takes the form of a civil action, or is one of administrative regulation, or even of an informal nature, it is still the place of the wrong that determines whether the government will move to take the steps it deems necessary under the circumstances.

In other words, when dealing with violations of the antitrust laws, the criminal, the civil, and the regulatory remedial aspects of antitrust enforcement have to be kept in mind; on the other hand, the determination of the *place of the wrong* deserves full attention because of the concomitant problems determined by the place where the wrong was committed.

Yet, when the various authors are consulted, one cannot help but come to the conclusion that the writers treat the problem as if it were one too difficult to grapple with. Instead of coming to grips with it, the authors point out that problems dealing with *locus delicti* have forced the States to abandon the principle of territoriality in favor of protection, nationality, or universality. But resort to a formula of expediency is not tantamount to solving the problems connected with the concept of *locus delicti.*

For instance, the following statements may be an indication of the problem caused by insufficient analysis of the *place of the wrong* and the concomitant problem of jurisdiction:

> 'According to international law, a State ought only to exercise jurisdiction over such persons and property as are within its territory...
>
> '... many States hold the view that a State may not try foreigners for offences committed outside its territorial jurisdiction...
>
> 'Hence the activity of a nation's criminal courts is mostly confined to those persons who have committed offences on its own soil or in one of its own ships.'[10]

However, one fails to find an interpretation of what constitutes 'an offence committed on its own soil.'

9. *Public Prosecutor* v. *L.L.*; H.R. April 6 (1915), *Nederlandse Jurisprudentie* 1915, p. 427, cited by VAN BEMMELEN, J. M., ONS STRAFRECHT, vol. 1, 3rd rev'd ed., Haarlem 1968, p. 60, adding that the Supreme Court specifically stated that the place of the wrong would not be determined by the place where the results of the acts of the actor manifest themselves.
10. TURNER, J. W. C., KENNEY'S OUTLINES OF CRIMINAL LAW, 18th ed., Cambridge, 1962, p. 532 § 641.

We will therefore, attempt to arrive at a satisfactory solution of the concept of *locus delicti.*

The Determination of the Locus Delicti in Civil Actions

We will try to indicate what criterion is (or should be) applied to determine the place of the wrong in civil actions. To do so we have selected two cases, respectively involving a request for injunctive relief (equity) and one aimed at treble damages (tort).

(1) *Steele* v. *Bulova Watch Co.*[11]

Some of the aspects of this case were used in our preceding chapter. We will now turn to those elements that deal with the place of the wrong; in the process we may have to repeat some of the pertinent facts.

Some time after 1926, mr. Steele, a resident of San Antonio, Texas, moved his watch business from San Antonio to Mexico Discovering that the trademark 'Bulova' was not registered there, he procured, in 1933, the Mexican registration of that trademark. He assembled Swiss watch movements and dials and cases (imported from Switzerland and the United States), and stamped, in Mexico City, his watches with 'Bulova' and sold them as such. The trademark 'Bulova' was, in the United States, for many years the property of the Bulova Watch Company. Some of the 'Bulova' watches sold by Mr. Steele found their way to American retail jewelers along the American-Mexican borders. The Bulova Watch Company sued for injunctive relief in the federal district court for the Western District of Texas.

The trial court dismissed the suit because Mr. Steele 'had committed no illegal acts within the United States.' The Court of Appeals reversed; the Supreme Court affirmed. The opinion of the Supreme Court reveals the following considerations:

(a) the 'operations and their effects were not confined within the territorial limits of a foreign nation;'

(b) the 'competing goods could well reflect adversely on Bulova Watch Company's trade reputation;'

(c) the 'spurious "Bulovas" filtered through the Mexican border' into the United States.

If we compare the opinion of the trial court with the opinion of the Supreme Court, it appears that they only differ with regard to the place of the wrong: the former holding that no wrong had been committed within the United States, the latter coming to a different conclusion. They have in common however, the underlying principle that in order to have a cause

11. 344 US 280, 73 S Ct 252 (1952). The case is cited and discussed in STEINER & VAGTS, *op. cit.*, pp. 886, *seq.* SCHWARTZ, I. E., *op. cit.*, p. 234, cites the case as authority for the departure from the principle laid down in the *Banana* case.

of action the plaintiff must show that a wrong was committed within the United States.[12]

(2) *Continental Ore Co.* v. *Union Carbide & Carbon Corp.*[13]

Continental Ore brought an action for treble damages against the Union Carbide & Carbon Corporation and Vanadium Corporation of America, because of an alleged concerted attempt on the part of defendants to exclude the plaintiff from the vanadium business, as a result of which it could no longer participate in the sale of this product in the Canadian markets. Vanadium is a product made in the United States, and exported from there to other countries. By obtaining substantially complete control over the ore deposits from which the vanadium was processed, the defendants had allegedly obtained a monopoly position. The trial court held (and the Court of Appeals affirmed) that no recovery would be allowed, because the harm was done by an arm of the Canadian Government (the purchasing agent in Canada). The Supreme Court vacated the judgment and remanded the case for a new trial. The following considerations are important to our present topic:

(a) 'the activities of the defendants had an impact within the United States and upon its foreign trade';
(b) 'the conspiracy was laid in the United States, was effectuated both here and abroad;'
(c) the plaintiff should be given an opportunity to show that its exclusion from the Canadian market resulted from action 'in concert with or under the direction of' the defendants.

Much like in the preceding case, we can conclude that in order to have a cause of action the plaintiff must show that a wrong was committed within the United States, even though the conduct complained of occurs in foreign countries.

If we construe from the above cited cases a broader framework we find that a plaintiff brings an action because he perceives certain practices as 'bad' or 'unfair': he is harmed; he is not concerned where the action occurs.[14] The courts,

12. As an interesting aside we should like to mention the following *dictum* in the opinion of the Supreme Court: 'We do not deem material that petitioner affixed the mark 'Bulova' in Mexico City. . . or that his purchases. . . when viewed in isolation do not violate any of our laws. They are essential steps. . .; acts in themselves legal lose that character when they become part of an unlawful scheme.' Thus, the United States Supreme Court evidenced a similar attitude as expressed by the Supreme Court of The Netherlands in the case of the horse that was pulled across the Dutch-German border; *cf. supra*, p. 136.
13. 370 US 690, 82 S Ct 1404 (1962). For an interesting discussion of some of the implications, see STEINER & VAGTS, *op. cit.*, pp. 930, *seq.*
14. *cf.* STEINER & VAGTS, *op. cit.*, p. 914: '. . . the defendant's conduct is readily perceived to be 'bad' or 'unfair' to the plaintiff (in the sense of being consciously injurious to another person and in violation of accepted business mores) rather than injurious to the economy as a whole.'

on the other hand, require that there be a *nexus* with the United States, because they must localize the place of the conduct: only if the harm is committed within the United States will an action lie. This should not be so difficult to determine: the *nexus* is there because there is an American plaintiff; conversely, if there were no American plaintiff, there would be no *nexus*. By the same token, if the plaintiff is a foreign businessman, and the defendant is an American corporation or person, the *nexus* is there, because one of the litigating parties is there. On that basis, *the place of the wrong is where harm is felt or done.*

If we take this one step further we may say that the place of the wrong is the place where the plaintiff says he is injured. But this is an economic determination, not a political or juridical one. For that reason, we submit that the extra-territorial reach of antitrust actions should be determined by different criteria. As long as the jurisdictional reach is based on principles of territoriality, or objective territoriality, or protection, we are, in effect dealing with political, or legalo-political considerations. In antitrust enforcement, on the other hand, we are concerned with the functioning of free competition in open markets. The businessman is not concerned with doctrinal principles which have, basically, undertones of power, pseudo-legality, or expediency. He wants a determination on economic considerations, because he is injured in his business. It is for that reason that he seeks injunctive relief or damages. In view of the functional aspects of antitrust enforcement we therefore, should like to formulate:

> *The place of the wrong in civil actions is the place where the plaintiff perceives that he is injured.*

This leaves to the judiciary the duty to determine whether the claim is correct, and what relief is in order.

The Determination of the Locus Delicti in Regulatory Actions

For the determination of the criterion applied to the place of the wrong in regulatory jurisdiction we have selected one case: *Branch* v *F.T.C.*[15] In this case, Branch had been ordered by the Federal Trade Commission to cease-and-desist from its allegedly false and deceptive advertising of its correspondence courses in newspapers in Latin America, as well as from its mailing of advertising materials to solicit customers throughout Latin America. The Court of Appeal denied the petition to set the cease-and-desist order aside. The court made the following observations:

(a) 'much of the objectionable activity occurred in Latin America;'
(b) the conduct was 'conceived, initiated, concocted, and launched on its way in the United States:'
(c) the Federal Trade Commission seeks to 'protect foreign commerce', not

15. 141 F 2d 31 (1944); the case is cited in STEINER & VAGTS, *op. cit.*, pp. 914, 915

the (prospective) customers in Latin America;

(d) competitors in the United States have a right that foreign commerce be protected 'from defilement.'

On the basis of this case, the place of the wrong in regulatory actions is apparently the place where the reprehensible conduct is 'conceived, initiated, concocted, and launched on its way'. The *nexus* with the United States – which provided the jurisdictional reach – is that it be done within the United States.

If we combine the results of this case with the decision of the *Swiss Watchmakers* case, where the conduct was 'conceived, initiated, concocted and launched on its way' in Switzerland, and where the jurisdictional reach was based on the harmful effects within the United States, we might just as well conclude that it is not necessarily where the wrong occurred, but where it was *felt* that is considered the place of the wrong.

The parallel with the place of the wrong in civil actions seems clear. The difference is that in civil actions an individual plaintiff acts, while in regulatory actions the Federal Trade Commission acts on behalf of the aggregate business community. The injured business interests are the real basis for the legal proceedings. We therefore, arrive at the following formulation:

> *The place of the wrong in regulatory actions is the place where the enforcement agency of the government perceives that the vital interests of its aggregate business community are injured.*

The Determination of the Locus Delicti in Criminal Actions

Finally, we turn to the determination of the criterion applied to the place of the wrong in criminal actions.

VAN BEMMELEN has pointed out that it is a cardinal principle of the Dutch criminal law that art. 2 of the Dutch Penal Code applies primarily to punishable behavior committed on Dutch territory, even though articles 4, 5, 6 and 7 of the Dutch Penal Code extend its jurisdiction over punishable actions committed outside the Dutch territorial boundaries, if Dutch interests have been affected.[16] However, no definition is given as to the place where an act is considered to have been *committed.*

The Norwegian Penal Code has at least attempted to overcome the difficulty by stating in article 12, last paragraph:

> 'In cases where the punishability of the act depends on, or is influenced by an actual or intended effect, the act is considered to have been committed also where the effect has occurred or was intended to occur.'[17]

16. BEMMELEN, J. M. VAN, ONS STRAFRECHT, Vol. I, Haarlem, 1965, pp. 20, 31.
17. *cf.* ANDENAES, J., THE GENERAL PART OF THE CRIMINAL LAW OF NORWAY (transl. OGLE, T. P.), London, 1965, p. 320. Article 12 is cited as a direct response to the question: 'Where shall the offence be deemed committed?'

BECKETT has properly pointed out that the phrase 'offences committed within the territory' is an ambiguous one, because it may refer to 'two entirely different classes of cases:

(a) Where a man physically present inside the boundary commits an act which is a criminal offence by the law of the country where he is at the moment.

(b) Where a man, without even entering the territory himself, commits an act, which produces harmful effects inside the State.'[18]

He therefore comes to the conclusion that in order to determine the place of the wrong, to the effect that a State can assume jurisdiction, 'The harmful effects must be in a legal sense the direct results of his criminal activity.'[19]

This statement by BECKETT might be used to counter the suggestion made by SARKAR that 'the *locus delicti* might be fortuitous so far as the harm flowing from a crime is concerned,' because, 'a strict interpretation of the territorial principle would create a "gap" in jurisdiction.'[20]

We do not think that the term 'gap' properly identifies the problem. It is not so much a matter of a *gap* in jurisdiction as it may be a matter of *overlapping* jurisdiction. We say this advisedly because the term 'gap' conveys to the mind the existence of a *lacuna,* a missing part, whereas the term 'overlapping' conveys to the mind the occurence of more than one agency asserting authority to deal with the problem. What we have to be aware of is that wrongs with multiple contact points should not lead us to the conclusion that these wrongs were committed in more than one *locus,* to wit, the place where the wrong was planned, or set in motion, and the place where the result was felt, or intended to be felt.

This is precisely the problem we are facing with regard to the extraterritorial reach of national legislation. Particularly in the area of antitrust enforcement we may find that a particular conduct disturbed the social or economic order in one State (i.e., in the State where the results of the conduct are felt, or intended to be felt), while the social fabric of the State where the conduct was planned, or set in motion, has not been disturbed. In fact, it may even happen that the latter State encourages, or even compels, the conduct that produces the harm in the former and which that State therefore properly reprehends.[21]

KATZENBACH has pointed out that 'exploitation of foreign markets has almost never been viewed as harmful to domestic interests.'[22]

It is particularly where national policies conflict, that the jurisdictional problems may become troublesome.

18. BECKETT, W. E., 'The Exercise of Criminal Jurisdiction over Foreigners,' in VI *British Year Book of International Law* 44, 52 (1952)
19. *ibid.*, p. 57.
20. *l.c.*, p. 53.
21. 'Conduct we proscribe is elsewhere tolerated and even positively approved,' *cf.* KATZENBACH, *l.c.*, p. 1150.
22. *ibid.*, at p. 1149.

In Chapter V we have alluded to the situation that no single body of law has been developed yet that could satisfactorily deal with problems of this order.[23] KATZENBACH has pointed out that 'through redefinition of both crime and its locus' the anomalistic result has been that a plurality of laws become applicable to the same offense.[24]

At the same time, he recognized that 'power to enforce locally through unilateral determination of appropriate policy is unlikely to prove a mutually satisfactory solution.'[25]

It seems to us that KATZENBACH has suggested two important points of departure by stating:

(a) 'There is little hope for an effective implementation of Sherman Act philosophy without foreign assistance in investigation and enforcement.'[26]

(b) 'Territoriality is a synonym for reasonable notice, venue and legitimate sovereign concern.'[27]

But even then, we are still at the threshold of the determination of where the wrong occurred. It is our contention that the proper definition of *locus delicti* is the key to the problem.

We can speak of a wrong only when the act complained of is wrong in the eyes of the complainant. This suggestion would enable us to almost disregard the presently existing distinction between crimes which are commonly so considered and crimes which are only criminal in a particular State.[28]

We have purposely stated that this would *almost* disregard the distinction referred to, because we would not go so far as to leave it entirely up to one State what foreign behavior it will consider criminal. The political history of the thirties seems to support the view that the determination of what foreign conduct constitutes reprehensible (i.e., criminal) behavior, still needs to be limited by internationally acceptable rules of policy determination.[29]

What mechanism will be needed in order to obtain agreement as to these limitations does not concern us at this time, as long as some mechanism necessary for the implementation of policy determination will be established.

This brings us back to our earlier statement that we can speak of a wrong only when the act complained of is wrongful in the eyes of the law-enforcing state, limited by the generally accepted rules of international law.

Once we have determined that is it the prerogative of the law-enforcing State to

23. *supra*, p. 127.
24. *l.c.*, p. 1142.
25. *l.c.*, p. 1147. The identical observation can be found in KAPLAN & KATZENBACH, *op. cit.*, p. 188.
26. *l.c.* at p. 1150
27. *l.c.* at p. 1151. For our criticism with regard to (b), see *infra*, p. 152.
28. We suggest that this is the same distinction as sometimes is made between *mala in se* and *mala prohibita; cf. Hanauer* v. *Doane*, 79 US (12 Wall) 342 (1870)
29. *infra*, p. 156.

determine what behavior is reprehensible, we come to the second phase, i.e., to pinpoint the *locus delicti.* As pointed out above, we should not, because of theoretical niceties, have to do so in a way in which we find ourselves placed in a position that more than one *locus delicti* can be identitied.

In other words, regardless of where the criminal act was planned or set in motion, as long as the harmful effects which directly result from the criminal activity are (intended to be) felt in a certain place, then that is the place of the wrong.

Accepting this view would no longer necessitate a juggling with doctrinal principles in order to assure that the jurisdiction of a court fits into some nicely designed theoretical structure, in order to avoid the stigma of being judicially (or juridically) unreasonable.

HOLMES once stated that 'To rest upon a formula is a slumber that, prolonged, means death.' This statement might well apply to the topic at hand.[30]

Sometimes the desire to keep the doctrine in tact causes people to lose sight of the fact that the nature and function of law is not to erect theoretical structures, but to provide a mechanism for problem solving.[31]

Thus it should not come as a surprise that HOLMES states: 'The law threatens certain pains if you do certain things, intending thereby to give you a new motive for not doing them. If you persist in doing them, it has to inflict the pains in order that its threats may continue to be believed.'[32] 'All law is directed to conditions of things manifest to the senses.'[33]

Criminal law, as part of law in general, purports to combine 'ought' and 'is' in rules that primarily provide a mechanism for maintaining generally accepted norms of social conduct.[34]

In view of the above, we should like to suggest: *the locus delicti over which a given criminal law enforcement agency may extend jurisdiction is the place where the harmful effects which directly result from the criminal activity are felt, or intended to be felt, regardless of the place where the criminal act was planned or set in motion.*[35]

30. HOLMES, O. W., 'Ideals and Doubts,' 10 *Illinois Law Review* 1, 3 (1915).
31. *cf.* BEMMELEN, *op. cit.*, pp. 3, *seq.* and the different views there presented. Also, see BERMAN and GREINER, *op. cit.*, pp. 16, *seq.*
32. HOLMES, O. W., THE COMMON LAW (HOWE, M. DE W., Edit.), Cambridge, 1963, p. 40.
33. *ibid.*, p. 42.
34. *cf.* BEMMELEN, *op. cit.*, p. 3.
35. The Supreme Court of the Netherlands has stated that the place of the wrong would not be determined by the place where the results of the acts of the actor manifest themselves; *cf. supra*, p. 136, *n.* 9. This statement was *obiter dicta,* since the case at hand did not require the Court to express itself on the subject. Furthermore, we submit that antitrust enforcement might have to follow different rules of *locus delicti.*

The Concept of Territoriality

Traditionally, territoriality has been associated with territorial boundary, because a State is empowered to have sovereign supremacy only within its own territory. Thus, we find in the *case of the ss. Lotus*[36] the frequently quoted statement:

> 'Now the first and foremost restriction imposed by international law upon a State is that – failing the existence of a permissive rule to the contrary – it may not exercise its power in any form in the territory of another State. In this sense jurisdiction is certainly territorial; it cannot be exercised by a State outside its territory except by virtue of a permissive rule derived from international custom or from a convention.'

Those familiar with principles of case analysis in the Anglo-American law are acquainted with the distinction between *holding, dictum*, and *obiter dicta:*

> the *holding* is the decision of the particular case before the court;
> the *dictum* is the judicial statement which may lead to the decision of the case, but not necessary to arrive at the final result;
> the *obiter dicta* are the wayside remarks made by the judge which are wholly off the point at issue.[37]

Applying this distinction to the *Lotus* case, we may state that the above quoted statement pertaining to the territorially limited jurisdiction of a court was not absolutely necessary to arrive at the decision; but neither was it a wayside remark wholly off the point at issue. Consequently, we may classify the statement as *dictum.* The same could be said with regard to the dissenting opinion of Justice LODER when he addressed himself to the problem of territoriality:

> 'The criminal law of a State may extend to crimes and offences committed abroad by its nationals since such nationals are subject to the law of their own country; but it *cannot* extend to offences committed by a foreigner in foreign territory, without infringing the sovereign rights of the foreign State concerned, since in that State the State enacting the law has no jurisdiction.'

It is clear that both in the case of the majority opinion and the dissenting opinion the judicial remarks are made to pave the way for the decision, but they are not the decision-as-such. Therefore, one can follow the views expressed, or one can reject them, in either instance without violating the authority, i.e., the holding of the case.

More difficult to classify are the statements of the Swiss court in the case *Kaiser and Attenhofer* v. *Basle,*[38] where the Court rejected an appeal of two Swiss

36. P.C.I.J., Sec. A., No. 10 (1927).
37. *cf.* LLEWELLYN, *op. cit.*, p. 42.
38. Federal Tribunal of Switzerland, 1950, *Int'l L. Rep.*, 1950, p. 189, quoted in KATZ & BREWSTER, *op. cit.*, p. 523.

nationals, tried and convicted for crimes committed abroad, on the grounds that Switzerland had independent authority to try its nationals for offences committed abroad. With regard to this aspect of the case, the Court stated:

> 'States do not limit their jurisdiction to acts committed on their territory.' To an extent, this statement can be reconciled with that part of the opinion in the *Lotus* case where we find the observation made that 'the territoriality of criminal law is not an absolute principle of International Law, and by no means coincides with territorial sovereignty.'[39]

It is evident that the concepts of territory and jurisdiction are closely if not imperceptibly interwoven[40]: on the one hand the jurisdiction of a State can only be exercised within the territorial boundaries of a State; on the other hand we find that this limitation does not seem to inhibit States to (criminally) prosecute a defendant for acts committed abroad.

We can arrive at a satisfactory solution only by a complete separation of the concepts of 'territory' and 'territorial jurisdiction.'

> *Territory, in our opinion, is any given location where an act is planned, set in motion, perpetrated, or completed, the results of which occur (or are intended to occur) either in the same location or elsewhere.*

This view would have as its concomitant the implication that it is the ultimate effect that is reprehended, rahter than the person committing the act. At the same time, it is the person responsible for this ultimate effect who will be subject to prosecution (be it civil or criminal) and punishment (or liability, or regulation).[41]

Of course, while we have suggested that the concepts of 'territory' and 'territorial jurisdiction' are to be separately viewed, this does not mean that one can disregard the context in which we have framed our statement. Indeed, the definition of 'territory' as suggested above would be entirely unacceptable if not used in its relation and context with territorial jurisdiction; in fact as a definition of territory it would hardly make sense. But when taken in its perspective of finding a solution to the question of what the concept 'territory' is all about, so that jurisdiction can properly be asserted, we think that our definition is helpful. We submit that our approach (and we hope, solution) will be less likely to lead to a 'catch-as-catch-can' system of law enforcement than currently appears to be the case. As we have stated earlier, the present system is not a matter of principle, but rather one of expediency. While expediency cannot always be avoided,

39. *cf.* OPPENHEIM, L., *op. cit.*, p. 334.
40. *cf.* 'Harvard Research in International Law', (hereinafter referred to as 'Harvard Research'), 29 *Am. J. International Law Supplement* 435, 470 (1935) (Vol. II, 'Jurisdiction with Respect to Crime'): 'the scope of the term "territory" in this Convention in thus the same as the scope of the term "territorial jurisdiction"...'
41. With regard to the views of the Supreme Court of The Netherlands (*cf. supra*, p.136. *n.* 9) this could conceivably be interpreted as 'the location where the instrument "worked".'

it should only be used as *ultimum remedium,* certainly not as long as other avenues are open.

The Application of the Concepts of Locus Delicti and Territory to Jurisdiction

In order to verify whether the concepts of *locus delicti* and territory as developed by us have any practical value we shall apply them to the exercise of jurisdiction. It goes without saying that we need not to concern ourselves with the jurisdiction *in personam,* because it only determines whether a defendant has properly been brought under the jurisdiction of the court: *locus delicti* and territory have nothing to do with venue and service of process.
The question is different with regard to the jurisdiction over the subject matter. In fact, it is precisely with regard to the jurisdiction over the subject matter that our concepts gain relevance. In order to prove this, we will demonstrate the application of our concepts to respectively, the civil, the regulatory and the criminal jurisdictional aspects of the extraterritorial reach of the antitrust laws.

(1) The Civil Jurisdictional Aspects.
As test case we have selected *Pacific Seafarers, Inc.* v. *Pacific Far East Line, Inc.*[42] The facts of the case are the following: Plaintiffs and defendants were American shipping companies. Under a United States Agency for International Development sponsored program, money was loaned to South Vietnamese importers to import a.o. fertilizer and cement from Taiwan and Thailand, on the condition that at least 50 percent of the goods would be transported by American-flag ships. Both the plaintiffs and defendants were competing for this business of carrying the goods. The defendants attempted to secure the trade by lowering their prices (in concerted action); by so doing they forced the plaintiffs out of business. For the damages sustained the plaintiffs brought an action in the federal district court of the District of Columbia. The trial court held that no damages could be awarded; although it dismissed the suit without opinion, the inference can be drawn that there was insufficient effect on the foreign commerce of the United States to warrant jurisdiction under the *Sherman Act.*[43] The Court of Appeal held that there was sufficient *nexus* between what the parties did and the United States to bring the practices under the reach of the *Sherman Act*, because:
(a) the restraints occurred in a market dominated by Americans;

42. 404 F2d 804 (1968), *cert. denied.* US, 89 S Ct 872 (1969). The case is cited and discussed in 1 *Case West. J. of Int'l Law;* the facts have been taken from there. The docketing of the case was cited in SUPPLEMENT, p. 55, *n.* 3.
43. According to the *Sherman Act* the restraint of trade must be either a restraint of trade or commerce among the several States, or with foreign nations (Section 1).

(b) the market was solely a creation of American foreign policy.
We submit that the reasoning of the Court of Appeals was wrong; it is unfortunate that the Supreme Court did not grant *certiorari* so as to review the basis on which the decision of the Court of Appeals rests.
The *locus delicti* was not the United States, but South-East-Asia. The territory was not the United States, but South-East-Asia. The parties were private litigants, who happened to be United States citizens.[44] The decision might lead to strange results. For instance, if the plaintiff had been a Norwegian corporation, who in order to obtain a share of the business would register in the United States, would the Court still hold that the foreign commerce of the United States had been affected? All that can be said is that a private litigant lost out on business somewhere in the Far East. No vital American interests were threatened.[45]
On the other hand, if we consider the *Bulova*[46] and the *Continental Ore*[47] cases, we submit that we would have come to the same results as the Supreme Court: the *locus delicti* in each case was the United States; and so was the territory. This provided the basis for the jurisdiction over the subject matter.

(2) The Regulatory Jurisdictional Aspects.
As test cases we have selected the *Swiss Watchmakers*[48] case and *Branch* v *FTC*[49]. With regard to the former, we find that the *locus delicti* was the United States; and so was the territory. We therefore, do not quarrel with the assertion of jurisdiction over the subject matter.
With regard to the latter, we have reservations about the correctness of the court's assertion of subject matter jurisdiction. While it is true that the conduct was 'concocted and launched on its way in the United States', the objectionable activity occurred largely in Latin America. Suppose that Branch had established a branch office in Latin America to launch the campaign, while the mechanics (the actual correspondence school courses) were maintained in the United States, would the threat to other American correspondence schools have been less? Would they not have been 'defiled'? And what if Branch had moved his headquarters to a foreign country while only maintaining a branch office in the United States, to carry

44. We have earlier pointed out that corporations are citizens; *cf.* Chapter IV, supra, p. 104, *seq.*
45. For a review of contrasting viewpoints with regard to the nature of the protected interest under the antitrust laws, see REHBINDER, *op. cit.*, pp. 115, *seq.*
46. *Steele* v *Bulova Watch Co.*, 344 US 280, 73 S Ct 252 (1952), see *supra*, p. 137
47. *Continental Ore Co.* v *Union Carbide & Carbon Corp.*, 370 US 690, 82 S Ct 1404 (1962), see *supra*, p. 138
48. *U.S.* v *Watchmakers of Switzerland Information Center, Inc.*, 1963 Trade Cases, nr. 70, 600
49. 141 F 2d 31 (1944), see *supra*, p. 139

out the mechanics of the correspondence course; would then, the commercial interests of American (would-be) competitors not have been 'defiled' or threatened? Now, if Branch had given out false information, for instance, to the effect that in the United States all educational institutions had to be licensed; and that this licensing was based on thorough subject matter competency of the instructional staff; and that strict standards of eductional performance were elements of considerations in the licensing process; now, if all that had been stated, when in fact Branch was not licensed, or that the licensing procedures were falsely misrepresented; then, the *locus delicti* (in regulatory jurisdiction) would be the United States, because that is where the enforcement agency of the government perceives that the interests of its aggregate business community are injured. In that case, the territory would also be the United States, and there would be jurisdiction over the subject matter. Absent these conditions, there is not.

(3) The Criminal Jurisdictional Aspects.

As test case we have selected the *Alcoa* case[50], because (a) it is the most commonly cited case; (b) it is the case which lead to the doctrine that liability can attach, even to non-nationls, for conduct abroad if the conduct produces results within the United States,[51] (c) it is one of the heavily disputed cases,[52] (d) it involved a foreign defendant.[53]

Inasmuch as we have discussed the case in detail in an earlier chapter, we need not repeat the facts and the reasoning of the court. As will be recalled, the criterion used by the court was that there had to be (1) intent to affect the foreign commerce of the United States, and (2) actual effect upon that foreign commerce.

It is furthermore, generally recognized that *some* American participation is required, too.[54]

If our definition of *locus delicti* were to be accepted, the participation by Americans would be immaterial. We consider this important, in the first place because it sounds too much like a pious declaration of concern that a foreign culprit is being accused of a violation of the antitrust laws; in the second place, the possibility of prosecuting a foreign defendant would depend on whether enough evidence can be produced showing American participation: this is in our

50. *U.S.* v *Aluminum Co. of America*, 148 F 2d 416 (1945), see Chapter V, *supra*, p. 118
51. *cf.* 1 *Case West. Res. J. of Int'l law* 132, 136 (1969)
52. *cf.* REHBINDER, *op. cit.*, p. 49, *n.* 6; SCHWARTZ, I. E., *op. cit.*, p. 245, *n.* 1, and the literature there cited.
53. Aluminium, Ltd., a Canadian corporation
54. *cf.* SCHWARTZ, I. E., *op. cit.*, p. 245, *n.* 1,; 1 *Case West. Res. J. of Int'l Law* 132, 136 (1969), *n.* 22.

opinion an unreasonable (and sometimes most difficult) requirement.

We submit that if the intent to produce harmful effects is proved beyond a reasonable doubt there is little reason to require that the conspiracy was entered into with an American co-defendant.

Our concept of *locus delicti* combined with that of territory provide sufficient safeguards to protect the honest foreign defendant facing a scrupulous judge; in the hands of an over-zealous judge pre-existing requirements will be bent anyway, by the process of extensive interpretation. Furthermore with the safeguard of Courts of Appeal and a Supreme Court we do not feel that one needs to be apprehensive about the possibility of over-zealous judges.

Our concept of *locus delicti* combined with that of territory would also protect foreign combinations that were established with a market other than the United States in mind, but which happen to direct part of their activity to the United States. We consider this an attractive feature of using our definition as criterion to determine whether the criminal sanctions of the American antitrust laws should be applied to foreign defendants.

We submit that application of our definitions as criterion to, e.g., the *Aniline* case[55] would also be possible: the *locus delicti* and the territory were such that the jurisdiction over the subject matter could be asserted and a decision rendered.

A solution as proposed by us could even lead to a more expeditious method of unification of the area of international criminal law. For substantiation we refer to the following statement:

> '. . . the principle of territoriality of jurisdiction is not a universal notion of penal law among civilized nations. Quite to the contrary, most nations adhere to further-reaching jurisdictional principles. . .'[56]

SILVING has properly pointed out that the 'preservation of a basically "positivistic" approach is essential in international law.' She finds support for this view in the modern concept of 'supra-statutory law,' as accepted by the German courts by the referral to 'a central core of law' which 'is present in the consciousness of all civilized nations,' and which 'must not be violated by any statute or by any other authoritative action.'[57]

Formulating the concept of 'territory' as suggested by us would create a basis for such a basically positivistic approach, because it would denote a frame of reference to which certain phenomena must be related in order to legally qualify.

As long as the *locus delicti* has been determined in such a way that the (intend-

55. *cf. Publikatieblad van de Europese Gemeenschappen,* Vol. 12, L-195/11 (August 7, 1969)
56. MUELLER, G. O. W., 'The United Nations Draft Code of Offences Against the Peace and Security of Mankind: An American Evaluation,' in MUELLER & WISE, *op. cit.,* p. 608.
57. SILVING, H., 'In re Eichmann: A Dilemma of Law and Morality,' in MUELLER & WISE, *op. cit.,* pp. ,338, 339.

ed) results occur in a given territory, then, the connection with that territory is sufficient to recognize the territorial jurisdiction of the affected State. We therefore, formulate the following principle:

> *A person who engages in a criminal activity, the directly resulting harmful effects of which are felt, or intended to be felt, in a certain place, is considered to have committed that criminal activity within the territory of that place, and, therefore, subject to the criminal law enforcement of that place.*

The Extent of the Concept of Territoriality in Criminal Prosecution

One major problem in accepting the preceding formula for territoriality, by relating 'territory' to *'locus delicti,'* is that sooner or later the term criminal activity needs to be elaborated upon.

To an extent this flows from the increasing and complex interdepency of 'human activities that know no State boundaries.'[58]

But the problem has a different aspect, too. KATZENBACH has properly pointed out, 'Criminal behavior goes to the very root of social organization. . .'[59] This holds particularly true for antitrust violations: 'Conduct we proscribe is elsewhere tolerated and even positively approved.'[60] In other words, what is considered criminal activity in one country, is not so regarded elsewhere. It is in this area that problems can easily arise.

We have already noted[61] that the majority opinion in the *Lotus* case stated that, 'The territoriality of criminal law. . . by no means coincides with territorial sovereignty.'

HANBURY mentions how a number of maritime countries require that a *wine ration* be carried on board ship; but during the Prohibition era, intoxicating liquor found on board any ship, foreign or domestic, within American territorial waters, could be seized. This could result in the situation that a British ship, eastbound, could carry no liquor till she had quitted United States waters and, westbound, had to get rid of it all before entering them.[62]

Indeed, this was exactly the conclusion reached in *Cunard Steamship Co.* v.

58. KATZENBACH, N. deB., *l.c.*, p. 1092 (1956).
59. *ibid.*, p. 1146, also *cf.*, KAPLAN & KATZENBACH, *op. cit.*, p. 186.
60. *ibid.*, p. 1150.
61. *supra*, p. 144. Whether this is really what HANBURY calls 'establishing' a rule may be questioned if one keeps in mind the distinction between 'holding' and *dictum'*; *cf.* HANBURY, H. G., 'The Territorial Limits of Criminal Jurisdiction,' 37 *Grotius Society-Problems of Public and Private International Law* 171, 177 (1952). We rather suspect that the citation should be qualified as *judicial dictum; cf.* LAUTERPACHT, H., 'Allegiance, Diplomatic Protection and Criminal Jurisdiction over Aliens,' in Vol. IX, nr. 3, *Cambridge Law Journal* 330, 343 (1947), cited by HANBURY.
62. *l.c.*, p. 177.

Mellon,[63] where the United States Supreme Court stated that the prohibition of transportation of intoxicating liguors within, or the importation thereof into the United States was equally applicable to foreign vessels carrying liqor as part of a ship's sea stores.

Even where, subsequent to a court's decision, diplomatic steps are taken to undo or mitigate the results of judicial application of domestic laws to foreign subjects (as was the case in the aftermath of *Cunard Steamship Co.* v. *Mellon*), this does not take away that, at first, without much ado, the highest Court holds a domestic ban applicable to a situation which by the foreign law might have been compulsory (such as the requirement of carrying a wine ration).[64]

One may wonder whether the Court still would follow the same reasoning, in view of the following *dictum* in *Hines* v. *Davidowitz:*[65]

> 'One of the most important and delicate of all international relationships, recognized immemorially as a responsibility of government, has to do with the protection of the just rights of a country's own nationals when those nationals are in another country. Experience has shown that international controversies of the gravest moment, sometimes even leading to war, may arise from real or imagined wrongs to another's subjects inflicted, or permitted, by a government.'

Whether the above statement indicates an enlightenment on the part of the Court is hard to judge. If nothing else, it demonstrates, as KAPLAN and KATZENBACH have pointed out, that 'it is not easy to relate formal authority to territory in any comprehensive way.'[66]

In his discussion of the *Joyce* case,[67] and the problem of territoriality in relation to crimes committed by aliens abroad, LAUTERPACHT states that, 'if a person acts in such a manner as seriously to threaten the security of another State, he must be deemed to act at his peril. . . The test cannot properly be whether such acts are permitted by the law of the State where he resides.'[68]

KATZENBACH goes still further when he states:

> 'An individual traveling abroad is conscious of an obligation to obey local laws, and generally knows that they may differ somewhat from those to which he is accustomed. A business enterprise is perhaps even more aware of potential prescriptions with regard to 'business done' in a foreign coun-

63. 262 US 100, 43 S Ct 504 (1923).
64. The fact that there was a dissenting opinion does in no way nullify the binding power of the decision.
65. 312 US 52, 61 S Ct 399 (1941)
66. *op. cit.*, p. 173. As an example they mention the difficulty of determining the geographical limits within which an event occurs, such as the restriction of production, the pooling of patents, or the price fixing of radios undertaken by a world-wide cartel; *ibid.*, p. 174.
67. *Joyce* v. *Director of Public Prosecutions,* 173 L.T. 377 (Court of Appeal), 1945 and A.C. 347, 1946 (House of Lords).
68. LAUTERPACHT, *l.c.*, pp. 347, 348

try, at least where it is more than incidental and isolated...
'Where the "impact" within a foreign state is reasonably foreseeable and the matter is one that is often subject to criminal sanction, even though not so regulated at the place of acting, it may be sufficient to subject the actor to the legal process of the place of impact if he can be there taken into custody, without objection by other states. The case is, of course, even stronger where the particular actor intends to violate the law in question, for here the general interest in order and respect for law is put in issue.'[69]

KATZENBACH recognizes however, that the government regulation of business and economic activity by an extension of police power may pose a perplexing situation, thereby emphasizing that 'The extra-territorial application of our anti-trust laws, the administration of exchange controls and nationalization of industries are among the more important current problems.'[70]

He then comes to the conclusion that 'there is no very useful purpose in cataloguing physical acts within the United States, or using verbal formulae such as the locus of the conspiracy, the requirement of local act, and so forth, save as they have some factual relevance to the notice question.[71]

We question KATZENBACH's views. On the contrary, we feel that as long as no clarity exists with regard to the concept of territoriality, some 'cataloguing' of physical acts, or the use of 'verbal formulae' are very useful.

We furthermore question his statement that 'Territoriality is a synonym for reasonable notice, venue and legitimate sovereign concern.'[72] While we agree that territoriality finds its roots and justification in legitimate sovereign concern, that does not make the one a synonym for the other.

Furthermore, notice and venue are jurisdictional aspects, while we have tried to show that the jurisdictional aspects come into play only after requirements such as impact and effect on territory and persons have been satisfied. Again, we should like to stress our earlier suggestion that there is a need to separate the concept of territoriality from territorial jurisdiction, no matter how closely the two are intertwined in judicial practice.

It is in our opinion the criminal activity of the perpetrator that determines the extent given to the concept of territoriality. Territoriality itself is determined by the intended impact of the criminal activity, by considering the perpetrator to have committed his activity within the territory of a State when the directly resulting harmful effects are (intended to be) felt in that State.

WISE has suggested that the application of a substantive criminal law requires an

69. KATZENBACH, *l.c.*, p. 1145. The identical statements can be found in KAPLAN & KATZENBACH, *op. cit.*, p. 185.
70. *l.c.*, p. 1147. The identical statement can be found in KAPLAN & KATZENBACH, *op. cit.*, p. 187.
71. *l.c.*, p. 1151.
72. *l.c.*, p. 1151.

adherence to 'seven ultimate notions, expressing the concepts of legality, harm, conduct, *mens rea,* concurrence of conduct and *mens rea,* causation and proportionate punishment.'[73]

Of these notions we do not concern ourselves with the aspect of proportionate punishment; the other notions, however, seem to be directly at issue.

Of these, we consider the concurrence of conduct and *mens rea* the pivotal one. Particularly when antitrust enforcement is the basis for the prosecution it becomes essential to realize that antitrust violations have not reached (and probably will not in the near foreseeable future) the qualification of a *common crime* (such as murder or piracy).

Consequently, an investigation into the *mens rea* of the violator becomes an important part of law enforcement; in other words, whether there is an element of *Zumutbarkeit*[74] in the perpetrator of the reprehended act.

KRONSTEIN has pointed out: 'A quick review of the American cases, then, makes it clear that American courts will apply American antitrust laws "extra-territorially" only when one or both of two conditions are met. These conditions are: First, American firms or their subsidiaries must have participated in the challenged cartel; or, second, the companies participating in the cartel must have executed the agreement within the United States to a significant degree.'[75] Indeed, in each of the given examples there was a *Zumutbarkeit* on the part of the foreign defendants.

Although KRONSTEIN does not say so explicitly, it might well be for this very reason that he takes issue with the conclusion drawn by SEIDL-HOHENVELDEREN 'that American courts must apply American antitrust law whenever two foreign nationals make an agreement in Switzerland not to export to the United States or to export only under restrictive conditions,' a conclusion which KRONSTEIN submits to be derived from a misreading of the holding in *Alcoa.*[76] We make our assumption because it seems that SEIDL-HOHENVELDEREN's view is based on the statement made by Judge HAND in the earlier cited *Alcoa* case, reading as follows:

73. WISE, E. M., 'Note on International Standards of Criminal Law and Administration,' in MUELLER & WISE, *op. cit.*, p. 147. For a similar view, *cf.* BEMMELEN, *op. cit.*, pp. 61, *seq.*
74. For a concise explanation of the term, *cf.* BEMMELEN, *op. cit.*, p. 64. One explanatory interpretation of the term might be: whether the perpetrator can be properly reproached or held accountable for his conduct.
75. KRONSTEIN, H., 'Conflicts Resulting from the Extraterritorial Effects of the Antitrust Regulation of Different Countries,' in XXth CENTURY COMPARATIVE AND CONFLICTS LAW, Leiden, 1961, p. 437. He substantiates his statement by referring to the underlying factual situations in *U.S.* v. *Sisal Sales Corp.* (274 U.S. 268, 47 S. 592 (1927)), *U.S.* v. *Aluminum Company of America* (148 F 2d 416 (1945)), *U.S.* v. *General Electric Co.* (the Phoebus Cartel case) (82 F Supp 753 (1949)), *U.S.* v. *Imperial Chemical Industries, Ltd.* (105 F Supp 215 (1952)), *U.S.* v. *Holophane* (19 F Supp 114 (1954); aff'd 352 U.S. 903, 77 S. Ct. 144 (1956)), and *U.S.* v. *Watchmakers of Switzerland Information Center, Inc.* (133 F Supp 40 (1955)).
76. *l.c.*, p. 436.

> '... it is settled law... that any state may impose liabilities, even upon persons not within its allegiance, for conduct outside its borders that has consequences within its borders which the State reprehends; and these liabilities other states will ordinarily recognize.'[77]

This is, of course, *judicial dictum, not holding.* Even so, the sentence clearly states that a State may *impose* liabilities; the significance becomes more accentuated when read in conjunction with the preceding sentence of Judge Hand's opinion, stating:

> 'We should not impute to Congress an intent to punish all whom its courts can catch, for conduct which has no consequences within the United States.'

The relevance of the judicial *dictum* becomes still greater when seen in conjunction with the sentences which follow the above cited ones:

> 'Two situations are possible. There may be agreements made beyond our borders not intended to affect imports, which do affect them, or which affect exports. Almost any limitation of the supply of goods in Europe, for example, or in South America, may have repercussions in the United States if there is trade between the two. Yet when one considers the international complications likely to arise from an effort in this country to treat such agreements as unlawful, it is safe to assume that Congress certainly did not intend the Act to cover them. Such agreements may on the other hand intend to include imports into the United States, and yet it may appear that they have no effect upon them.'
>
> '... we shall assume that the Act does not cover agreements, even though intended to affect imports or exports, unless its performance is shown actually to have had some effect upon them.'

We feel that Judge HAND clearly limits the applicability of the American legislation to those acts which actually had an impact within the United States, and where there was intent on the part of the perpetrator to bring about the reprehended result. In other words, the element of *Zumutbarkeit* has to be satisfied before a foreign defendant can be successfully prosecuted.

In fact, all through the case Judge HAND shows how the actions of the Aluminum Co. of America must be of such a nature that there is reason to impute some degree of guilt, at least enough to hold the company liable for its conduct. We mention by way of illustration the following passages:

> '... the correspondence between those interests and 'Alcoa' ... even though it may not justify the conclusion that the two were acting in conjunction, leaves no doubt that they were not to be competitors at arms length.[78]
>
> '... at least as early as 1930 the complaints charged it with notice of the

77. *cf. supra,* p. 118.
78. *l.c.,* at p. 431.

effect of what it was doing; and yet it kept on until the Department began to move, when it at once found means to cure the situation.'[79]

'Both agreements... were unlawful, though made abroad, if they were intended to affect imports and did affect them.'[80]

Similarly, we find in the *Holophane* case such statements as:

'... the restrictive agreements were designed to eliminate competition...'

'The intended effects of the agreements... will continue unless prevented by this court.'[81]

The question then, how far we should extend the concept of territoriality when dealing with antitrust enforcement, can be answered as follows:

The territory in which a person engages in an activity which he knows to be wrongful as to the effect this activity will have in the place where these wrongful effects are felt, or intended to be felt, is considered the territory to which the criminal laws of the country where these wrongful effects are felt, or intended to be felt, extend.

The principles Underlying Criminal Jurisdiction

To show how far ahead of its time the Dutch Criminal Code of 1881 was, the statement has been made that the same principles which formed the foundation of the Code are still in force today.[82]

MULDER lists those basic principles as follows:[83]

(1) the principle of territoriality;
(2) the principle of (active) nationality;
(3) the principle of personality (passive nationality);
(4) the protective principle;
(5) the universality principle.

The *Harvard Research in International Law,* in its exhaustive study, lists pretty much the same principles in its 'Draft Convention on Jurisdiction with Respect to Crime.'[84]

The reasons necessitating varied bases to justify prosecution for offences commenced or put in motion outside a State are aptly summarized by SARKAR:

'... changes in social structure during the last few hundred years have

79. *l.c.*, at p. 438.
80. *l.c.*, at p. 444.
81. *U.S.* v. *Holophane Co.*, 119 F Supp 114 (1954), at p. 119.
82. *cf.* MULDER, A., 'De extra-territoriale werking van het strafrecht,' in 51 *Mededelingen van de Nederlandse Vereniging voor Internationaal Recht,* 12 (1964). Of course, one might use the same phenomenon to come to the conclusion that between 1881 and 1964 no new thinking had gained momentum, sufficient to provide a different foundation for criminal jurisdiction. (The term 'jurisdiction' is here used both in the sense of 'power to render a binding decision' and 'subject matter jurisdiction.')
83. *l.c.*, p. 12.
84. 29 *Am. J. of International Law Supp.* 435, 439, 440 (1935).

> been accompanied by altered conceptions of crime and, hence, of criminal jurisdiction. Until the late sixteenth century, crime was still regarded as a local wrong. . .'
>
> 'In the early seventeenth century. . . criminal jurisdiction began to be based rather on the principle of territoriality. In a pre-industrial age. . . it was a reasonable presumption that the preparation and completion of a crime, and the presence of the criminal would coincide in one place. . .'
>
> 'It was inevitable that the growth of technology would cause crimes to become increasingly complex. . .'
>
> '. . . international law has dealt with the changed situation by creating new principles. In the course of such dealings the old established concepts have been so encrusted with exceptions and engrafted with legal fictions that the old concepts may be said to be fairly buried under them.'[85]

The examples cited by SARKAR to illustrate the extent to which States may go to justify jurisdiction based on the nationality principle or the protective principle seem only to substantiate our claim.

For instance, when 'an Italian court convicts an Italian national for violation of the Italian law against criminal association, even though the offence was committed in the United States and was not there regarded as a crime, and even though Italy was not harmed by it,' then, the assertion of jurisdiction seems to us on rather shaky grounds.[86]

Or when a French court convicts 'a Spanish national, who was captain in the Spanish merchant marine, to a long term of imprisonment for corresponding in Spain, during the First World War, with subjects of an enemy of France,'[87] then again the assertion of jurisdiction can only find justification by applying a charitable(?) and flexible(!) yardstick.

The *Harvard Research in International Law* suggests that the seeking of a solution to the admittedly often intricate problems pertaining to the assumption of jurisdiction in criminal prosecution cases becomes, 'primarily a matter of the avoiding or resolving of conflicts.'[88]

It is on the basis of 'An analysis of modern national codes of penal law and penal procedure, checked against the conclusions of reliable writers and the resolutions of the jurisprudence of national courts' that 'five general principles' of jurisdiction, as claimed by States, are discerned:[89]

85. SARKAR, *l.c.*, pp. 50, 51. The article purports to 'indicate a solution. . . which may be a possible way of improving the basis of criminal law administration in international law,' by recognizing the law 'which has the most significant contacts with the crime' as the 'proper law of crime' (*l.c.*, p. 76).
86. *cf.* SARKAR, *l.c.*, p. 63, citing *RE Di Lisi,* Court of Cassation of Italy; *Annual Digest* 193 (No. 9), 1933.
87. *ibid.*, p. 69.
88. 'Research in International Law,' *cf.* 29 *Am. J. of Int'l Law Supp.* 443 (1935).
89. *ibid.*, p. 445.

(1) The territorial principle, determining jurisdiction by reference to the place where the offence is committed;
(2) The nationality principle, determining jurisdiction by reference to the nationality or national character of the person committing the offence;
(3) The protective principle, determining jurisdiction by reference to the national interests injured by the offence;
(4) The universality principle, determining jurisdiction by reference to the custody of the person committing the offence;
(5) The passive personality principle, determining jurisdiction by reference to the nationality or national character of the person injured by the offence.

Of these, SARKAR only reviews the first three, although the fifth one is in some way brought into the discussion.[90]

Addressing himself to the special problems of American antitrust enforcement, VERZIJL recognizes the following instances where a State might claim competence to assume jurisdiction:[91]

(1) Jurisdiction based on unlawful conduct concluded in the United States itself.
(2) Jurisdiction based on unlawful conduct by Americans anywhere in the world aimed at unlawful interference with United States interests.
(3) Jurisdiction based on conduct 'performed outside the United States,' but with 'effect within its borders.'
(4) Jurisdiction based on 'acts wheresoever and by whomsoever committed, which directly injure U.S. nationals or residents or, more broadly, affect certain vital American interests.'

MULDER has properly pointed out that the introduction of the principle of 'territorial effect,' as suggested by VERZIJL, is a departure from the commonly accepted nomenclature and, furthermore, in reality rather a qualification of what should be understood to be included in a State's 'own territory.'[92]

We rather agree with JESSUP that, 'When a State wishes to find and punish the "Whodunit" it follows strange fictional clues to territoriality.'[93]

It seems as if conformity with an abstract doctrine, presumably covering all situations that might present themselves, has been the prime concern of legislative and judicial authorities. This, in turn, has led to the introduction of 'fictions.' However, as JESSUP has observed, 'As soon as one passes from the reality

90. *op. cit.*, pp. 51, *seq.*, 61, *seq.*, 67, *seq.*
91. VERZIJL, *l.c.*, p. 6.
92. MULDER, A., 'De extra-territoriale werking van het strafrecht,' 51 *Mededelingen van de Nederlandse Vereniging voor Internationaal Recht* 12, n. 11 (1964).
93. JESSUP, Ph. C., TRANSNATIONAL LAW, New Haven, 1956, p. 45, and the examples there given; thereby following the examples cited by the *Harvard Reserach,* pp. 485 and 494.

to the fictional basis. . . one has opened the door to wide extensions of jurisdiction.'[94]

Our personal concern is that it appears that jurisdiction has been the sole concern of the legal writers and researchers. Yet, it seems that precisely on that issue much greater clarification is needed.

We have earlier had an opportunity to point out the necessity of distinguishing between the so-called legislative and the judicial jurisdiction.[95] Failure to do so would make it appear that if there is judicial jurisdiction there must be legislative jurisdiction, *vice versa.*

The 'Draft Convention' is almost typical. Thus, we find in Article 1, sub (b), the statement that 'A State's "jurisdiction" is its competence under international law to prosecute and punish for crime.'[96] And Article 2, dealing with the scope of the 'Draft Convention,' specifically states that the above mentioned jurisdiction 'is defined as limited by this convention.'[97] However, nowhere does one find a limitation of a State's legislative jurisdiction under international law. Yet it seems paramount that such power ought to be recognized and spelled out in the 'Draft Convention,' lest international friction emerge at a later date.

The problems pertaining to this aspect of jurisdiction, i.e., a State's legislative jurisdiction, do not appear to be of such formidable dimensions that a complete lack with regard thereto can be justified.

The *Harvard Research* does not stand alone in this error of omission.[98]

While we do not pretend to suggest a definitive formulation, we suggest that the *Harvard Research in International Law,* rather than leaving its 'Draft Convention' the way it stands now, might have done well to amend its Articles 1 (b) and 2,[99] so that these would read as follows:

Article 1 – USE OF TERMS

(b) A State's 'jurisdiction' is its *legislative and judicial competence* under international law to legislate and to prosecute and punish for crime.

Article 2 – SCOPE OF CONVENTION

(a) (1) A State's *legislative jurisdiction* with respect to crime committed by foreigners is limited to those acts or omissions which

94. *op. cit.,* p. 46. Writers may have a natural tendency to construct doctrinal edifices; this tendency is not, however, typical of courts and legal draftsmen.
95. *supra,* Chapter IV, p. 96.
96. *cf. Harvard Research, op. cit.,* p. 439.
97. *ibid.,* p. 439.
98. *cf.* FRY, Th. P., 'The International and National Competence of Australian Parliaments to Legislate in Respect of Extra-Territorial Crime (Including War Crimes),' *Univ. of Queensland Papers,* Faculty of Law, Vol. I, Nr. 2 (1947), p. 1.
99. The above suggested amendment of the Articles 1 (b) and 2 of the 'Draft Convention' would be an attempt to delimitate the powers of a State to legislate behavior that either in whole or in part occurred outside that State's territorial boundaries, but the effect of which was felt, and intended to be felt, within the State's territory.

are either in whole or in part set in motion or concluded within a State's territory, including those acts or omissions which are intended to affect that State's territorial or economic structure.

(2) A State's *legislative jurisdiction* with respect to crime committed by its nationals is regulated by the State's sovereign power to so regulate the conduct of its citizens as it sees fit, provided that the conduct is reprehensible both where committed and in the State itself.

(b) A State's *judicial jurisdiction* with respect to crime is defined as limited by this convention.

(c) Nothing in the provisions of this Convention shall preclude any of the parties to this Convention from entering into other agreements, or from giving effect to other agreements.

While the above suggested amendments would separate legislative from judicial jurisdiction, and open the way to take a more careful look at a State's legislative jurisdiction, we still have to deal with the phrase 'competence under international law' as state in Article 1 (b), both in the existing, as well as in our suggested amendments to the 'Draft Convention.'

The Concept of 'International Law'

The Comment of the *Harvard Research in International Law* states that 'The Convention is concerned only with the international capacity of States. . .'[100] However, if the competency of a State under international law is interpreted as a State's international capacity to prosecute and punish, then, it should be said that this capacity in turn is contingent upon a State's capacity to legislate under international law.

It is precisely here that the crux of the problem lies. As long as the term 'international law' remains as vague as it is, the question what a State's legislative capacity under international law is will remain unanswered.

Particularly the phrase 'general principles of law recognized by civilized nations,' as used in Article 38 of the Statute of the Court of International Justice[101] is

100. *l.c.*, p. 647, and the literature there quoted. Since the word 'capacity' has a technical meaning in legal terminology, referring to the rights and obligations of the parties, we wonder what can be meant by this statement, particularly in view of the existing uncertainty with regard to the binding rules of international law.

101. Art. 38-1, Statute of the Court of International Justice, annexed to the Charter of the United Nations, San Francisco, June, 1945. We are not unmindful that the definition given to the term is 'principles which find expression in the *municipal laws of various nations;*' *cf.* SCHLESINGER, R. B., COMPARATIVE LAW, Brooklyn, 1959, p. 25, and the literature there cited, but this is known only to those initiated in the special jargon, and even then there is no certainty with regard to the quantitative aspects of the term *municipal laws of various nations.*

subject to varied interpretation. Some of the questions that may come up with regard thereto are the following:

(a) Does a principle become 'international law' only if *all* of the civilized nations recognize it as a principle of law?

(b) Will a principle become 'international law' if the majority of the civilized nations recognize it as a principle of law? If so, are nations awarded one vote each, or are nations awarded votes on a population basis (thus giving China a strong vote and The Netherlands, or Belgium, or Luxemburg, a minuscule vote)?

(c) By what standards shall it be determined whether a nation qualifies as a 'civilized nation'? When its citizens are properly dressed or eat their food with western eating utensils? Or will the culture of a nation (in terms of centuries) be the determining factor? Or will admission to the United Nations be sufficient evidence of having reached civilization?

(d) What happens if the great number of newly emerged and emerging nations promulgate that murder is not such an act as to make it a criminal offence? Does that mean that there should be a shift in the general principles of law recognized by civilized nations?

(e) Who will be designated to determine which nations can qualify as civilized nations? The United Nations? The Court of International Justice? Or will the mere existence of statehood (implying national sovereignty) be sufficient to qualify?

We might be able to raise some more questions, but for our purpose the above ones will suffice. All we meant to show is that the phrase 'general principles of law recognized by civilized nations' is no longer a phrase susceptible of simple interpretation.[102]

In defense of the phrase we should add that in 1945, at the time of its inclusion in Article 38 of the Statute of the Court of International Justice, the world situation had not yet become as complex as it appears to be in 1970, even though in 1945 the situation was more complex than in say, 1927, or in 1830. For the present purpose we do not deem it necessary to dwell any longer upon this issue.

Suffice it to state that the theoretical foundation upon which extra-territorial criminal jurisdiction (both legislatively and judicially) should be based, can be found only if some new formula for 'international law' can be found.

We submit as a formula:

International law is the body of rules and principles that since time im-

102. *cf.* JESSUP, *op. cit.*, p. 58. 'Differences in social customs and standards prevent a unified world view on the criminality of bigamy, or the sale and consumption of alcohol, or the smoking of opium; what is justifiable homicide in one country may be murder in another.' Here, too, the formula *municipal laws of various nations* will not provide much guiding light as to which principles should be considered 'general principles of law recognized by civilized nations.'

memorial have occupied the minds and actions of legislatures, courts and legal writers, and which in the absence of a common consensus can acquire the force of authority only by a world-wide recognized legislative or judicial agency.

It is within the context of such body of rules and principles that a State's legislative competency should be limited and can be judged as to its legality.

The International Law Aspects of the Extraterritorial Reach

At the beginning of this chapter we intimated that there are theoretical-juridical problems connected with the extraterritorial reach of the antitrust laws which need to be solved in accordance with the generally recognized and accepted principles of international law. This is necessary for any State if it does not want to run the risk of being accused that it flouts those principles, no matter how vague they may be. Certainly the United States should not want to expose itself to this accusation.

The question then, which needs to be answered is: Is the assertion of extraterritorial jurisdiction in antitrust cases by the United States in accord with the principles of international law?

In order to find an answer to that question we have identified four pivotal points of consideration, because any controversy invariably centers around these points. They are: (a) the determination of the *locus delicti;* (b) the determination of the territory over which a State can be said to have jurisdiction; (c) the extent to which a State may go for the assertion of jurisdiction over persons or conduct outside the territorial boundaries of that State; (d) the essence of international law.

Whether the principles of international law sanction or disapprove of what a State is doing with regard to the assertion of jurisdiction depends on the interpretation of those four points.

We concede that the weakest point in the link is caused by our own view of international law. However, with all the uncertainty that exists with regard to the essence of international law, there are certain principles about which a common consensus may safely be surmised. These, we will on the basis of our own definition accept as belonging to the body of rules and principles which will find general acceptance and therefore, qualify as sources of international law. One of these is fairness, another one is justice. We need no more for our purpose. We have framed our definition of *locus delicti* and territory in such a way that they focus on the place where the injury is perceived, the intention of the actor, and the geographical area where the intended acts operate. As a criterion for the assertion of jurisdiction (legislatively and judicially) this appears to us to be fair, and leading to just results.

While the argument may be raised that our two-fold criterion (*locus delicti* and territory) leads to nothing but a re-wording of the objective territoriality principle, we reject such an argument in advance. It may be true that the objective territoriality principle will lead largely to the same results. But there are differences. In the first place, that principle has traditionally been introduced specifically with regard to criminal jurisdiction, not to other areas; whereas we wanted to find generally acceptable criteria that could equally apply to civil and regulatory jurisdiction. Furthermore, we were not so much after a classification of principles to be applied to jurisdictional problems as we were interested in suggesting guidelines which would be fair and just to both actor and injured. Third, we had to reckon with the possibility that suggestions to adopt a well-known principle that has a known connotation (even if modified) runs the risk of being lost in a shuffle of arguments over competing principles. By avoiding any label and stressing the aspects of fairness and justice, we think that we have achieved what we set out to examine: the necessary link between the extraterritorial reach of antitrust enforcement and the requirements of fairness according to the principle of international law. We submit that our criteria of *locus delicti* and territory answer that requirement.

CHAPTER VII

CONCLUSIONS

In our introductory chapter we alluded to the statement that the application of the antitrust laws to foreign commerce is still somewhat of a 'frontier area of the law'.

The extraterritorial reach of restrictive trade legislation is by necessity a conflicts-evoking type of legislation and regulation; this is caused by the existing differences with regard to the organization of the national economic systems in the various countries around the world. When commercial practices, resulting from different national regulations of business activity, are extended into the international community a collision course is often inevitable.

Particularly in view of the increased (and continually increasing) participation by businessmen all over the world in, and the resulting expansion of transnational business, the dangers of a collision are becoming a greater likelihood.

It was with a view thereto that we undertook our examination of the extraterritorial reach of the American antitrust laws, so far the most developed of restrictive trade legislations in the world.

We were particularly interested in examining to what extent the application of the American antitrust laws to the area of foreign commerce was moving into the right direction, what shortcomings could be observed, what corrective steps could be suggested, so that attention thereto could be directed before the law in its often apparent propensity to become rigid would be too firmly entrenched to allow for modification.

In order to gain a proper insight into and perspective of the American antitrust laws we approached these laws first, from their historical and philosophical development bases.

This approach lead us to the conclusion that the origin of antitrust enforcement was characterized by a litigation by private parties, based on either tort or contract. It was not a government regulation of business relationships. Even the first government regulation pertaining to restrictive trade practices (the *Statute of Monopolies* of 1623) was in fact the authorization of treble damages to private litigants, therefore, still a regulation of private litigation. This is markedly different from restrictive trade legislation elsewhere. The appearance of the Government into the area of the regulation of private enterprise did not occur until the turn of the 19th century, with the enactment of the *Sherman Act* of 1890, some 489 years after the *Schoolmaster* case of 1411 had been decided, and some 267 after the *Statute of Monopolies* of 1623.

It is this possibility of being faced with an action for treble damages, in a private litigation, by a competitor who claims to be injured by the alleged commercial practices, that may come as a surprise to many a foreign businessman who finds himself caught in this type of lawsuit. In fact, in a recent article in a German publication (previously mentioned at p. 18) businessmen were particularly warned against this danger.

The second conclusion to which we arrived is that the apparent confusion caused by the concurrent existence of civil, criminal and regulatory (administrative) remedies resulted from the functional aspects of the antitrust laws, i.e., the mechanics of implementation of the purported objectives. This is of particular importance because the American antitrust laws are characterized both by a positive (i.e., the promotion of free competition in open markets) and a negative aspect (i.e., the prevention of excessive concentration of economic power in private hands).

Because the remedial aspects of the litigation are determinative both of the relief asked for and the character of the proceedings (i.e., whether the action is a civil, a criminal, or a regulatory one) we approached and analyzed the problems that may arise primarily from their remedial vantage points.

We felt that this would be of particular importance and advantage to the foreign businessman who might not be aware of the peculiar character of the American antitrust laws. Indeed, not doing so would only lead to a perpetuation of the conclusion that the multiplicity of legal provisions, enacted in different laws, and the concomitant remedies available to litigants (be they private parties or the Government) are confounding. Also, the method of approaching a legal system entirely from its remedial vantage points may be a new experience to those who are not sufficiently familiar with the common law legal system, characterized by its maxim 'there shall be no wrong without a remedy.' Indeed, it has often been stated that the common lawyer is primarily geared to remedy, while the civilist lawyer is more attuned to doctrinal principle.

It was on the basis of the functional aspects of the American antitrust laws, resulting in the availability of multiple remedies, that we arrived at our conclusion that it would be necessary to consider the entire area of antitrust enforcement as a separate area of the law, answerable to its own jurisdictional rules. Not doing so would only lead to international friction and feelings of injustice, particularly in cases involving the extraterritorial reach of the law.

As an illustration in point we mention the modern merger movement which increasingly acquires global proportions. What a foreign businessman considers sound commercial policy may well run counter to the policies embodied in the American antitrust laws. Thus, the European businessman who enters into a relationship with an American corporation to explore jointly, say the African market, may find himself caught unawares in an antitrust suit (instigated either by an American competitor in a private litigation, or by the American antitrust enforcement agencies) because of alleged violations of the American antitrust laws, resulting in an extraterritorial reach of these laws.

Having recognized the functional character of the American antitrust laws, we considered which steps had to be taken at the point of implementation to bring the purported objectives to its fullest fruition. We singled out two necessary steps:

(1) First, the compilation and enactment of a unified comprehensive Antitrust Code. This would enable the (foreign) businessman to consult in a relatively easily accessible manner the regulation of private enterprise in the United States, including the instances of assertion of extraterritorial jurisdiction (both legislatively and judicially) over persons and subject matter. We consider this a minimum requirement of fairness.

(2) Second, because the antitrust laws should be considered as a separate area of the law, answerable to its own jurisdictional rules, we considered it necessary that a special judiciary be established to deal with the proper functioning of antitrust enforcement. Much like the Bankruptcy Courts we recommended that Antitrust Courts be attached to the various federal District Courts.

Also, in view of the possibility of conflict situations caused by transnational business relationships, we recommended that a special judiciary be established at the supra-national level. This Supra-National Tribunal for Antitrust Matters could conceivably be attached to the Court of International Justice. The functions of this tribunal would be: (a) to settle disputes with transnational aspects; (b) to develop new rules and principles of international antitrust law; (c) to serve as a guide to courts elsewhere in the world where problems related to the extraterritorial reach of restrictive trade legislation is emerging. As an illustration in point we mention the recent decree of the Commission of the E.E.C. regarding the collusive price increases of aniline pigments.

Because of the uncertainty with regard to the principles of international law, i.e., the absence of firmly recognized and accepted principles to which States must submit themselves, and in view of the necessity to develop new rules and principles of international antitrust law, we recommended that the extraterritorial reach of restrictive trade legislation be guided by a two-fold criterion, to wit, a special concept of *locus delicti* and a special concept of *territory*. This would give antitrust enforcement a global aspect and still be in accordance with the requirements of fairness and justice.

While it may be true that our proposed two-fold criterion would be perceptibly little different from what is commonly known as the objective territoriality principle, we intentionally rejected to follow that terminology; we did so for the following reasons:

(a) the objective territoriality principle has traditionally been applied only to the area of criminal law enforcement, not to the area of private litigation or regulatory jurisdiction. We submit that our criterion will be susceptible to application to all forms of jurisdiction, civil, criminal and regulatory.

(b) the application of 'principles' to cases may evoke objections in countries

> that profess not to be interested in the settlement of disputes by the application of principles but only in the settlement of disputes on an *ad hoc* basis. However, the use of 'yardsticks' (a criterion) is universally acceptable in the settlement of disputes.
>
> Consequently, we submit that our proposal will better serve as a guide to the expressed desire to arrive at a harmonization of restrictive trade legislation at the international level.

Our proposal is also important to the foreign businessman: he is in a better position to determine in advance the consequences of the possible effects of his commercial practices and policies, both locally and transnationally.

Thus, a consideration to engage in a joint venture with an American corporation in a far away country, or a proposal among foreign corporations to join hands in an effort to establish a firm foothold on the American market, can be analyzed with regard to the effects on the foreign commerce (or the domestic commerce) of the United States. If the effects are such that they will run counter to the principle of free competition in open markets, combined with the principle of prevention of excessive concentration of economic power in private hands, he better think twice before he acts.

Finally, our examination of the extraterritorial reach of the American antitrust laws has led us to conclude that by and large the American courts have displayed great circumspection when dealing with foreign defendants. This was not, however, necessarily the result of what the legislative jurisdiction allowed the judiciary to do; rather, it appeared at times that this circumspection came about in the form of a modification of a decree, thus leaving the impression that what was done was more a matter of expediency than the application of law.

We submit that the foreign businessman is entitled to know clearly in advance what practices are allowed and what practices will expose him to an encounter with the American antitrust enforcement authorities; this is possible only by clearly defined and delimited legal criteria.

SELECTED REFERENCES

AMERICAN

American Bar Association, 'Impact of Antitrust Laws on Foreign Trade', Chicago, 1953

American Bar Association, 'Section on International and Comparative Law', Chicago, 1953

Anderson, R. A., 'Law A.D. 2067', *American Business Law Journal* 249 (1967)

Antitrust Developments 1955–1968, A supplement to the Report of the Attorney General's National Committee to Study the Antitrust Laws, Chicago, 1968

Beckett, W. E., 'The Exercise of Criminal Jurisdiction over Foreigners', in VI *British Yearbook of International Law* 44 (1952)

Bemmelen, J. M. van, ONS STRAFRECHT, Part I, 2nd ed., Haarlem, 1965

Bemmelen, J. M. van, ONS STRAFRECHT, Part I, 3rd rev'd. ed., Haarlem 1968

Berman, H. J. & Greiner, W. R., THE NATURE AND FUNCTIONS OF LAW, 2nd ed., Brooklyn, 1966

BLACK'S LAW DICTIONARY, 4th ed., St. Paul, 1951

Blake, H. M., & Pitofsky, R., ANTITRUST LAW – Cases and Materials, Brooklyn, 1967

Brewster, K., Jr., ANTITRUST AND AMERICAN BUSINESS ABROAD, New York, 1958

Cheatham, E. E., Griswold, E. N., Reese, W. L. M., Rosenberg, M., CASES AND MATERIALS ON CONFLICT OF LAWS, 5th ed., Brooklyn, 1964

Cohen, M. R., 'The Basis of Contract', 46 *Harvard Law Review* 553 (1933)

Delaume, G. R., AMERICAN-FRENCH PRIVATE INTERNATIONAL LAW, New York, 1961

Edwards, C. D., CONTROL OF CARTELS AND MONOPOLIES – An International Comparison, New York, 1967

Edwards, C. D., TRADE REGULATION OVERSEAS, New York, 1966

Ehrenzweig, A. A., A TREATISE ON THE CONFLICT OF LAWS, St. Paul, 1962

Emmerglich, L. J., 'Antitrust Jurisdiction and the Production of Documents Abroad', 11 *The Record* of the Association of the Bar of the City of New York 122 (1956)

Fortas, A., 'American Antitrust', 45 *Progress* – The Magazine of Unilever 244 (1957)

Foster, R. S., 'Jurisdiction', in ENCYCLOPEADIA OF THE SOCIAL SCIENCES, Vol. VII, p. 471, New York, 1959

Friedmann, W., LAW IN A CHANGING SOCIETY, Berkely, 1959
Fugate, W. L., FOREIGN COMMERCE AND THE ANTITRUST LAWS, Boston, 1958
Goodrich, H. R., HANDBOOK OF THE CONFLICT OF LAWS, 3rd ed., St. Paul, 1949
Haight, G. W., 'International Law and Extra-Territorial Application of the Antitrust Laws', 63 *Yale Law Journal* 639 (1954)
Handler, M., TRADE REGULATION – Cases and Materials, 4th ed., Brooklyn, 1967
Hanna, J., & MacLachlan, J. A., THE BANKRUPTCY ACT, Brooklyn, 1958
'Harvard Research in International Law', 29 *American Journal of International Law Supplement* 435 (1935), Vol. II, 'Jurisdiction with Respect to Crime'
Holmes, O. W., 'Ideals and Doubts', 10 *Illinois Law Review* 1 (1915)
Holmes, O. W., THE COMMON LAW, (Howe, M. DeW., Edit.), Cambridge, 1963
Houghteling, J. L., & Pierce, G. G., THE LEGAL ENVIRONMENT OF BUSINESS, New York, 1963
Jessup, Ph. C., THE USE OF INTERNATIONAL LAW, Ann Arbor, 1959
Jessup, Ph. C., TRANSNATIONAL LAW, New Haven, 1956
Kanazawa, Y., 'The Regulation of Corporate Enterprise: The Law of Unfair Competition and the Control of Monopoly Power', in Von Mehren, A. T., LAW IN JAPAN, Cambridge, 1963
Kaplan, M. A., & Katzenbach, N. deB., THE POLITICAL FOUNDATIONS OF INTERNATIONAL LAW, New York, 1961
Katz, M., & Brewster, K., Jr., THE LAW OF INTERNATIONAL TRANSACTIONS AND RELATIONS, Brooklyn, 1960
Katzenbach, N. deB., 'Conflicts on an Unruly Horse: Reciprocal Claims and Tolerances in Interstate and International Law, 65 *Yale Law Journal* 1087 (1956)
Kaysen, C., & Turner, D. F., ANTITRUST POLICY – An Economic and Legal Analysis, Cambridge, 1965
Kennedy, R. F., 'This Case is a Reflection on All of Us', *Life* Magazine, February 24, 1961, p. 30
Kessler, F., & Sharp, M. P., CASES AND MATERIALS ON CONTRACTS, Boston, 1953
Kronstein, H., 'Conflicts Resulting From The Extraterritorial Effect Of The Antitrust Legislation Of Different Countries', in XXth CENTURY COMPARATIVE AND CONFLICTS LAW, Leiden, 1961
Kronstein, H., 'The Nationality of International Enterprises', 52 *Columbia Law Review* 983 (1952)
Lawson, F. H., A COMMON LAYER I OOKS AT THE CIVIL LAW, Ann Arbor, 1953
Letwin, W. L., 'Congress and the Sherman Antitrust Law 1887–1890', 23 *University of Chicago Law Review* 221 (1956)

Letwin, W. L., 'The English Common Law Concerning Monopolies,' 21 *University of Chicago Law Review* 355 (1954)

Llewellyn, K. N., THE BRAMBLE BUSH, New York, 1951

Massel, M. S., COMPETITION AND MONOPOLY, Washington, 1962

Mc Cracken, R. T., 'The Federal Antitrust Laws From the Viewpoint of a Business Lawyer,' *Antitrust Law Symposium – 1953,* Chicago, 1953

Mueller, G. O. W., 'The United Nations Draft Code of Offences Against the Peace and Security of Mankind: An American Evaluation,' in Mueller, G. O. W., & Wise, E. M., Edit., INTERNATIONAL CRIMINAL LAW, London, 1965, p. 608

Neale, A. S., THE ANTITRUST LAWS OF THE UNITED STATES OF AMERICA, Cambridge, 1960

Note, 'An Introduction to the Extraterritorial Application of the American Antitrust Laws', 1 *Case Western Reserve Journal of International Law* 132 (1969)

Oliphant, H., CASES ON TRADE REGULATION, St. Paul, 1923

Oppenheim, L., INTERNATIONAL LAW, 8th. ed. (Lauterpacht), Vol. I, New York, 1963

Oppenheim, S. C., 'Federal Antitrust Legislation – Guideposts to a Revised National Antitrust Policy', 50 *Michigan Law Review* 1139 (1952)

Oppenheim, S. C., & Weston, G. E., FEDERAL ANTITRUST LAWS, 3rd. ed., St. Paul, 1968

Rabel, E., THE CONFLICT OF LAWS, 2nd. ed., Vol. I, Ann Arbor, 1958

Report of the Attorney General's National Committee to Study the Antitrust Laws, Washington, 1955

Restatement of the Law (Second), Conflict of Laws, Proposed Official Draft, Part II (1968)

Restatement of the Law (Second), Foreign Relations of the United States (1965)

Reynolds, W. B., 'Extraterritorial Application of Federal Antitrust Laws: Delimiting the Reach of Substantive Law Under the Sherman Act,' 20 *Vanderbilt Law Review* 1030 (1967)

Schlesinger, R. B., COMPARATIVE LAW, Brooklyn, 1959

Schwartz, L. B., FREE ENTERPRISE AND ECONOMIC ORGANIZATION, 3rd ed., Brooklyn, 1966

Shartel, B., OUR LEGAL SYSTEM AND HOW IT OPERATES, Ann Arbor, 1951

Silbiger, T., 'Dutch Antitrust Laws – Some Developments and Comparisons,' 1 *American Business Law Journal* 35 (1963)

Silving, H., 'In re Eichman: A Dilemma of Law and Morality,' in Mueller, G. O. W., & Wise, E. M., INTERNATIONAL CRIMINAL LAW, London, 1965, p. 338

Smith, L. Y., & Roberson, G. G., BUSINESS LAW, UCC EDITION, 2nd. ed., St.

Paul, 1966
Smith, R. A., 'The Incredible Electrical Conspiracy,' *Fortune* Magazine, April, 1961, p. 132, and May, 1961, p. 161
Steiner, H. J. & Vagts, D. F., TRANSNATIONAL LEGAL PROBLEMS, Mineola, 1968
Thorelli, H. B., THE FEDERAL ANTITRUST POLICY – Origination of an American Tradition, Baltimore, 1955
Timberg, S., 'Extraterritorial Jurisdiction under the Sherman Act,' 11 *The Record* of the Association of the Bar of the City of New York 101 (1956)
Time Magazine (European Edition), January 5, 1970 and February 9, 1970
Tocqueville, A. de, DEMOCRACY IN AMERICA (Reeve, H., transl.), 6th ed., vol. I, Boston, 1876
Trautman, D., 'A Study of the International Environment: The International Reach of American Regulatory Legislation Other Than the Sherman Act,' in Brewster, K. Jr., ANTITRUST AND AMERICAN BUSINESS ABROAD, New York, 1958, p. 309
Statistical Abstract of the United States, 1968, U.S. Department of Commerce, Washington, 1969
Van Cise, J. G., THE FEDERAL ANTITRUST LAWS, Washington, 1955
Von Mehren, A. T., & Trautman, D. T., 'Jurisdiction to Adjudicate: A Suggested Analysis,' 79 *Harvard Law Review* 1121 (1966)
Waite, J. B., THE CRIMINAL LAW AND ITS ENFORCEMENT, Chicago, 1947
Wengler, W., 'Laws Concerning Unfair Competition and the Conflict of Laws,' 4 *American Journal of Comparative Law* 167 (1955)
Wilcox, C., PUBLIC POLICIES TOWARD BUSINESS, Homewood, 1960
Wise, E. M., 'Note on International Standards of Criminal Law and Administration,' in Mueller, G. O. W., & Wise, E. M., INTERNATIONAL CRIMINAL LAW, London, 1965

FOREIGN

Andenaes, J., THE GENERAL PART OF THE CRIMINAL LAW OF NORWAY (Ogle, Thos. P., transl.), London, 1965
Donnedieu de Vabres, H., LES PRINCIPES MODERNES DU DROIT PENAL INTERNATIONAL, Paris, 1928
Donnedieu de Vabres, H., TRAITE DE DROIT CRIMINEL ET DE LEGISLATION COMPAREE, 3ième ed., Paris, 1947
Drion, J., STARE DECISIS – HET GEZAG VAN PRECEDENTEN, 's-Gravenhage, 1950
Dubbink, A., 40 *Mededelingen van de Nederlandse Vereniging voor Internationaal Recht* 7 (1959)

Ellis, J. J. A., 'De extraterritoriale werking van het nationale strafrecht,' 51 *Mededelingen van de Nederlandse Vereniging voor Internationaal Recht* 29 (1964)

Fry, Th. P., 'The International and National Competence of Australian Parliaments to Legislate in Respect of Extra-Territorial Crime (Including War Crimes),' *University of Queensland Papers,* Faculty of Law, Vol. I, nr. 2 (1947)

Gleiss, A., 'Die Gefahren des US-Antitrustrechts für europäische Unternehmen,' *Auszenwirtschaftsdienst des Betriebs-Beraters,* Vol. 15, nr. 12, p. 499 (1969)

Hanbury, H. G., 'The Territorial Limits of Criminal Jurisdiction,' 37 *Grotius Society – Problems of Public and Private International Law* 171 (1952)

Handelingen der Nederlandse Juristen Vereniging 1966, Vol. 1, Zwolle, 1966

Holland, Th. E., THE ELEMENTS OF JURISPRUDENCE, 6th ed., Oxford, 1893

Jennings, R. Y., 'The International Law Covering Antitrust Jurisdiction,' in *Report of the Fifty-First Conference of the International Law Association Held at Tokyo,* London, 1965

Kahn-Freund, O., 'English Contracts and American Antitrust Law; The Nylon Patent Case,' 18 *Modern Law Review* 65 (1965)

Langemeyer, G. E., 'Le Principe de Territorialité,' in LE DROIT PENAL INTERNATIONAL, Leiden, 1965

Lauterpacht, H., 'Allegiance, Diplomatic Protection and Criminal Jurisdiction over Aliens,' *Cambridge Law Journal,* vol. IX, nr. 3, p. 330 (1947)

Macassey, L., 'Controlling Cartels Under the Rule of Law,' 31 *Grotius Society – Problems of Public and Private International Law* 232 (1946)

Maitland, F. W., FORMS OF ACTION AT COMMON LAW, Cambridge, 1962

Mulder, A., 'De extra-territoriale werking van het strafrecht,' 51 *Mededelingen van de Nederlandse Vereniging voor Internationaal Recht* 14 (1964)

Mulder, A., DE HANDHAVING DER SOCIAAL-ECONOMISCHE WETGEVING, 's-Gravenhage, 1949

Mulder, A., & Mok, M. R., KARTELRECHT, Alphen aan den Rijn, 1962

Oliver, C. T., 'The Harmonization of Laws and the Development of Principles for the Resolution of Conflicts of Enforcement Jurisdiction as to Transnational Monopolistic and Restrictive Trade Practices,' in *Report of the Fifty-First Conference of the International Law Association,* London, 1965, p. 554

Oliver, C. T., 'The Range of Effect of the Anti-trust Laws of the United States,' *Report of the Fifty-Fist Conference of the International Law Association,* London, 1965, p. 544

Pompe, W. J., 'Comment,' *Nederlandse Jurisprudentie* 1952, nr. 42, p. 123

Rehbinder, E., EXTRATERRITORIALE WIRKUNGEN DES DEUTSCHEN KARTELLRECHTS, Baden-Baden, 1967

Riedweg, A. J., 'The Extra-Territorial Application of Restrictive Trade Legislation – Jurisdiction and International Law,' *Report of the Fifty-First Conference of the International Law Association,* London, 1965, p. 385

Sarkar, L., 'The Proper Law of Crime in International Law,' in Mueller, G. O. W., & Wise, E. M., INTERNATIONAL CRIMINAL LAW, London, 1965, p. 52

Schwartz, I. E., DEUTSCHES INTERNATIONALES KARTELLRECHT, Köln, 1962

Sociaal Economische Wetgeving, vol. 15 (1967)

The Economist, vol. 165, p. 556 (1952), 'Comity and the Oil Companies'

Turner, J. W. C., KENNEY'S OUTLINES OF CRIMINAL LAW, 18th ed., Cambridge, 1962

Van der Grinten, W. C. L., & Bieger, K. S., 'Internationale aspecten op het gebied van de economische mededinging,' 39 *Mededelingen van de Nederlandse Vereniging voor Internationaal Recht* 6 (1959)

Van Gerven, W., PRINCIPES DU DROIT DES ENTENTES DE LA COMMUNAUTE ECONOMIQUE EUROPEENNE, Bruxelles, 1966

Verloren van Themaat, P., 'Les Cartels Internationaux devant les Législations Nationales d'un Point de Vue Juridique,' 3 *Sociaal Economische Wetgeving* 18 (1955)

Verzijl, J. H. W., 'The Controversy Regarding the So-Called Extraterritorial Effect of the American Antitrust Laws,' VIII *Nederlands Tijdschrift voor Internationaal Recht* 3 (1961)

Wiarda, G. J., 'Drie Typen van Rechtsvinding,' in EEN BUNDEL GEDACHTEN, Zwolle, 1963

TABLE OF CASES

FOREIGN CASES

GPSR Compliance

The European Union's (EU) General Product Safety Regulation (GPSR) is a set of rules that requires consumer products to be safe and our obligations to ensure this.

If you have any concerns about our products, you can contact us on ProductSafety@springernature.com

In case Publisher is established outside the EU, the EU authorized representative is:

Springer Nature Customer Service Center GmbH
Europaplatz 3
69115 Heidelberg, Germany

Batch number: 10844623

Printed by Printforce, the Netherlands